THE DIVINE DEFAULT

THE DIVINE DEFAULT

WHY FAITH IS
NOT THE ANSWER

J.J. DYKEN

Algora Publishing
New York

Library of Congress Cataloging-in-Publication Data —

Dyken, J. J.
  The divine default: why faith is not the answer / J.J. Dyken.
     pages cm
  Includes bibliographical references and i2ndex.
    ISBN 978-1-62894-006-0 (pbk.: alk. paper) — ISBN 978-1-62894-007-7 (hc: alk.
paper) — ISBN 978-1-62894-008-4 (ebook) 1. Religion—Controversial literature. 2.
Christianity—Controversial literature. I. Title.
  BL2775.3.D95 2013
  230—dc23
                             2013027605

Printed in the United States

Acknowledgements

No other topic has been or will ever be as ubiquitous and at the same time contentious as religion. For much of human history, a contrarian point of view expressed in a book like the one you hold in your hands would not have been possible. With this in mind, I would like to express my sincere gratitude and appreciation to all of the freethinkers and skeptics who came before me and to those who will invariably come after. Your efforts to speak your mind have paved the way for me to speak mine.

There are many people who have helped me during this process. To my good friends Ron and Andrea—thank you for your feedback and encouragement. I would also like to thank the fine folks at Algora Publishing for their patience and for giving me a voice. Above all I wish to thank my family with special appreciation for my wife Jodie, who may not always agree with me, but whose support and encouragement never wavered. To my beautiful children Taylor and Alex, thank you for always making me smile. If I could impart just one piece of advice to my children, it would be to always think for yourselves. Ask. Search. Explore. Exercise your mind. It is the greatest tool that you will ever own.

TABLE OF CONTENTS

Chapter 1. Introduction

> "It was, of course, a lie what you read about my re-
> ligious convictions, a lie which is being systematically
> repeated. I do not believe in a personal God and I have
> never denied this but have expressed it clearly. If some-
> thing is in me which can be called religious then it is the
> unbounded admiration for the structure of the world
> so far as our science can reveal it."—Albert Einstein

This book will not take a position on whether or not there is a God. Plenty of other people have already made passionate arguments for both sides of
this question, and the only real, honest answer is that we don't know. While
I cannot prove or disprove the existence of a prime mover, the evidence sub-
mitted thus far on behalf of God requires us to use words like "faith" and
"belief" in order to substantiate the claims. To be religious is to believe that
the creator of the universe has authored a number of books and that these
books are deemed to be so profound as to completely dismiss the possibility
of human authorship. One need only page through any of these texts to see
the implausibility which results from that kind of claim, yet the majority of
the people living on our planet find these texts to be not just worthwhile,
but rather essential documents on which to base their lives upon. As I intend to demonstrate, this type of ideology is not only naïve and divisive, it is
dangerous.

I began the book with a quote from Albert Einstein, not just because it
refutes the religious who erroneously claim Einstein for themselves, but because it's the perfect umbrella under which to present a case for the Divine
Default. The idea of a divine being isn't new and the concept of God isn't necessarily the problem. It's what we do with that belief that has serious con-

sequences. For all of the good that has been attributed to God and religion, rarely as a society do we recognize and acknowledge the associated dangers and pitfalls. For many of us, our worldviews are built upon a foundation of religion—a foundation that isn't as solid as we are led to believe. We treat ancient texts as rigid instructions on how we are to live our lives and many of our fellow neighbors fail to think critically about these claims instead treating them as infallible truths. We attempt to find meaning in the world by looking to the divine and we frequently use these "divinely-inspired" ancient texts as justification for our beliefs and actions. By virtue of their place in history, the most advanced and knowledgeable person in the first-century would be considered merely elementary by today's standards. You and every person that you have ever met have more scientific knowledge of our world than the most advanced first-century person could possibly have dreamed of. Even the average tribal elder living today in the most remote parts of Afghanistan, Iraq, and Egypt are more knowledgeable about our world than any of the figures from the times of Moses and Jesus and yet the words written thousands of years ago by these primitive people hold tremendous and irrational influence over contemporary society. It is an eye-opening experience to read the Bible from this perspective. The authors of Genesis for example gave us dominion over animals but clearly had no idea that this dominion wouldn't include germs—organisms that they didn't know existed and that we still don't have complete dominion over. Any assertion of historical or biological significance by the people who wrote our holy books should be open to scrutiny. Any scientific claim, whether cosmological, biological, or geological, made by a pre-scientific culture should be scrutinized. Because of its pervasive nature, the roots of religion and the resulting beliefs and actions shouldn't be glossed over or dismissed, and yet religion has and continues to be the only area of our discourse that remains systematically protected from criticism. Is this protection justified? If beliefs directly impact our actions, then it should be of utmost importance to each of us that we reduce the amount of false beliefs that we accept as fact. When a belief can influence an action, we should want to have as many true beliefs as possible. We have to be open to change in order to accomplish this.

When discussing religion, it's important to ask ourselves what it would take to change our minds. This very simple question goes right to the heart of determining how open one's mind is on this topic. Before you read another sentence, ask yourself what would it take for *you* to change your mind? You could be steadfast in your conviction, but do you remain open to changing your belief if the appropriate evidence warrants such a change? If you could visually see or verbally speak to God, would that cause you to believe? If science could physically prove abiogenesis, would that be enough to convince someone that divine creation stories are false? I ask these questions because it is important to know where you draw your own line. How sincere are you at finding the "truth," whatever that may be? If you are ultimately unwilling to listen or consider any side other than your own, the chances of finding the truth become no better than the odds of finding a pot of gold at the end of a rainbow. As a former believer, I know where my line in the sand is. An omniscient god would know exactly what is needed to convince me of its existence, and being omnipotent, it could easily produce such evidence. That didn't happen while I was a believer and it hasn't happened since.

If someone wants to believe that Jesus was the son of God or that Brahman created our world, so be it. I happily support their right to believe anything they like, as long as they keep their thoughts within the privacy of their own home and their belief doesn't hurt anyone. It's when those beliefs escape that privacy and enter the public realm that I begin to take issue. Beliefs all too easily become actions and therein lies the problem. If religions and their followers were able to keep their beliefs to themselves, this book wouldn't exist. Sadly, that is simply not the world that we live in. Many of our brothers and sisters truly believe that the creator of the universe desires us each to adopt certain beliefs and practices. Many of these beliefs require actions taken in this life that will purportedly influence the next life, and we have been cowed into not criticizing either the belief or the action. We are told that these unjustified beliefs are sacred and off the table for rational discourse. As Salman Rushdie once said, "the moment you declare a set of ideas to be immune from criticism, satire, derision, or contempt, freedom of thought becomes impossible." We can openly criticize and expostulate our neighbor's position on politics, history, fashion, or finances but we must somehow respect his/her beliefs about invisible realities, even when their certainties of the next life are often discordant and incompatible with acceptance in this one. When people speak about their faith in glowing terms, they are essentially saying that they are prepared to believe in almost anything on little/no evidence. Is the most appropriate response to a statement like that one of respect, or suspect?

When parents are advocating the teaching of creationism or pushing for prayer in our public school classrooms, these actions require a response. When folks elevate Canon Law or Sharia over secular laws, these actions require a response. When religious belief influences laws preventing the scientific advancement of initiatives like stem cell research, these actions require a response. When condoms are considered morally evil, actions taken because of this belief require a response. When homosexual couples are denied the rights and privileges enjoyed by heterosexual couples, these actions require a response. Every time religion attempts to tear down the wall separating church and state, each of those attempts requires a response. If the various religions and their billions of followers were truly capable of keeping their beliefs to themselves, folks like me would have no reason to raise our voices in response. Again, this is simply not the world that we find ourselves living in.

If there is a purpose to this book, it is to elevate this millennia-old discussion by putting the "common" back into common sense using simple logic and rationality instead of superstition and bad evidence. None of the concepts I put forth requires the reader to hold a Ph.D. to understand. Common sense and common knowledge are enough to highlight religious contradictions. If you are religious, my hope is that you'll become more aware of these contradictions by the end of the book. If you are not religious, it is my sincere desire and hope that you will finish this book having learned something new. I'll attempt to do this by applying commonly-held religious beliefs to real-world examples. I'll try to stay away from philosophical arguments where possible, which tend to confuse those unfamiliar with the many varied methods and terminology, and instead stay with common sense and common language. I want this book to be thought provoking as well as easy to read. When quoting the Bible, I'll further that theme by primarily using the New International Version. I am aware that the translations from the King James Bible to the New International Version are often not perfect, but the latest translations are certainly the easiest version for most contemporary people to understand. I'll do my best to be fair and give a higher weight to the intent behind the passages.

I acknowledge that it is nearly impossible to avoid philosophical arguments when discussing religion, but I will try and limit those arguments only to where it is truly necessary and in terms that are easy to understand. It is often said that philosophy is questions that may never be answered while religion is answers that may never be questioned. The reason why a dedicated ontological chapter will not be found in this book on the potential for God is because I believe that philosophy of this sort is purely speculative and ultimately irrelevant. I will gladly concede the philosophical potential for God. This concession in no way validates the existence of a personal God. It simply leaves open the possibility. I have read and listened to many persuasive arguments for the existence of a universal "creator" from both historical minds like St. Augustine and St. Thomas Aquinas to modern-day religious minds like David Wolpe and William Lane Craig. None of these folks can provide conclusive evidence of an uncaused cause, but just as thousands have done before them, they use various methods of inductive reasoning to infer one. Conceding the potential for God is not the same as saying that revealed knowledge has been imparted to any human being.

There is a time and place for philosophical debates, however, debating religion on purely philosophical grounds is like a rocking chair—it gives us something to do but it doesn't really get us anywhere. Let me give you an example. One of the most talented contemporary Christian philosophers in my opinion is William Lane Craig. During his opening remarks in a debate with the late Christopher Hitchens at Biola University, Craig discussed the cosmological argument by saying:

> "The question of why anything at all exists is the most profound question of philosophy. The philosopher Derek Parfit says no question is more sublime than why there is a universe—why there is anything rather than nothing. Typically atheists answer this question by saying that the universe is just eternal and uncaused."

While the debate itself was fantastic, the last part of that statement highlights my concern and supports my position that philosophy isn't as solid a ground to stand on as evidential arguments. Craig belittles the atheistic assertion that "the universe is just eternal and uncaused" but never takes the time to realize the implications of the Christian assertion that God is equally "just eternal and uncaused." He does a fine job inferring a creator of both time and space, but misses the irony of the creator in the first place. If God can be uncaused, why can't the universe? The definitive answer as to whether or not God exists (and the more specific question of which god) can never be answered on philosophical grounds alone. That kind of declaration requires an evidential argument. Make no mistake about it, we have been presented with an abundance of "evidence" on behalf of every religion and yet a sufficient, compelling evidential argument does not exist to warrant rational belief in any of them. For me, an evidential argument trumps a philosophical argument every time. We're going to be looking at some of this evidence throughout our time together.

One of the most important messages I hope to impart from our time together is this: it is certainly conceivable to believe in the possibility of the "Einsteinian" God as I referenced at the beginning of this chapter without falling victim to the dogma that this being cares about what we eat, wear, do, say, or even think. It is a tremendous leap from deist to theist. Extraordinary claims truly do require extraordinary evidence. Imagine for a moment that we were to all wake up tomorrow morning and find that our knowledge of religion was completely wiped out. How would we go about determining the validity of the religions presented to us in the various books we have? How would we determine that the virgin birth of Jesus Christ is more plausible than Zeus perched upon his throne or that the sun god Ra rising in the sky is more plausible than Apollo favoring a specific side in battle or Poseidon churning the seas? We would have to evaluate each claim based upon its associated evidence, even though evidence of this sort is almost universally inconceivable. This is why any leap from deist to theist is truly a Kierkegaard leap of unsubstantiated faith. After thousands of years, we have yet to find any evidential argument presented on behalf of any religion to be of sufficient quality to not only dismiss all other religions as false but also to conclusively anoint just one as true. The actual evidence is either terrible or nonexistent, which is why the word "faith" exists in this context. It seems like a rather obvious point to make, but if the evidence for any religion was conclusive, we would have no further need for the word "faith." If the theme of this book is to provide an easy to read assessment of religion, favoring philosophical arguments over real, practical examples would defeat the purpose of putting pen to paper. At every opportunity, I will abandon philosophical arguments for evidential arguments where possible. Theological claims with practical, mortal implications being made by fallible men on behalf of the creator of the universe should be open to scrutiny and even ridicule where appropriate. Asking for evidential arguments instead of philosophical arguments seems to me to be the best platform from which to have these types of discussions.

You'll find that when I make specific religious references throughout the course of this book, I will usually make them about Christianity. This isn't to single out Christianity in favor of other religions, but rather due to the fact that Christianity is the religion that not only constitutes the largest percentage of my fellow Americans, but is the one that most often tries crawling over our secular walls. When I make reference to God, I will generally capitalize any applicable pronoun. I do this out of respect for the religious reader—not because I respect the belief itself but rather because I conscientiously recognize that the belief is a cherished one. Be forewarned that I enjoy using a great deal of satire and at times sarcasm, particularly when analyzing the plausibility of asserted stories. I find that these literary tools can be effective in highlighting the inane and illogical. Using this technique allows me to do what millions of my brothers and sisters do on a daily basis and personalize the statements. Millions believe in a personal god and attributing things to Him often allows me to show the absurdity of the attribution.

You'll also notice that when I make references to specific passages from the Bible, I give equal weight to both the Old Testament and the New Testament. For those religious readers who believe that the New Testament fundamentally repealed the laws of the Old Testament, I would offer up the fact that when Jesus and the apostles referred to the "Scriptures," they were in almost every case referring to what Christians now call the Old Testament. The Old Testament is still considered the word of God, and just like the Abrahamic covenant, it is neither conditional nor temporary. If God is eternal and unchanging, then there is no expiration date on His word.

Many Christians contend that the teachings of Jesus in the New Testament fundamentally annulled and replaced Mosaic Laws. This argument is presented anytime Christians say that they do not have to adhere to the Old Testament, but is this a valid position to take? The Sermon on the Mount comprises three chapters of Matthew's Gospel and is the longest recorded statement of Jesus' teachings, so it is here that I want to address this common misperception. Please keep in mind that the teachings of Jesus Christ were very different than those of the Sadducees and Pharisees. These groups were prominent Jewish sects who practiced and preached a strict adherence to the Laws of Moses. They and many others believed that Jesus was attempting to subvert the authority of God by replacing God's laws with his own teachings. Jesus clears this up early on, as we find in Matthew 5:17-19:

> "Do not think that I have come to abolish the Law or the Prophets; I have not come to abolish them but to fulfill them. For truly I tell you, until heaven and earth disappear, not the smallest letter, not the least stroke of a pen, will by any means disappear from the Law until everything is accomplished. Therefore anyone who sets aside one of the least of these commands and teaches others accordingly will be called least in the kingdom of heaven, but whoever practices and teaches these commands will be called great in the kingdom of heaven."

Jesus compares the permanence of heaven and earth to God's laws. The heaven and earth have not yet disappeared nor will everything be accomplished until the Day of Judgment. Jesus clearly had no intention of eliminating the law. He makes it pretty clear that he came to "fulfill the law." He not only validates and reaffirms the laws; he lays out the expectation that we should do so as well. The New Testament was never intended to render the Old Testament obsolete. "Fulfilling the law" simply means that Jesus came to complete the law and perfect it. "Thou shalt not kill" didn't just mean the obvious, but also that the evil and negative thoughts leading up to the physical act of murder are also against the law. "Thou shalt not commit adultery" didn't just mean the obvious, but also that the lust leading up to the physical act of adultery violates the commandment. Jesus preached that we must not only obey God's laws outwardly but also inwardly. He charged the Sadducees and Pharisees with only paying attention to the outward laws (Matthew 23:25). In the Sermon on the Mount, Jesus not only proclaims the permanence of God's law, he proclaims his respect for it. It would be highly problematic to suggest that Jesus' intentions were anything but refuting the wrong interpretations of the law by the religious leaders of the time.

There is also the rather obvious contradiction of the authorship of the laws. If we are to believe in the concept of the Holy Trinity, Jesus and the Father are one. In John 8:58, Jesus proclaims himself to be one with the Father by saying that he was around before Abraham. If Jesus and the Father are one, then the laws are from the same author. From this perspective, there simply cannot be such a fundamental conflict between the laws where one set is rendered obsolete. In fact, the underlying morality must be consistent and unchanging. God is quite explicit in Deuteronomy 13:1 when He says, "Whatever I am now commanding you, you must keep and observe, adding nothing to it, taking nothing away." In Malachi 3:6, God clearly tells us "I the LORD do not change." Throughout Leviticus, God makes multiple references to a "lasting ordinance for the generations to come." Throughout the New Testament, Jesus, Paul, and others reference the Old Testament in an authoritative manner. It was understood that God's laws can only be fulfilled. They cannot be dissolved. John 14:15 says, "If you love me, keep my commands." The Father gave Moses His commands and the vast majority of Christians today continue to keep those commands. When we look around our world, we readily find references to the Ten Commandments and many other Old Testament topics. For these reasons, I will treat the Old Testament as authoritatively as I do the New Testament.

I've already mentioned the religious influences of historical figures like St. Augustine and St. Thomas Aquinas as well as contemporaries like William Lane Craig and David Wolpe. I have enjoyed reading and listening to the varied religious opinions from these men in addition to other contemporary apologetics like Ken Ham, Lee Strobel, Kent Hovind, and Frank Turek. While each makes a compelling case for God, the other side of the argument makes a more intellectually honest case against the proposition. I am proud to say that contemporary folks like Richard Dawkins, Sam Harris, Neil deGrasse Tyson, Daniel Dennett, Matt Dillahunty, and the late Christopher Hitchens are my intellectual heroes. I've devoted a great deal of time over the years to both sides of this debate, and while I may not always agree completely with any one side (particularly the pseudoscientific accounts presented by Strobel, Hovind, and Ham), I do appreciate the balanced yet contrarian views. Every word that I've listened to or read has been thought provoking and I have been influenced at one point or another by each of these men—religious and atheist alike. You will find their influences throughout this book. As Bernard of Chartres might say, I find myself merely a dwarf standing on the shoulders of giants.

As you'll quickly discover throughout this book, I generally hold pseudoscientists like Lee Strobel and Ken Ham in contempt. These are the folks who try to fly under the banner of science instead of faith. Christian figures like St. Augustine, John Calvin, and Martin Luther urged people not to use the Bible as a scientific instrument or scientific proof, yet pseudoscientists are doing this every day. They have a very clear religious agenda and try to make science fit that agenda. This is perhaps my biggest gripe with them. Pseudoscientists already have an unassailable conclusion. The conclusion that they want to end up with is their starting point. They take great liberties with established scientific principles, introduce assumptions as evidence, and make critical use of the Divine Default in order to work backwards from their foregone conclusion. They tend to ignore or explain away any evidence that would lead them in a different direction because the thought that the Bible could be inaccurate is simply inconceivable to them. Because they project an air of scientific authenticity, they are able to prey upon the gullibility of a large and growing audience that is already predisposed to accepting any evidence supporting their preconceived notions while at the same time unable to critique the evidence itself. My contemptuous attitude towards these individuals is derived from their hypocritical use of scientific principles and misleading conclusions. They willfully disregard their burden of proof and their conclusions have been largely refuted time and time again by the actual scientific community, yet they are able to continue their pseudoscientific barrage with impunity while raking in millions of dollars in the process. They give an appearance of scientific credibility but lack any and all scientific responsibility. This confirmation bias held by most Christians certainly makes the inconvenient facts more easily dismissible. I want to change that.

Unfortunately, there is no shortage of customers for the pseudoscientists. Sadly, far too many people around the world cling to pseudoscientific beliefs and these beliefs extend well beyond religion. Depending on the survey, anywhere from 33%[1] to 88%[2] of all Americans believe that astrology is a science. Frankly, I am ashamed and embarrassed that so many of my fellow Americans believe that horoscopes, tarot cards, and psychic readings are considered legitimate science. It deeply saddens me that some in our society are content to dwell in the trenches of stupidity but it no longer surprises

---

1 National Science Board. *"Science and Engineering Indicators 2006"* (PDF). p. A7–14. Retrieved 3/15/2012

2 "The popular perception of science in North America." *Transactions of the Royal Society of Canada.* V IV: 269–280. 1989.

me. Depending on the survey, between 40% and 50% of Americans believe the Earth was created sometime in the last 10,000 years[1] and this view has persisted within that range for decades. Considering the scientific consensus that the Earth is approximately 4.5 billion years old, this is not a trivial error. When I combine this with the fact that 1 in 5 Americans still believes that the Sun revolves around the Earth, I'm not surprised that Ken Ham, Kirk Cameron, and Lee Strobel have found a following. There are people, and far too many apparently, who will virtually believe almost anything on little to no evidence.

You'll find that I place a much higher value on evidence than I do faith. Perhaps this is why I am an agnostic. If agnosticism deals with knowledge and atheism deals with belief, I could also be described as being an agnostic atheist. I am agnostic in that I don't have any knowledge of God's existence and I am an atheist in that I don't believe in any of the gods presented by our organized religions. I am not alone. In fact, every single person on this planet is an atheist as it relates to every religion for which they don't profess belief in. Whether you are a believer or a nonbeliever, you know exactly what it feels like to be an atheist. Every Christian is an atheist as it relates to Hinduism. Every Jew is an atheist as it relates to Islam. Taking a cue from Stephen Roberts, I just take it one god further. I find that there is something highly irrational about those who make untenable claims of certainty about invisible realities and I choose not to be part of that crowd. I have devoted a great many years to the topic of religion, and as I see it, agnosticism and rationalism are the only honest and humble positions to take in this matter. I do not believe that Jesus was the son of God any more than I believe that the archangel Gabriel appeared to Muhammad. The particular religion is actually irrelevant because the simple fact remains that not a single follower of Christ, Brahman, Yahweh, or Xenu has met their burden of proof. These religions are all equally bizarre and impractical with a burdensome dependency on unsubstantiated faith and their influence on our world cannot be ignored.

Any belief should be accompanied by evidence substantiating it; otherwise the belief should be subject to change. For example, I subscribe to the cosmological model known as the Big Bang theory because sufficient evidence, including cosmic microwave background and redshift, has been presented to justify such a belief. It is a comprehensive theory that explains a great deal about our universe while remaining consistent with a wide range of observed phenomena. While I subscribe to this theory, I will always keep my mind open to change if and when sufficient evidence is presented that contradicts it. If a religious person could provide sufficient evidence beyond mere assertions that God willed everything into existence over the course of a few days, I would be open to changing my views. The evidence needs to be superior to that of the evidence we have for the Big Bang, however. Additionally, I will be the first to admit that I don't know what caused the singularity and this gap in our knowledge is the only thing tenuously holding the door open for God. It's important here to note the distinction between pre and

---

1 "Evolution, Creationism, Intelligent Design." Gallup. May 2012

post bang. The Big Bang Theory does not address the initial cause of the universe—only its development and expansion over time. What caused the Big Bang in the first place? I don't know and I doubt whether or not we will ever definitively know. Many theists take that opportunity to attribute the bang to a deity. Many truly believe that this deity instantly created everything exactly as it is today, while folks that I refer to as skeptical theists take a hybrid approach and attribute the Big Bang to God and then let science take over from there. Regardless of which side of the fence you happen to be on, the only true statement is that we don't conclusively know what started the universe. To say that a deity is or isn't responsible for the Big Bang is to argue from a position of ignorance. When we really think about it, the Big Bang is a tremendous concept in and of itself. It is quite burdensome to try and scientifically account for everything in our universe once fitting into a spot as tiny as the head of a pin. We have absolutely no evidence whatsoever to conclusively explain what started the expansion of the universe. Any proclamation of its source or pre-existence is foolish because insufficient evidence exists to make such a proclamation. This premise is applicable to both theists and atheists. Whether we're theorizing about multiple universes, holographic universes, or divine creation, the undeniable truth is that you do not know what (or who) created the universe any more than I do.

Agnosticism and atheism are not without their difficulties. A recent poll conducted by the University of British Columbia showed that non-believers are among the least trusted people in our society ranking just ahead of rapists. Imagine that! Is this perception of non-believers accurate or fair? Is this perception grounded in fact or mistrust? The poll was disturbing, particularly in light of a March 2009 academic article by Phil Zuckerman of Pitzer College in *Sociology Compass* that compared social behaviors among believers and non-believers in relation to the overall religiosity of their environment (i.e., religious nations to less religious nations and religious states to less religious states).[1] The study found that "murder rates are actually lower in more secular nations and higher in more religious nations where belief in God is widespread." If we were to look at the top 50 safest cities in the world, nearly all of them are in "relatively non-religious countries." Even though it's a bit of a religious enigma itself, the United States showed the same trends. "Within America the states with the highest murder rates tend to be the highly religious, such as Louisiana and Alabama, but the states with the lowest murder rates tend to be the among the least religious in the country, such as Vermont and Oregon." If non-believers were truly worthy of having earned the distinction of being the least trusted people in our society, we should find a correspondingly high rate of incarceration, yet non-believers make up a disproportionately small percentage of those in prison. The trends extend well beyond just murder and can be found consistently in so many different facets of our lives. For example, violent crime tends to occur more frequently in the more religious states. Globally, the more secular nations tend to donate

---

[1]   http://www.pitzer.edu/academics/faculty/zuckerman/Zuckerman_on_Atheism.pdf
Retrieved 8/4/2012

more money and aid per capita to poorer nations than highly religious nations. Zuckerman pointed out that during the Holocaust, "the more secular people were, the more likely they were to rescue and help persecuted Jews." The populations of less religious nations tend to report the highest levels of happiness.

The same misperceptions of non-believers can be found when discussing sex and family. Young adults who took the religiously-inspired "virginity pledges" were found to not only engage in premarital sex as frequently as their non-pledging peers but were actually more likely to engage in unprotected intercourse. A 1999 Barna study showed that non-believers in America tend to have lower divorce rates as well as a much lower rate of domestic violence than their religious peers. A 2005 study[1] showed that the least religious societies on Earth tend to be the healthiest in terms of life expectancy, adult literacy, education, homicide rates, gender equality, and infant mortality. None of this should be used to declare the moral superiority of either believers or non-believers but rather to demonstrate that religiosity is perhaps not the best indicator of social morality. As such it simply isn't fair to paint non-believers as untrustworthy. We deserve much more credit than that.

It's not easy being a skeptic, doubter, nonbeliever, atheist, agnostic, or whatever label society places upon us. Religion is absolutely everywhere. To demonstrate just how pervasive religion is in our society, I conducted an informal experiment over the course of one normal week. I simply counted the number of occurrences where I was being exposed to some type of religious message and tallied them up. On average, I was exposed to 78 religious messages each day. Whether it was a billboard along the highway, articles in the local newspaper, online postings from friends and family, or television and radio shows/commercials, we are inundated by religious propaganda so often that it has literally become ubiquitous. It is simply amazing how inescapable religion has become, and yet you won't find atheists blowing themselves up over it. A cartoon depicting atheists in a negative fashion will hardly warrant a yawn let alone mass demonstrations and the burning of embassies. You won't find the kind of backlash from the nonbeliever community that we regularly see from the believers whenever their cherished beliefs are put in check. Using just the Ten Commandments as an example, we have seen disagreement elevated to death threats when the secular public objects to the Ten Commandments being placed on government property. We saw tempers flare when former Alabama Justice Roy Moore was ordered to remove a giant granite replica of the Ten Commandments from his courthouse. In a complaint filed against the New Kensington-Arnold School District in Pittsburgh in September 2012, a mother received multiple threats after challenging the legality of a Ten Commandments monument at the local Valley High School. In response, U.S. District Judge Terrence McVerry declared that this mother's "decision to be identified has resulted in threats and harassment. A number of the threats referenced in her affidavit have extended beyond ad hominem rhetoric, although they certainly appear

---

1 United Nations' Human Development Report

to include threats of violence and ostracism." He continued, saying, "there is a substantial public interest in ensuring that litigants not face such retribution in their attempt to seek redress for what they view as a constitutional violation, a pure legal issue." In each of these cases, the response from the religious community was not what we should ever hope for and certainly not something that any of us should be proud of. The secular community is offended daily, and yet you will be hard pressed to find scathing threats of violence aimed at the religious majority by the non-religious minority. Do we not get any credit for our peaceful and dignified response to religious bombardment? I have 78 opportunities every day to be offended by the religious, and yet it doesn't provoke anything more than a rare word here or there. I recognize the rights of individuals to speak freely, spread their ideas, and share those beliefs as long as there is a clear delineation between faith and government sponsorship of that faith. The rules are clear and have been well known for more than two hundred years. There are certain lines that mustn't be crossed, and when those lines are crossed, the last thing we should see are the religious surprised and up in arms.

Besides being frowned upon by a religiously dominated society, atheism and agnosticism require effort. I'm speaking from experience when I say that it would be so much easier to simply chalk everything up to God. The Divine Default has been a wonderful excuse for so many people throughout the history of mankind because it allows religious people to take the path of least resistance in searching for that elusive concept of "truth." Frankly, religious faith is the easy way out. As I'll show in this book, the path of least resistance allows things as arbitrary as geographic location to overwhelmingly influence what religion one believes to be "true." While I believe in the *possibility* of a "creator" and I fully understand the consequences of this position (i.e., who created the creator), that doesn't mean that a creator has anything to do with us personally. Religion introduces this concept to us. Religion gives us names for our gods. Organized religion is a man-made facade with a legacy of undeserved power and influence.

For centuries, religion was the authoritative voice about everything in our world. As Bob Dylan once said, "the times they are a-changin'." We no longer need God to explain how or why many things happen. There are so many things that have been attributed to God over the course of thousands of years that science has systematically snatched out of the hands of religion and rightfully laid claim to. Science allows us to gain a greater understanding of our world, but even with all of our advancements, I will readily admit that it's not perfect. Unlike religion though, science doesn't claim to have all the answers and I believe this is both a defining characteristic and an admirable quality. A scientist is not afraid to say "I don't know." A scientist may read hundreds of books throughout the course of his/her life and still be left with the knowledge that there is more to be learned. Most religious people will never fully read their one book and yet they will think they know it all.

The scientific method has been the most consistently reliable way of determining fact from fiction. Science may not currently have all the answers about things like dark matter, dark energy, black holes, string theory, or quantum mechanics, but no other method, including religious revelation, has been as useful or accurate in helping us learn the many truths about our world and universe. Physics, for example, has helped us uncover a tremendous amount of knowledge into how the universe behaves, but there's still more to learn. Even with that acknowledgement, there is nothing in physics that would lead us to believe in a god who not only built everything as we see it, but who has taken a personal interest in what we think, what we eat, who we sleep with, and what we say. Using nothing but the known laws of physics, we can show that the cosmos can and does function without the precept of God.

Religion often accuses science of only being able to deal with the "how" and not the "why," which I have always found to be misleading even when I was a believer. The problem here lies with the definitions. "How" generally refers to the process by which something happens. "Why" is often used as a personalizing reference to an intent by a creator. Things can be created without intent by a designer. Many of the mountain ranges we find on Earth were created by tectonic plates. An apple falls to the ground because gravity is pulling on it. In these cases, the "how" and "why" are often the same because we don't feel the need to personalize those explanations. Science deals with the "how" because it is the only area that can be feasibly studied. Religious people feel the need to personalize the events that brought us into existence, thus the explanation for "why" has to be different than the one for "how." Why are there mountains? We could give a geological answer as to how mountains are created, but that's not what religious people want to know when they ask "why." They want to know the purpose, and the idea that there may not be a purpose for mountains—or even humans—is abhorrent to them.

I'm no stranger to religion having been raised Catholic. Some of my earliest religious memories from childhood involved the church services where in one moment we're being told how terrible we sinners are and the next moment we're shaking the hands of those around us uttering "Peace be with you." I've been to services where we've been told that we're loved and saved, but 5 minutes later we're reminded about the risk of eternal damnation. I've stood. I've knelt. I've prayed. I've read. I've sang. My friends and family will confirm that I do not have a particularly good singing voice; however that didn't stop me from attending service each week and singing in the choir at Fort Jackson during my Army Basic and AIT (Advanced Individual Training) days. As a child, I wasn't presented with religious options. There was no religious buffet where I could sample the various flavors with the final choice left up to me. My religion was chosen for me. We didn't have any Jews, Muslims, or Hindus living among us, so it would be many years later before I even knew that there were alternatives to my god. As an adult, I started to question some of the "facts" about my chosen religion. A large number of those "facts" seemed out of touch with reality and the more I began questioning religious assertions, the more I realized just how delicate of a balance this house of cards was built upon. The cards really began to crumble the day we were told that 19 pious Muslims hijacked airplanes on September 11, 2001, and used them as missiles to show our pious nation the value of religious certainty. The news stories about that day brought religious fanaticism into our living rooms in a way that past events had not and this spurred my interest in learning more about the Muslim faith. Had this happened a decade earlier, my ability to find a wide range of opposing viewpoints about Islam would have been negligible.

The world is a very different place than it was even a few decades ago. Just as the printing press proved extremely beneficial to the Protestant Reformation, we too have an even more powerful medium to share information. The rise of the Internet makes information sharing ubiquitous. The only items required to research anything today are a computer and an Internet connection. Compare this situation to when many of us grew up. If we wanted to know more about any topic, it usually involved a trip to the library where we were limited to what the library physically had. For those of us who had experience with the Dewey Decimal System, it's readily apparent that no library today could ever possibly hold the breadth and depth of information that exists on the Internet. The barrier to the world's information has been forever lowered. Anything that we want to know can now be retrieved in a fraction of a second. This open access to the collective knowledge of the world has forever altered our view of the world. The news of the world is literally at our fingertips as is its history. I can research the tenets of Islam just as easily as I can research the tenets of Christianity. The world's religions are also just a click away and this allows people of all faiths to share information, debate, and discuss their differences. Unlike my situation as a child, the barrier to exposure from other faiths has been lowered as well. In this age of information, ignorance truly becomes a choice and not an excuse.

This fundamental change in how we share information is a threat to the information gatekeepers of old. Not unlike the trial of Galileo Galilei, who disputed the Aristotelian view of the universe during the 1600s in favor of Copernican astronomy, religion has had to continually cede ground that was once its sole domain. That pace of yielding ground continues to intensify, and many religious leaders openly say that there's very little room left to give. What they fail to understand is that progress will not be stopped. The truth will always find a way to break through. Consider Cardinal Robert Bellarmine, one of the most respected Catholic theologians of his time, who urged caution on adoption of heliocentrism. He was appalled at the very notion that our sun was the true center of our solar system and that our planet revolved around it. He wrote to Paolo Foscarini, who publicly supported Galileo's theory that the earth was not the center of the universe, and said:[1]

> But to want to affirm that the sun really is fixed in the center of the heavens and only revolves around itself (i.e., turns upon its axis) without traveling from east to west, and that the earth is situated in the third sphere and re-

1 http://www.fordham.edu/halsall/mod/1615bellarmine-letter.asp Retrieved 7/7/2012

volves with great speed around the sun, is a very dangerous thing, not only by irritating all the philosophers and scholastic theologians, but also by injuring our holy faith and rendering the Holy Scriptures false.

And if Your Reverence would read not only the Fathers but also the commentaries of modern writers on Genesis, Psalms, Ecclesiastes and Josue, you would find that all agree in explaining literally (ad litteram) that the sun is in the heavens and moves swiftly around the earth, and that the earth is far from the heavens and stands immobile in the center of the universe... It would be just as heretical to deny that Abraham had two sons and Jacob twelve, as it would be to deny the virgin birth of Christ...But with regard to the sun and the earth, no wise man is needed to correct the error, since he clearly experiences that the earth stands still and that his eye is not deceived when it judges that the moon and stars move.

Let's not forget that most religious men at this time truly believed that the Earth was the center of the universe. To be fair, this view was consistent with general observations at the time as well as in line with what the Bible asserted; however, Cardinal Bellarmine felt that any concession would render "the Holy Scriptures false." He pleaded with Foscarini to reconsider a cosmology that was Biblically supported. He proclaimed this with great conviction fueled by a confidence instilled into him by the seemingly undeniable authoritativeness of the Bible. If the Bible indicates that the Earth is immovable (Psalms 92, 95, and 103), then any suggestion to the contrary is as unbelievable and incorrect as denying the virgin birth of Christ. To Bellarmine, and indeed the overwhelming majority of the Church's leadership, the mere thought that the Bible would be incorrect was tantamount to heresy and Galileo was thus labeled a heretic. If God could command the sun and moon to stand still in the sky for 24 hours (Joshua 10:12-13), the Earth simply had to be the center of the universe. This is one of many examples in which science has disproved long-held religious beliefs. It would take 200 years before the Church finally treated a heliocentric view of our world as physical fact[1]. It would take more than 350 years after Galileo's trial for the Church to finally vindicate Galileo[2] and it wasn't until the year 2000 that the Church would formally apologize for their mistakes. While it may take centuries, scientific truths eventually win out. When they do, it makes believing in religious assertions about our world that much harder.

A recent and extensive survey conducted by the Pew Forum on Religion and Public Life[3] shows that 16% of Americans now claim no affiliation with any particular faith. Among adults ages 18–29, that number increases to 1 in every 4 who do not affiliate with any specific religion. It's important to note that the 16% is more than double the number of people who did not have a religious affiliation as a child. This is a trend that will likely continue. These

---

1 Heilbron (2005, pp.279, 312–313)

2 Daniel N. Robinson citing John Paul II in *Human nature in its wholeness: a Roman Catholic perspective,* edited by D. N. Robinson, G. M. Sweeney and R. Gill, Front Cover

3 http://religions.pewforum.org/pdf/report-religious-landscape-study-full.pdf   Retrieved 3/15/2012

folks do not want the dogma of organized religion. The values espoused by religion are often in direct conflict with the values of subsequent generations. Religion emphasizes conformity while younger generations tend to value individuality. Religion values tradition and superstition while younger generations tend to value creativity and reasoning. Religion values exclusivity and authority while younger generations tend to value diversity and personal freedom. Combined with the now ubiquitous nature and availability of information, it shouldn't come as a surprise to see nearly 25% of adults under the age of 30 rejecting the dogma of organized religion. On a global basis, Pew has identified those with no religious affiliation (including atheists and agnostics) as the 3rd largest "religious group" after Christians and Muslims. The stigma of unbelief is quickly losing its potency.

When I discuss organized religion, it will quickly become evident (if it hasn't already) that I don't place religion on an untouchable pedestal like the faithful do. To question its legitimacy on the truth is something that I wish more people did. I think we've made great progress historically. At various points throughout history, it would have been unthinkable to question religion. A book like the one you're holding would have meant a death sentence for both you and me, and in some parts of the world it still does. The church has had an arrogant monopoly on the "truth" for centuries, often with disastrous consequences. Every religion has a holy book that is considered infallible and inerrant. Religious people consider it a virtue that their holy book doesn't change. I think that's naive, detrimental, and, by the purest definition of the word: stupid. Perhaps this is a defining characteristic between the religious and nonreligious. To a religious person, the original story is all that's needed. Conversely, if I believe something, but I'm presented with new facts, I retain the right to change my mind based upon new evidence. We can illustrate this point by looking at the Native American ritual of rain-making. This ceremonial dance was intended to bring out rain to places that needed it. There is nothing to suggest that dancing in particular fashions while chanting and wearing large, ornate headdresses will cause rain clouds to appear any faster than not dancing at all. That doesn't mean that people didn't believe in it though. Through time and research, we now know how to more reliably cultivate crops under those types of conditions and it can be done without a shaman. We changed our minds based upon new evidence and rainmaking is now a more ceremonial ritual with no real expectations for an outcome. Being open to changing our beliefs because new evidence warrants such a change is a virtue that gets lost in the religious discussion. I would challenge anyone to name me any other area of human discourse where we actively deny incremental improvements in favor of keeping the status quo. For example, if we treated medicine like we do religion, we'd still be employing bloodletting, amulets, and animal dung.

Faith allows a religious person's standard of proof to be exceptionally low. In the previous rain dancing example, proof of its effectiveness would be shown the next time it rained—regardless of whether it was a day, a week, or a month later. The proof is arbitrary which begs the question what kind of all-powerful deity is incapable of producing direct, verifiable evidence of its existence or influence? What kind of god would instead force us to try and interpret normal events to ascertain "clues" or "proof" of divine intervention? In the event that we can't read the tea leaves or we find evidence to the contrary, we are told that we must simply believe the original proposition or risk eternal damnation. In this risk/reward scenario, religion is fundamentally no different than our holiday tradition of telling young children that they won't receive any gifts if they don't believe in Santa Claus. The difference here is that children eventually grow out of Santa Claus.

In every discussion I've ever had with religious people, it can be determined rather quickly that I do not possess the "correct" understanding of the Bible or the Qur'an. As is the case every time, I'm fortunate enough that the person I'm speaking with usually does possess that critical ability to render the *correct* interpretation even though the correct interpretation can and does vary by believer. For example, some folks choose to interpret the Genesis story of creation literally while others will say that it wasn't ever meant to be taken in that fashion. If I read the Bible as it is written, the creation story reads like a literal telling of how the universe, our planet, and life itself began. Because of the knowledge that we have gained over the past millennia, this account would be much more plausible in the year 200 than in the year 2000. When the plausibility of a literal interpretation finally fades into absurdity, we are told that these stories were actually meant to be parables or metaphors. Let's try and put some of this into perspective. How believable would the story of Jesus be if it occurred in a 21st-century United States instead of a 1st-century Roman Empire? How believable would the story of Muhammad be if it occurred today instead of the 7th century? What kind of evidence do you think our society would require today to warrant belief in these stories? What rational person would believe that a man put to death three days ago was able to rise from the grave this morning while the graves in the city opened and the dead freely walked about town? If a man reported that he flew to heaven on a Buraq (a winged horse), what kind of evidence would you ask for? Try and imagine these kinds of stories being reported on CNN and what kind of reaction they might provoke. How serious would we take these stories if the CNN reporter asked for evidence and the eyewitnesses responded that instead of evidence, we should simply take them on their word? It's as if we're saying that the stories from the Bible or the Qur'an are somehow more credible because they occurred in pre-scientific times.

The sad fact is that while I think a scientifically-literate society would question some of these assertions, the truth is that not everyone in our society today is scientifically-literate or apt to think critically. We have far too many "Honey Boo Boos" among us. I would like to say that few if any would actually believe those stories today, but the reality is that there will always be those who are gullible enough to do so. I make that claim using the South Indian guru Sathya Sai Baba as evidence of mankind's ability to believe in almost anything. In similar fashion to Jesus Christ, Sai Baba was allegedly born of a virgin and performed many miracles throughout his life. He sang in Sanskrit (a language he apparently knew nothing of) after being stung by a scorpion. He made Prasad and flowers magically appear for various family members, which prompted his father to think his son was possessed. Sai Baba performed many miracles in front of many eyewitnesses, some of whom claim him to be a living god. His picture graces millions of homes and his ashrams (religious retreats) once dotted nearly 126 countries, yet few people in the United States or the rest of the world have ever heard of him. Does the simple fact that his followers made claims about miraculous healings, appearances in multiple locations at the same time, and the conduction of other acts of omnipotence, make any of those claims true? If we are to take the claims of early Christians, Muslims, and Jews as true, using faith as our litmus test, who are we to say that the claims of Sai Baba's eyewitnesses are false? Who are we to say that someone in the 20th century is more or less apt to attribute sleight of hand or simple conjuring tricks to divine actions any more than someone from the first century? If any of Sai Baba's claims were real, how many scientific laws would they violate? If any of Jesus' or Muhammad's claims were real, how many scientific laws do you think those would violate? I'm reminded of Arthur C. Clarke's Third Law which says that any sufficiently advanced technology is indistinguishable from magic. David Copperfield and Lance Burton would have been gods if they had been born in the first century. When someone gives legitimacy to a miracle, regardless of whether it was conducted by Sai Baba, Jesus, or Muhammad, they are essentially saying that these people were able to violate the laws of physics. If we were to look up at the sky tonight and the stars suddenly arranged themselves into English words, that event would be a miracle. It would be a suspension of the laws of physics. That would be an unbiased phenomenon that we could document and study. To date, no documented experience has ever violated the laws of physics therefore there is no reason to believe in any of those "miracles." It is not only permissible to question any assertions of miracles, it is imperative that we do.

During the course of writing this book, I have been plagued with recurring thoughts about the kind of reception that it might receive, particularly among Christians. To some, the Bible is the literal word of God and to challenge this would be considered obscene. I have personally been "advised" by several people to get a bodyguard because I choose to challenge religious assertions—and this is from people I know and trust! I would think that unfathomable, yet we see this type of response frequently whenever the Establishment Clause is challenged. Lisa Herdahl received death threats for challenging prayer in her children's school. Tyler Deveny, an eighteen-year-old student, was beaten by eight other students when he challenged the legality of the invocation at his high school's graduation ceremony. When Vashti McCollum challenged the practice of allowing public school students to attend religious classes held in the public school, her house was vandalized and her sons were assaulted. High school student Jessica Ahlquist was so bullied and threatened for objecting to a "School Prayer" banner posted in the auditorium that she required police escorts to and from class. When

Joann Bell and Lucille McCord asked the courts to prohibit the distribution of Gideon Bibles in their children's school, harassment quickly followed. "More than once a caller said he was going to break in the house, tie up the children, rape their mother in front of them, and then 'bring her to Jesus'."[1] This harassment escalated all the way to Joann's house being burned to the ground. Against this backdrop, I find the stench of hypocrisy overwhelming when a Christian, a believer in a "faith of peace," suggests that bodily harm may come to me for my contrarian views. If faith can move mountains, certainly it should be able to withstand a little criticism.

I take solace in the fact that I am part of a growing trend as more people value rationality over superstition. Additional solace can be found in the fact that the vast majority of the religiously faithful blatantly ignore the parts of the Bible that they don't agree with. To them, the Bible is treated no differently than a modern-day software license. Nobody ever reads the whole thing, but that doesn't prevent us from scrolling to the bottom and clicking "I Agree." I'm confident that most of the people who would find my questioning of Christianity obscene would never consider forcing a girl who was raped to marry her attacker, stoning someone to death for breaking the Sabbath, or condoning slavery even though the very Bible I'm questioning clearly makes provisions for these actions. They tend to discard "those parts of the Bible," but at the same time, they will cherry pick the part of the Bible that calls homosexuality an abomination because they don't approve of the gay and lesbian lifestyle. Either the Bible is the infallible word of God or it isn't. If it is, shouldn't the whole thing be followed? It certainly was at one point in Christian history, and it is still followed to the letter by fundamentalists today.

"Fundamentalist" is an interesting word. Have you ever tried to determine what characteristics cause us to label someone a "fundamentalist" or an "extremist"? What characteristics cause us to label someone a "moderate" Christian or a "moderate" Muslim? By all accounts, the difference in the labels is directly proportional to the amount of the holy book that gets willfully ignored. The more of the book someone ignores, the more moderate they become. The religion is still the same however. This is what I would like religious believers to understand. A certain amount of hypocrisy exists when it comes to religion in modern society. Someone might find it virtuous to say "Yes, Lord. I will do whatever you want" in one breath, but never ask themselves in the next breath if they would be willing to sacrifice their child as Abraham was willing to do. I have spent a great deal of time witnessing the differences between what a Christian says versus what a Christian will actually do and reconciling that to what the Bible says. I devote an entire chapter of this book to that hypocrisy.

I devote several chapters to demonstrating and systematically debunking the myths about religion that have been perpetuated for millennia using nothing more than the power of common, real-life examples. We have been led to believe that faith is an essential component to our continued exis-

---

1 *Freethought Today.* Freedom From Religion Foundation. Vol 30 No 2. pp 12

tence. Without it, we would be helpless in determining right from wrong. Our moral compass would somehow be lost without faith in a higher being. Every preacher since the dawn of time has ingrained into us the belief that there are so many positive things to be derived from religion that cannot be obtained or fulfilled elsewhere. I will demonstrate how these claims are simply fallacious and casuistic. We have also been led to believe that the terrible things done in the name of religion are actually due to the fallibility of human beings and not the result of religious belief. The ultimate in credulity arrives when we're told that religion is not only inculpable but is actually the only antidote! Religion has been very creative in dismissing the criticism leveled against it. This is a smoke screen that desperately needs to be cleared.

Historically speaking, science and time have killed more gods than any single book could ever do. I'm under no illusion that this book will change every reader's mind, as that is a lot to expect. My goal is simply to apply religious assertions, beliefs, and actions to modern day examples and allow you, the reader, to ascertain whether or not the religious positions hold up. Whether you are a religious moderate, fundamentalist, or non-believer, your end of the bargain is simple. If you don't like my opinions or conclusions, it is my sincere hope that you dislike them because I have omitted glaring and overwhelmingly incontrovertible facts, not simply because you don't like the opinion stated, the conclusion drawn, or the question asked in the first place. I seek the truth—the ultimate truth—and rarely does that materialize without asking tough questions. As a former believer, I asked tough questions and have devoted years to searching for those answers. While the simple fact is that there exists so much information on the topic of religion that it is nearly impossible to have read or absorbed everything on every facet, it is my intention to lay my cards on the table and let the chips fall where they may. Please do not misinterpret any of my comments as personally insulting. Other than the pseudoscientists, none of my comments are meant to be taken in an offensive manner. If you believe in talking snakes, I may question (sarcastically, at times) your belief, but there is no malicious intent to disparage you personally. Many of my family and friends are religious and they are some of the most genuine, kind, and caring people I know. But most of those who are "born again" were just as genuine, kind, and caring before they found Jesus. It's inevitable that someone will be offended by what I've written. This is the risk that I'm taking, but hopefully by the time they reach the end of the book, they'll understand why.

God doesn't do. It means that God deemed something mundane and frivo-lous more important than saving any of the nine million children under the age of five who will die this year from preventable causes. If we are to believe that God intervenes in our daily lives, we must then believe that God has weighed the merits of someone asking for help for any arbitrary thing against the well-being of a child and a grieving parent beseeching Heaven for food or clean water—and God finding the starving child unworthy of interven-tion. There is nothing humble about this. In fact, this kind of thinking is the ultimate in narcissism. As I stated, the Divine Default is an excuse of convenience and ignorance and perhaps no other example makes this more perfectly clear.

When a woman named Marie took her children to see the July 20, 2012, midnight showing of the movie "The Dark Knight Rises" at a theater in Col-orado, she could not have envisioned the evil that was to befall them that evening. A very sick individual named James Holmes opened fire in the the-ater, killing 12 people and injuring 58 others. When the shooting started, she threw herself over her 14-year-old and began praying. When the shooting subsided, she and her children dashed out of the theater past a lifeless body until they safely reached their car. According to Marie, she and her children felt the presence of God more closely at that time than at any other. Pierce O'Farrill also survived the shooting that night; however, unlike Marie and her children, he was shot twice in his left foot and once in his upper arm. As he lay on the ground, his head was mere inches away from the gunman's boot. Pierce would later say, "There is no doubt in my mind that God saved me. I believe that He saved me out of that theater so that I can just show the world that there is light." For Marie, Pierce, or any other survivor, what possible explanation could exist for attributing anything positive about the experience to God? Like many who survived Hurricane Katrina in 2005, the devastation wrought didn't soften their belief in God—it actually strength-ened it! When Pierce invokes the Divine Default to explain God's desire for him to "show the world that there is light," the corollary to this line of think-ing is that he is callously implying that God either didn't find the twelve who died worthy of the same mission or that the twelve had to die so that Pierce would have purpose. The invoking of the Divine Default is religious egotism masquerading as humility.

As Bertrand Russell once said, "Where there is evidence, no one speaks of 'faith'. We do not speak of faith that two and two are four or that the earth is round. We only speak of faith when we wish to substitute emotion for evidence." That becomes quite apparent when we hear the story about a woman who was 12 weeks pregnant when she discovered through ultra-sound that her son had a lower urinary tract obstruction that would prevent the baby from processing amniotic fluid, and thus he would be unlikely to develop properly. The outlook for the baby was dire and ranged from dying in the womb to being born with organ damage. She claimed that in light of the diagnosis, the doctors immediately urged her to end the pregnancy. She decided to pray instead and even enlisted the help of others to pray for the baby. When she finally delivered the baby via Caesarean, a specialized team of doctors was standing by ready to whisk him into emergency surgery. They were astounded to learn that the tiny baby's organs were working perfectly. This, according to the woman, was evidence that God not only exists but that He responded to their prayers and personally intervened on her behalf. This, as so often is the case in medical situations, is a great example of the Divine Default. She drew a theological conclusion where one could not have been conclusively drawn. By doing this, she ignores the vital role that her own body plays or any of a thousand other reasons as to why the baby survived, including any chance of misdiagnosis by the doctors. There is no quantifiable proof for the direct intervention by God, and by invoking the Divine Default she is obscenely implying that God deemed her and her child so worthy as to require divine intervention while any family in the same situation experiencing the opposite result was just unworthy of saving.

When God intervenes, the intervention seems to always be conducted on an intimate level. I once read the story about a young man named Matthew Needham who felt such personal desperation that he took his father's gun out of the cupboard in his room, went to a spot where he had privacy, and put the gun to his head with the intention of ending his life. When he went to pull the trigger, nothing happened. It turns out that the gun had a safety on it and Matthew didn't think to turn it off. The experience convinced him that God has created each of us for a special purpose and that it is up to us to find that special calling. On what logical basis could he arrive at that conclusion? When he invokes the Divine Default, he is essentially saying that his lack of firearm knowledge translated to proof not only of the existence of a Supreme Being but also of a direct intervention conducted on his behalf by this Supreme Being. If we are to give this attribution any degree of legitimacy, we have to then believe the corollary that God didn't feel it necessary to intervene on behalf of the 38,000+ people who will sadly take their own lives this year in the United States. Are we to believe that Matthew is so important to the functioning of our universe that God would personally come down from the heavens, make sure that the gun's safety was engaged, and save this man's life? The hubris here should be both appalling and obvious.

Oftentimes the invocation of the Divine Default combines both a personal component with the God of the Gaps. For example, if you could rewind time to the Fifth Dynasty and visit ancient Egypt, you would find that society worshiping the sun god Ra. The sun was a phenomenon that was unexplainable to the populace at that point in human history, and without a viable explanation, they concluded that it must be divine. The people created Ra to help them understand this bright, hot object clearly visible in the sky. By the fourth dynasty of ancient Egypt, the pharaohs were often regarded as manifestations of Ra in human form—not unlike the future concept of Jesus as the manifestation of God himself. This gave pharaohs unarguable power because what peasant would dare challenge the gods? Ra provided light and warmth—things that could be seen and felt by every Egyptian. Ra cared for man. Today we would laugh at the idea of attributing both human and divine characteristics to a massive sphere of hot gases, but that doesn't negate the fact that ancient Egyptians "knew" it to be true in much the same way that people today "know" God to be true.

Consider for a moment what would happen if you could travel back in time to ancient Egypt with the knowledge that you have today. Regardless of your religious affiliation, imagine trying to explain to the high priests that Ra was not an actual god. Imagine trying to use logic and reasoning to explain the true source of their "god." Besides being labeled blasphemous, the odds are slim that you would survive such an encounter. The rulers and religious leaders would have considered you mad and perhaps opted to incarcerate you...or worse. There is little reason to believe that anyone would have taken you seriously regardless of the logic that you were applying to the situation. This should tell us something about human nature. As a species, we are naturally adept in applying both confirmation bias to evidence and arguments that strengthen our beliefs and disconfirmation bias to evidence that contradicts those beliefs. It is an easily reproducible paradox that human beings, when presented with contradictory evidence, will often cling more tightly to their beliefs. It takes effort to overcome this.

Moving on from ancient Egypt, we can look through the pages of history at some of the most brilliant scientists that have ever walked the Earth and find them invoking the Divine Default once they reached the limits of their knowledge. If we read *Almagest* from the Greek mathematician and astronomer Claudius Ptolemy, we find one of the better early attempts at using geometry to help explain the movements of the sun, moon, and planets. Ptolemy's geometrical models of the heavens were laid out in a convenient format for determining what the position of planets would have been in the past along with where we could expect to find them in the future. He is often credited with coining the term "epicycle" which was used to describe the circular paths that these heavenly objects took in space. Once Ptolemy reached the limits of his knowledge, however, he invoked the Divine Default and we see this with comments he wrote in the margins of Almagest:

> I know that I am mortal by nature, and ephemeral; but when I trace at my pleasure the windings to and fro of the heavenly bodies I no longer touch earth with my feet: I stand in the presence of Zeus himself and take my fill of ambrosia, food of the gods.

Ptolemy really cemented the view that the Earth was the center of the divine universe. This Earth-centered model was consistent with the Genesis account of Earth being created before the sun and this view would remain cemented for at least the next 1,500 years. This view would slowly begin to change when Nicolaus Copernicus published his *On the Revolutions of the Celestial Spheres*, and it would forever be altered with the discoveries of Galileo Galilei. The invention of the telescope, for example, showed us that a divinely created universe of heavenly bodies was not as perfect as many believed. The moon was not blemish-free, the sun had spots that moved across it, and not all motions and rotations in the heavens were as perfectly envisioned.

Johannes Kepler came along and established the three scientific laws (now referred to as Kepler's laws of planetary motion) describing these motions in mathematical terms. Even though Kepler was a religious man, he didn't need to insert God into areas that he could explain because...he could explain them. While others at the time were convinced that a perfect creator of the universe would put the heavens in perfect circular orbits, Kepler infused astronomy with physics and showed the contradictory elliptical nature of the orbits. The mere hypothesis that orbits weren't perfect circles was disturbing to many. Sir Isaac Newton, perhaps the most brilliant scientist ever, built upon these advancements, including creating the first practical reflecting telescope. He also put the geocentric/heliocentric debate to rest for scientists. Newton was a deeply religious man but he didn't need to invoke Ptolemy's Divine Default, because he picked up where others had left off and figured it out. When he could finally answer questions for which "God" was the only answer earlier, God was no longer needed and the Divine Default fell to the wayside. Once the gap in our knowledge was filled with the truth, God was no longer deemed necessary for that explanation.

While Newton advanced science tremendously, he couldn't explain everything. For example, his universal gravitation law helped explain how gravity affected the sun and planets but it didn't quite hold up when additional planets were involved. Once the equation became too complex, the stability of the orbits could no longer be maintained and Newton feared that the planets could eventually crash into each other or be spun out into space. Once he reached the limits of his knowledge, we find him invoking the Divine Default by placing God as the force keeping everything in balance. He needed an explanation, and only when he was unable to produce a valid explanation was the Divine Default invoked. We can follow this to the French mathematician Pierre Simon de Laplace who built upon that knowledge to produce a mathematical approach to complex gravitational issues with celestial bodies. Once he did this, Newton's God explanation was no longer needed. By now, I hope you're starting to see a pattern here. We've seen this type of pattern occur throughout history and the single biggest lesson we should learn from this is to stop one another from rushing to apply the label of God to something we simply don't yet understand. A lack of knowledge does not warrant divine attribution.

Fast forward to modern day and we find ourselves in a similar situation. While we no longer worship Ra, 18% of Americans still believe that the sun revolves around the Earth. Our political leaders still ignore scientific discovery in favor of more divine answers. A Gallup poll in 2010 showed that 78% of Americans doubted evolution. The vast majority of these people can't adequately explain the principles that comprise Charles Darwin's Theory of Evolution, but that doesn't necessarily factor into their thinking when it comes to determining whether or not it's true. I could retire if I had a dollar for every time I've heard someone ask "if we came from monkeys, why are there still monkeys?" This misconception is often used as some form of justification to dismiss evolution. My sarcastic side has always been tempted to ask "If we came from dirt, why is there still dirt?" It has always struck me as odd that people will readily believe in talking snakes, the walking dead, and transubstantiation but have difficulty believing that man and ape are evolutionary cousins who share a common ancestral link.

Perhaps this disconnect in logical reasoning is due to the fact that the human brain has a difficult time with the concept of probability. Picture this scenario: a single mother of modest financial means spends money each week playing the lottery. The holidays are approaching and she is having a difficult time juggling the mortgage, utilities, medical bills, and Christmas shopping for three children. When things look most bleak, she breaks down crying and prays to God for help. Can you envision this person? Now imagine that the next week she wins the lottery and in an instant becomes entitled to $25 million. All of her financial worries have vanished. One would be hard pressed to find someone more deserving of that money. Inevitably, people, upon hearing the story, will find a way to attribute this to God. God *must have* answered her prayers.

What if the woman in that scenario did not win the lottery, as she hadn't won for all of those previous years? What if three wealthy gentlemen pitched in one dollar on a lark and won the lottery as Greg Skidmore, Brandon Lacoff and Tim Davidson did when they won the $254.2 million Connecticut Lottery in 2011? What conclusion would you draw then? Would God forsake this struggling single mother or the hundreds of thousands just like her in favor of someone more "deserving"? What could the struggling woman have done better?

The human brain has difficulty with the concept of probabilities. For many, it's much easier to invoke the Divine Default as the reason when probabilities become too much for us to understand. Keep in mind that a 1 in a million chance is not so staggering if there are a million chances. In a lottery system where six numbers are drawn from a range of 49, the odds of getting the drawn numbers are 1 in 13,983,816. Given enough time and chances, someone will eventually win. Sometimes people win more than once. For example, in early 2013 Stephen and Terri Weaver of Stuttgart, Arkansas, won a $1 million jackpot and a $50,000 jackpot in the same weekend! The odds of winning two large jackpots only days apart by the same people are astronomical, but it can happen and there is a lesson here. At no point in our history has anyone ever been able to prove that God circumvents the mathematics to favor someone deemed "deserving," but yet it's permissible in our society to attribute the act to God. God *must have* answered their prayers.

People will naturally use motivated reasoning to come to the conclusion that they want. If the woman deserved the money and prayed for it, surely it had to be divine intervention. If she doesn't win, it must be God's will that she didn't win, because as every good Christian knows—God has a plan for each and every one of us. People will find a reason that fits their mind's predisposed outcome. They will often make the facts fit the situation that they want and ignore the ones that don't support their conclusion.

Here's another great example of people making things fit their predisposed outcome. A survey conducted by the Public Religion Research Institute showed than nearly 3 out of every 10 Americans believes that God "plays a role in determining which team wins a sporting event."[1] More than half of Americans believe that God rewards athletes who have faith with success and good health. There is nothing to suggest that the creator of the universe cares or intervenes in a sporting contest, but that doesn't prevent the majority of Americans from giving into this type of gullibility. We saw this extensively with Tim Tebow—the new favorite NFL player for Christians worldwide. He lives a life devoted to Jesus and makes it a point to express his faith frequently in public. During the 2011 football season, Tebow made a name for himself with a number of impressive 4th-quarter comebacks. The most impressive, however, came on January 8, 2012, in the AFC wildcard playoff game against the Pittsburgh Steelers. On the first play of overtime, Tebow threw an 80-yard touchdown to give the Broncos the win. Tebow was not known for his passing abilities (this was his first 300+ yard game), but with that score, he managed to throw for 316 yards. The comparisons started immediately because Tebow famously wore 3:16 (in reference to John 3:16) in the black under his eyes when he led the Florida Gators to victory in 2009. Even more, he averaged 31.6 yards per pass, the TV rating from CBS peaked at 31.6 between 8:00 and 8:15 pm ET, and Pittsburgh's time of possession was 31 minutes and 6 seconds. Surely this must mean that Jesus blessed Tim Tebow, right? How could the numbers lie?

If someone was already a believer, they probably support the theory that God's intervention helped lead Tebow and the Broncos to victory. Perhaps others put their faith into the notion that God has more important things to do. Regardless of what camp you belong to, enough people gave in to the application of numerology that it was a hotly debated talking point for that following week. Why didn't anyone pay attention to Tebow's rushing stats? After all, he's much better known for his ability to scramble for rushing yards than he is for his ability to throw. He rushed 10 times for 50 yards in that game for an average of 5 yards per carry—stats that are not only fantastic for any quarterback but desirable for any running back. His completion percentage was 47.6%. The time of possession for his team, the Broncos, was 29 minutes and 5 seconds. Why would his opponent's time of possession be more important? If you don't cherry pick the 8:00–8:15 portion of the CBS ratings, the game itself had a TV rating of 25.9. The point is that the people who want to believe that Jesus had a part in the game, or that the outcome was divinely inspired, will find the facts that fit the conclusion that they want while ignoring the facts that do not.

Humans are pattern-seeking mammals. We want to have explanations, and in the absence of a legitimate explanation, we will find anything that satisfies this primal desire. This concept is not even debatable. We have thousands of historical examples verifying this basic human tendency. Be-

---

1 "Nearly 3 in 10 Americans Say God Plays a Role in Outcomes of Sports Events". *Public Religion Research Institute*. January 29, 2013.

fore we knew anything about tectonic plates, we attributed volcanic erup-
tions to the actions of gods and demigods. Each of the major outbreaks of
plague was attributed to God as punishment for the sins of man. Before we
knew anything about bacteria, many thousands of people believed that God
could rescind illness and disease if man repented and reformed. Before we
had acquired knowledge of meteorology, many historical accounts of localized flooding have been attributed to God as castigation for mans' wicked
ways. In every one of these cases, humans needed an explanation, and lack-
ing a legitimate one, we assigned supernatural causes. Religion is therefore a
natural product of this process.

When we try to figure out our place and purpose in the world, the Divine
Default is often the easiest way for us to do this. It's much easier to assign
the world and everything we see to an invisible force that cannot be proven
and yet cannot be unproven. Religion acts as a mental shortcut. The human
brain is a master at making these mental shortcuts. These shortcuts, called
heuristics, allow us to hit a fastball, drive a car, choose what to eat, and create impressions based upon limited information. This isn't necessarily a bad
thing. It allows the human mind to cope with an overwhelmingly complex
environment. Most of the time, these mental shortcuts work out quite well.
However, when it comes to reasoning about complex systems, these shortcuts go from being efficiently effective to downright misleading.

To demonstrate this I'm going to ask you two questions. I'd like you to
answer them as quickly as you can. Answer the first question before moving
on to the second one.

1. How many fingers does the typical man have on his hands?

2. How many on ten hands?

Good! Simple questions, right? If you are like most people, you answered
ten and one hundred. Your first answer would be absolutely correct; however your second answer would be wrong. Your mind took a mental shortcut
called conditioning by association. One man has ten fingers on his hands.
The typical hand (singular) has five fingers on each and when that is multi-
plied by ten hands, you have fifty fingers, not one hundred.

Here's another example. Please answer it quickly.

If a bat and a ball have a total cost $1.10 and the bat costs $1.00 more than
the ball, how much does the ball cost?

Most people would say that the bat costs $1.00 and the ball costs 10
cents. The mental shortcut that our mind takes allows us to quickly arrive
at an answer of 10, yet the real answer is 5 cents. The bat costs $1.05 and the
ball costs $0.05, giving us a total of $1.10 with the bat being $1.00 more than
the ball.

In 1974 researchers gathered 45 people to test the reliability of the human memory and whether or not mental shortcuts could alter the facts that
each person believed[1]. The people were all shown the same film of a car acci-

---

1 Loftus and Palmer (1974), *Reconstruction of Automobile Destruction*

dent and then asked questions after watching it. The researchers broke them up into groups of five. The first group was asked to estimate how fast the cars were traveling when they "hit." The second group had the same question posed to them but with the word "smashed" instead of "hit." "Collided," "contacted," and "bumped" were used for the remaining groups. The people in the "smashed" group estimated the cars to be traveling 10 mph faster than those who were given the word "contacted." The participants were asked a week later about the broken glass from the car accident. Those who were given the more violent words recalled seeing broken glass even though no glass was ever broken in the film. This simple experiment demonstrated that a single word has the ability to shortcut our memories. Instead of thinking through the situation, the group was easily manipulated into believing things that did not happen. If a single word one week later could influence what people "saw," try and imagine how this principle might impact the stories of Jesus or Moses which were initially spoken verbally and handed down over the course of many years by non-eye witnesses before finally being written down.

We still use mental shortcuts today, and we even do it on a large-scale basis. Consider the political environment that we find ourselves in. Mental shortcuts often lead to a polarization of our beliefs. It's easier to label someone a conservative, a liberal, a Republican, or a Democrat when most people, if they spent the time to actually understand all of the nuances for a given issue, would most likely not be on the extreme. It's simply easier for us in terms of both time and mental resources to take a stance based upon minimal knowledge. Using federal regulations on businesses as a stereotypical example, conservatives generally espouse a hands-off approach while liberals espouse a more regulated approach. Neither side readily accepts the fact that a completely hands-off approach will lead to monopolies while over-regulation leads to a significant decrease in competiveness and innovation. Once we get past the political rhetoric, we find that the mental shortcuts that we've taken haven't given us the outcome that we want or need.

I respectfully ask you to keep this concept in mind as you explore the chapters of this book that deal with Noah and his famous Ark, Jonah's fish tale, and the Genesis account of Cain's wife. As we go through the stories, try not to allow yourself to take mental shortcuts. Try to take the time to reason not only through each part of these stories, but also for any other story in the Bible. Only by removing the mental shortcuts and applying reason and knowledge can we ever hope to gain a better understanding of that elusive concept of truth.

CHAPTER 3. THE BURDEN OF PROOF

"What can be asserted without proof can just as easily be dismissed without proof."—Christopher Hitchens

Before we get into more specific areas of religion, it's important that we establish a foundation for moving forward. If you were charged with a crime, the prosecution has the responsibility to prove that you did what they claim you did. The prosecution carries the burden of proof, not you. In a court of law, the Latin phrase *"semper necessitas probandi incumbit ei qui agit,"* which means "the necessity of proof always lies with the person who lays charges." This is of paramount importance to our judicial system. The defense car-ries the benefit of assumption, meaning that the accused bears no burden of proof. Ironically enough, the benefit of assumption, used as a legal instru-ment, was first created by Jean Lemoine, a French cardinal, bishop of Arras and papal legate.

Whether you subscribe to the well-known legal version of the burden of proof or the philosophic burden of proof, the end result is the same. The responsibility for providing evidence to support something as true is owned by the person making the claim[1]. If Christians are presenting the Bible as true, Christians bear the responsibility of presenting sufficient evidence to back up their claim. If Muslims present the Qur'an as true, Muslims bear the responsibility of proving it.

If I were to tell a man that rubbing green Jell-O on his bald head will help him regrow hair, he's going to require some evidence and proof before rushing out to the store to purchase large quantities of green Jell-O. If I were

---

1 Michalos, Alex. 1969. *Principles of Logic.* Englewood Cliffs: Prentice-Hall. p 370—"usually one who makes an assertion must assume the responsibility of defending it. If this responsibility or burden of proof is shifted to a critic, the fallacy of appealing to ignorance is committed."

to tell the same man that the book he has in his hands on Sunday was written or inspired by an invisible entity with unimaginable powers and that he should believe everything in the book because of that assertion, he surprisingly requires no further evidence or proof. A comically-inspired example reinforcing this concept comes from the late, great comedian George Carlin. He once said, "Tell people that there's an invisible man in the sky who created the universe, and the vast majority will believe you. Tell them the paint is wet, and they have to touch it to be sure."

I've watched and participated in a number of religious discussions where the person making the case for their chosen religion is unable to adequately respond to contradictions and issues of logical deficiencies. Once they've reached their threshold of frustration, they often participate in a fallacy known as "Shifting the Burden of Proof" by suggesting that I or someone else prove them wrong. If this were the most appropriate way of determining truth, we would all bear the burden to prove that Jesus wasn't the son of God, Muhammad wasn't visited by the archangel Gabriel, and Vishnu, Brahma, Shiva, and Shakti do not exist. This is neither a practical approach nor an intellectually honest one. If you're a Christian, the responsibility to disprove your religion does not belong to the atheist, agnostic, Muslim, Buddhist, or Hindu. The responsibility to prove, or at the very least support, your assertion lies with you.

I'd like to share with you a remarkable and deeply personal story. I only ask that you read the following with an open mind. For the past 6,000 years there has existed a group of watchers who have been the guardians of mankind. They not only intervene in the lives of the humans in their charge but they also provide spiritual guidance in both our current lives and our afterlives. We don't know for sure how they came to be, but we do know that one of these beings is assigned to every human soul that walks this earth. We know this because they personally revealed this to our ancient ancestors and specifically highlighted the fact that we have free will to either accept or reject their guidance. These magnificent beings resemble pink unicorns that stand an impressive seven feet tall. My personal unicorn physically lives in my backyard and I look to him for guidance 24 hours a day. This guidance is dispensed in accordance with the UniBook—a divinely inspired text with instructions on how to live a righteous life. The UniBook clearly tells me that the world was created instantly the moment that the Great Unicorn rubbed his magical horn, willing mankind into existence. The Great Unicorn has commanded us not to make any graven image and it is therefore forbidden to depict the Great Unicorn in any manner. I can't show you a picture of the Great Unicorn, but I need you to have faith that he exists. I choose not to pay attention to those who say they can't see the unicorns because I know that those people are sinners and not true believers. They have rejected this amazing gift from the Great Unicorn. These sinners tell me that unicorns don't exist because science has been unable to measure or prove their existence. These people don't understand that the mere fact that we can't see the unicorns doesn't mean that they don't exist. It certainly doesn't negate the more important fact that I can feel the love and care resulting from the personal relationship that I have with my unicorn. I have seen evidence of my unicorn's influence in my life every day. Even when it feels like the world is about to crash around me, I know that my unicorn loves me unconditionally and that love gives me strength. I am a better person because of my unicorn and I know how to tell the difference between right and wrong because of the Great Unicorn and his divinely-inspired UniBook. I cannot imagine nor would I want to live in a world where unicorns do not exist.

I challenge anyone to prove that the pink unicorn does not exist. Until someone comes forth with evidence of the pink unicorn's non-existence, I demand that you respect my belief—not the right to have the belief but respect for the belief itself. In the meantime, I would like to have tax exempt status for unicorn-worshiping organizations and I would like to have the story of the Great Unicorn taught alongside evolution in our public schools.

You might consider me insane if I truly believed in the pink unicorn and you would have every right to do so. The pink unicorn story uses the same brilliant principle used by philosopher Bertrand Russell in *Russell's Teapot* to demonstrate where the burden of proof lies. If we take any religious claim and substitute the word "God" with "Unicorn," we can not only achieve the same logical result as the initial claim, but we can also demonstrate how arbitrary the supernatural beliefs and metaphysical claims of religion truly are. I would not expect anyone else to prove that the unicorn doesn't exist. If you are a religious person, please understand that this is exactly how your religion and the demands made on behalf of your religion appear to the rest of us. If a religious person could convince me that pink unicorns do not exist, I would gladly accept a successful refutation because it would mean that a model exists to prove the nonexistence of their god as well.

Anyone making a claim that they want others to rationally accept should provide rational support to help draw that conclusion. A conclusion without logical, supporting evidence does not warrant rational belief.

The default position in any argument should be disbelief until credible evidence is presented to support the claim. If someone wants to believe in miracles and claim that they are true, they can't say that miracles exist because nobody has proven that they don't. If someone wants to believe in angels and claim that they are real, they can't say that angels exist because nobody has proven that they don't. If someone wants to believe that God exists and claim that it is true, they can't say that He exists because nobody has proven that He doesn't. To do otherwise gives someone the ability to say with equal authority that leprechauns exist because we can't prove that they don't. Pink unicorns exist because we can't prove that they don't.

Whenever I ask someone why they believe what they do, I frequently get the response "because I do," "I have an inner conviction," or "I just know." Are any of these answers a satisfactory fulfillment of the burden of proof? If I gave the same type of answers when pressed to prove my unicorn's existence, would those types of answers be sufficient to warrant rational belief? A similar line of questioning has been posed to me regarding love. How do I know that my wife loves me? I can't see love, nor can I taste, touch, or hear love. For many Christians, this concept is frequently offered up as analogous proof or validation of their relationship with Jesus. This isn't a fair comparison because the difference lies in the evidence for each position. I believe that my wife loves me because 1) she has verbally told me, 2) she has indicated her feelings to me in written form, and 3) her actions are consistent with the concept of love. Could she have faked any of it? She certainly could have, but the evidence doesn't suggest such a conclusion. To the Christian, Muslim, or Jew, I would ask whether or not the same three criteria can be applied in their situation? Has God ever verbally spoken to them? Has God ever personally written something to them? Has God ever done something directly and specifically for them to demonstrate His love without the person having to read tea leaves to try and interpret the event? The honest answer to each of those questions is no. God does not verbally speak to us. God does not personally send us letters, manuscripts, banners, faxes, emails or any other type of written communication. God does not physically do anything to show us love in a way that can be directly and verifiably attributed to Him in the same manner that we can with a visible loved one.

It's not uncommon to hear people say that they've felt the presence of Jesus. I'm not going to deny that people truly believe this, nor would I ever cast any doubt upon their sincerity. To them, it was most likely a very real event. It was likely just as real to that Christian as it was to the Muslim who made a similar claim. If a Hindu has a religious vision, he/she believes with an equally strong passion that the vision was real. If someone wants to claim that they "just know," then under what authority is it permissible for that same person to discount someone of another faith who "just knows"? One (or both) of them is wrong. "Just knowing" is not sufficient to satisfy the burden of proof. For many years, people "just knew" that the world was flat. At one time, we "just knew" that fairy rings were caused by elves gathering and dancing. For centuries, we "just knew" that lightning and thunder were the work of gods. If someone is a religious believer and intends to tell another person that his/her chosen religion is true, they need to be prepared to do more than just assert their beliefs as true. They need to demonstrate it; support it; prove it.

Finally, I would offer the following suggestion. If a god is not just a spiritual god, but rather a personal god that answers prayers, intervenes, and can have a material impact in our world, I would propose that this can be measured and quantified. If there is a physical change in our world, we can measure that physical change. The chapter of this book that deals with prayer will pose this very question.

Carl Sagan, the famous astronomer and astrophysicist, once said, "Extraordinary claims require extraordinary evidence." Please keep this concept in mind as you not only progress throughout this book, but also as you progress through your daily life. If someone makes an amazing claim like an act of God, it is appropriate to expect amazing evidence in return to support that conclusion. The burden of proof is on them.

Chapter 4. Why is Faith Dangerous?

> "Science flies you to the moon. Religion
> flies you into buildings."—Victor Stenger

The real danger of religion is that it is mass delusion. Consider for a moment that more than 6 billion people right now believe in a god that cannot be physically seen, touched, or heard. Please also consider the very simple fact that the inherent conflicts between the religious claims made on behalf of each faith means that not every religion can be true. If it is impossible for every religion to be true then we can reasonably conclude that many billions of people around the world are praying to...nothing. The moment you realize this, the concept of god for so many people goes from being merely invisible to downright imaginary.

This is when it becomes readily apparent that literally billions of people are praying and carrying on conversations with themselves while believing that an invisible being is listening to them. Because beliefs directly influence actions, these same people are taking actions that they believe are consistent with the desires of an imaginary being. This is by its very definition delusional and it can make people who are normally rational, intelligent individuals believe in certain things that would appear very bizarre to those who don't share the same faith. For example, if you heard someone say, "The worst that a nuclear war could do would be to bring millions of people into paradise earlier than expected," you might be forgiven for attributing it to some kind of religious zealot. Sadly, that was uttered by the Archbishop of Canterbury Michael Ramsey. If you heard someone say, "AIDS is the divine punishment of a just God for improper sexual behavior," you might be forgiven for attributing it to a religious fanatic like Pat Robertson. Unfortunately, that was uttered by the Blessed Mother Teresa of Calcutta. Who else but the religious would look upon a newborn baby and consider it not only appropriate but profoundly imperative to ensure the act of genital mutilation known as circumcision takes place before the eighth day of this newborn's life? Who else but the religious would give serious consideration to murdering someone for imaginary crimes like witchcraft and feel completely justified in doing so based upon a belief that an invisible being has instructed us to do so? Faith allows rational people to rationalize some very irrational beliefs. History is littered with examples of mass delusion and they generally end badly.

Fortunately, most of the religious people that we come in contact with on a day to day basis lack the same level of devotion to their religion as their fundamentalist counterparts. They generally attend church services and participate in the occasional religious ceremony, but they are not consumed with a literal interpretation of their holy book. These people are religious moderates, which is a distinction gained when people take scripture less and less seriously. Whether we want to admit it or not, the hammer of modernity continues to make religious claims—claims believed, recited, and acted upon for centuries—less tenable. The literalness in which our holy scriptures are interpreted today is vastly different than a first-century Roman Empire or even a medieval Europe. So, if large swaths of contemporary people dismiss or marginalize equally large swaths of scripture as irrelevant, what's the harm in keeping the "good" parts of our scriptures? Isn't religion a good, moral guiding force in the world? The answer, if we're being intellectually honest with ourselves, is simply no (at least not by itself). If we're not being honest with ourselves, it's worth asking this question: what good things does religion bring us that *cannot* be achieved through *nonreligious* means? What is exclusive to religion that makes it "good"? Please try and keep this in mind as you progress through this chapter.

It would be disingenuous for me to paint religion as evil with a single broad stroke. I believe it is quite safe to say that the effects of religion are not all bad and I am not afraid to offer that up. Religion, as a social utility, can and does serve many positive purposes. Many of the world's most beautiful buildings, artwork, and stories are religiously inspired. As we'll discuss in more depth shortly, many people the world over are helped by charitable acts that are influenced in part by religion. Collectively, churches of all faiths contribute billions of dollars through charitable endeavors each year. Faith can also be a very personal thing. A person facing death, one of the most terrifying aspects of life, can find comfort in that faith. It's not uncommon for someone facing a hardship to find emotional strength in the belief that he/she isn't facing the hardship alone.

The most often cited argument for the virtue of religion is that it gives us a moral compass that we would be lost without. Religion, it is argued, strongly influences our ability to determine the difference between right and wrong, thus influencing our behaviors. As a force guiding our morality, surely religion can't be dangerous, can it?

A cursory glance around the world is all it takes to state with confidence that religion has had and will continue to have a positive influence in the lives of billions of people for the reasons just outlined. That same cursory glance however will also expose the fact that religion has had and will continue to have a negative influence in the lives of billions. To try and quantify the positives and the negatives for measurement purposes is an exercise in futility, yet it is important to put the declared contributions of religion into perspective. Too often, this discussion is marred by those who try to force behaviors that can exist secularly to become synonymous with faith. Since the dawn of man, the faithful in our society have tried to present their various religions in this type of mutually exclusive approach. Under that banner, they would have us believe that we are incapable of being good to one another without a divine mandate. For all intents and purposes, there are no positive contributions made to society in the name of religion that cannot also be made in spite of religion. I want to remove this false mask of humility by exposing the mutually exclusive façade.

It's also worth asking whether or not any of this ultimately lends itself to the legitimacy or authenticity of a religion. Do the positive contributions of the Church of Scientology translate into genuine evidence that Xenu was an intergalactic warlord? Do the positive contributions of the Church of Jesus Christ of Latter Day Saints translate into genuine evidence that Joseph Smith really found and was able to translate those golden plates? Do the positive contributions of the Roman Catholic Church translate into genuine evidence that Jesus was the son of God? Clearly, positive (and negative) contributions to society have absolutely no bearing whatsoever on the truthfulness of any faith, and yet the faithful use these contributions to present their religion in the most benign, most beneficial light possible.

Many believers inevitably point to their charities as a way to elevate the purity of their religion. When a religious group reaches out to the less fortunate in our society with food, blankets, money, or an open ear, the charitable act itself is deserving of praise. Many people are helped by these charitable acts, and I have no intention of degrading or belittling the charitable deeds themselves. With that being said, if charity is an example of the positive side of religion, it begs the question of whether or not it's exclusive to religion. Is it done because God has commanded it or are human beings capable of being compassionate without God? Can one exist without the other? The fact that there are thousands of charitable organizations around the world that are nonreligious in nature would lead me to believe that God isn't a required component for this argument. How is this any different than S.H.A.R.E., Goodwill Industries, Amnesty International, United Nations Children's Fund, Wheelchair Foundation, or Foundation Beyond Belief? As I discuss in the chapter of this book that deals with the Christian Reward System, billions (that's billions with a "B") of dollars have been donated through the Bill and Melinda Gates Foundation and all of their work is being done without God playing a commanding role. The Foundation believes "that every life has equal value." Note that they don't say that a life is worth any more or less because someone doesn't believe in Jesus, Allah, or Krishna; and yet religions like Christianity very clearly say that those souls who do not accept Jesus

Christ as savior are not only inferior to those who do but will spend an eternity in torment because of that disbelief.

Anytime we try to make charity exclusive to religion, we infect and pollute the basic integrity of any charitable act. Frankly, we don't need a religious reason to do what we should be doing anyway for our fellow man. The religious reason becomes superfluous. No one is incapable of acting charitably just because there is no divine being telling us that we must. This concept is insulting to secular charities and to the concept of charity itself. Additionally, this line of thinking does nothing to contribute to the defense of the moral claims made on behalf of religion. As much as the religious faithful might otherwise hope, there is absolutely no distinction between charity and "religious" charity, other than the ulterior motive involved.

Charity work may not be the exclusive domain of the religious, but missionary work most certainly is. The trouble is that the two deeds are often used in a religiously synonymous way. To a Christian missionary, there is no distinction. Mother Teresa was one of the world's most famous missionaries and a fantastic example highlighting the fruits and dangers of religion. As the founder of Missionaries of Charity, Mother Teresa ministered to the sick, poor, and dying for decades. In 1979, she was awarded the Nobel Peace Prize which enhanced her already impressive list of honors. As revered as she may have been, none of her awards can eliminate the criticisms leveled against her. Christianity shaped her views on suffering, leaving her with the conclusion that suffering actually brought people closer to Jesus.[1] She was criticized for not administering painkillers to people in extreme pain because the suffering they felt was "the most beautiful gift for a person, that he can participate in the sufferings of Christ".[2] The quality of care was consistently questioned—particularly when reports of hypodermic needles being reused surfaced or when medical decisions about patients were being made by people with no medical knowledge. Her theology of suffering actually embraced such misery which, to the non-indoctrinated, seems rather obscene, masochistic, and callous. This wasn't a position applied only to the already sick and dying, however. For example, Mother Teresa equated contraception to abortion and abortion to murder. In her Nobel Prize acceptance speech, she said that abortion was "the greatest destroyer of peace." Forbidding contraception has led to millions of unwanted births and additional hardships.

While Mother Teresa was undoubtedly a caring and courageous person, the suffering caused or compounded by her faith should not go unnoticed nor should the value of the millions of dollars spent on her missionary work be considered indisputable. Do good deeds make it appropriate for her to have accepted $1.25 million from Charles Keating, the man famously involved in the Keating Five scandal of fraud and corruption? She accepted donations from the corrupt Duvalier Family in Haiti as well. In both of these cases, she

---

1 Byfield, Ted (20 October 1997). "If the real world knew the real Mother Teresa there would be a lot less adulation." *Alberta Report/Newsmagazine* 24 (45).

2 "India has no reason to be grateful to Mother Teresa," Sanal Edamaruku." Mukto-mona.com. Retrieved 28 August 2011.

supported and praised each of them before and after the donations. Incredibly, the money was not always accounted for, and where it was, it was often used to open new convents instead of combating poverty (remember—she asserted that suffering was the mechanism by which man could know Jesus) or improving the safety and conditions of already existing hospices. This was a woman who truly believed that the aborting of an unwanted fetus was more morally damaging to the world than the suffering caused by denying abortions for families who could not support another child, or when having the child would destroy the mother's life. These criticisms are as valid today as they were when they were first made decades ago.

Her theology of suffering should cause additional pause when viewed against the backdrop of her grave doubts regarding the very existence of the God to which that suffering could bring us closer. Privately, Mother Teresa "felt no presence of God whatsoever ... neither in her heart or in the Eucharist" for many decades, even though all her deeds were conducted under the banner of missionary work. It is this same God whose compassion is nowhere to be found even today among the millions who are suffering unimaginable afflictions at this very moment.

Missionary work does not validate any of the core beliefs of a chosen religion and we don't have to look to icons like Mother Teresa to demonstrate this. We can find examples much closer to home. I'd like to share a story about my high school sweetheart recounting her experience in church one day where the congregation prayed for her father. I've been told that the Holy Ghost came down upon her father and he literally fainted from the weight. Apparently it was a moving experience. I remember asking the question "...and you give these people money?" Perhaps it was the delivery, but she didn't find my question quite as humorous as I did at the time. These days, her parents are both reverends and missionaries. They have traveled to numerous places around the globe to preach the message of Jesus Christ. Are they and others like them reaching out to the less fortunate people of the world simply because they are compassionate human beings whose only desire is to help those less fortunate? Could it really be that noble? It's difficult for me to put the noble label on them when I see photos of them holding up the Bible and preaching. I believe it is both fair and appropriate to ask how many of these trips have been or would be undertaken without the spreading of their faith? The answer to that question is indicative of the true purpose behind the trip. Is it possible to help people without giving them a Bible or trying to convert them? If it is, then I find it highly pretentious to say the word "charity" in the same breath as "missionary." I commend the helping, but doing missionary work under the guise of charity is misleading and disingenuous. It is not "charity work" but rather a religious marketing campaign with some charitable side effects. The mission isn't as noble and selfless, like organizations such as Doctors Without Borders, who donate their time and expertise without expecting anything in return—like souls, belief, allegiance, and eternal commitments.

So why is religion good? Perhaps it is the belief that it provides us with moral guidelines. I've heard this rationale many times and I cover it in greater depth in a later chapter. What actions deemed morally acceptable can be taken by a religious person that cannot be taken by a nonreligious person? Take some time and really think about that question. I think you'll find your own conclusion to be enlightening.

Perhaps religion is good because it purports to explain why we're here and how we got here. It's not uncommon for the religious to hold their faith up as an example of being able to answer a fundamental question that science cannot. Unfortunately, religious faith is the single worst excuse for objective discourse. For example, what verifiable, factual, and authentic evidence exists to conclusively support the Christian version of creation over the stories of Lord Brahma, Taiowa, or Izanagi and Izanami? Each of these stories and the many like them all begin the same: in the beginning there was nothing. They diverge quickly thereafter by proclaiming and attributing creation to their own personal deity or deities. I assure you that every basic argument that a Christian produces for his/her story will be met with an equally-passionate argument from someone of another faith. I know of no unbiased source that has conclusively and exhaustively weighed the merits of every religions' assertions. The only unbiased source we have to try and answer these types of questions is science. The scientific method has been the most consistently reliable way of understanding the world and universe that we inhabit. We have learned more about our place in the universe in the past 100 years than we have in the previous 1,000 years. When viewed in this light, there is no reason to believe that revelation is anything more than a red herring designed to placate the masses.

Perhaps faith is good because it purports to answer the crucial question about whether or not there is life after death. Let's be honest—the fear of death is a strong emotion and faith can be very comforting. What rational person hasn't at least given a few fleeting moments of thought to what happens to us after we die? We all want to believe that we'll continue to live in some fashion. Death becomes merely a speed bump and therefore a less scary prospect. In the past I have personally found comfort in the thought that a loved one is somehow still alive and happy in Heaven. I have for years kept the religiously-inspired memorial card from my great grandmother's funeral in the visor of my vehicle. I don't really believe that she is physically watching over me, but I find comfort in keeping her in my thoughts. That's not the case with everyone though as many of our neighbors truly do believe that our relatives are actively watching out for the living from the comfort of paradise. The problem is that religion is selling an invisible product, and the mere fact that it may provide comfort ultimately has no bearing whatsoever on the truthfulness of its claims. Wishful thinking does not lend itself to the truth and I don't feel remorseful for pointing this out. In fact, I am reminded of something that the author and screenwriter Rupert Hughes once said,

> As for those who protest that I am robbing people of the great comfort and consolation they gain from Christianity, I can only say that Christianity

includes hell, eternal torture for the vast majority of humanity, for most of your relatives and friends. Christianity includes a devil who is really more powerful than God, and who keeps gathering into his furnaces most of the creatures whom God turns out and for whom he sent his son to the cross in vain. If I could feel that I had robbed anybody of his faith in hell, I should not be ashamed or regretful.

Depending on which invisible product we buy, we may be greeted by virgins in the afterlife willing to do our bidding, or perhaps we'll get to see our loved ones again in a magical place called Heaven. Maybe we'll be reincarnated as something (or someone) else entirely. Again, it all depends on which invisible product we buy. Billions and billions of people have already died, and yet despite all of these opportunities, we still have no proof of an afterlife. It seems that when I bring this inconvenient fact up, I'm almost always met with the "evidence" put forth by those who have had a near-death experience (NDE). With little variation, we are given accounts of experiences that include

> feelings of peace and joy; a sense of being out of one's body and watching events going on around one's body and, occasionally, at some distant physical location; a cessation of pain; seeing a dark tunnel or void; seeing an unusually bright light, sometimes experienced as a 'Being of Light' that radiates love and may speak or otherwise communicate with the person; encountering other beings, often deceased persons whom the experiencer recognizes; experiencing a revival of memories or even a full life review, sometimes accompanied by feelings of judgment; seeing some 'other realm,' often of great beauty; sensing a barrier or border beyond which the person cannot go; and returning to the body, often reluctantly.[1]

But the subject of an NDE was "near death" and not in fact dead. This is a rather substantial difference. If the subject did not actually die, the experience is not one of death. Regardless, NDE enthusiasts embrace these stories as evidence that our consciousness can exist outside of the body without ever really considering what "outside of the body" truly means. Someone could suffer a heart attack and later recall these types of sensations. There have been reports of people who could vividly recall the events taking place around them while they lay on the operating room table. The problem with these reports is that the brain and body are still alive, thus making the association of these events to death somewhat of a misnomer. In cases where brain activity has completely shut down, it again seems like a rather obvious observation that the brain activity must resume at some point or else the subject wouldn't be able to tell us about the sensations in the first place. The difficulty here is in assigning those sensations to the brief moments of an inactive brain state instead of to the near/after death moments. NDE received a boost in 2012 when Harvard-educated neurosurgeon Dr. Eben Alexander wrote a book describing his religious experience while his cortex

---

1 E.F. Kelly et al., *Irreducible Mind: Toward a Psychology for the 21st Century.* New York: Rowman and Littlefield, 2007, p. 372

was "completely shut down" during a rare E. coli spinal meningitis infection. Finally, the NDE community had someone with solid scientific credentials explaining in medical terms what his body went through when he claims the experiences took place. Dr. Alexander's account is by far the most interesting account of NDE ever put forth, however I can't seem to get over the fact that in order for his brain to record these events to memory, the brain would have to have been functioning. Anything else would mean that memories are somehow stored outside of the brain. A complete understanding of consciousness eludes scientists even today, so that kind of assertion truly is audacious and demanding of evidence. I'm not ready to completely dismiss near-death experiences but I'm not likely to rush to supernatural explanations either. Regardless of our positions, it seems rather apparent that until human beings lose their fear of death, religion and religious experience will always have a place in our society.

The only real answer to the "BIG" question is: I don't know. It is the *only* answer that is both humble and honest. Just because someone believes that Heaven exists or that they'll be reincarnated doesn't automatically make their belief true. Belief on its own is neither a virtue nor a valid reason for substantiating any claim. Religion is dangerous because it lets people believe that they have all the answers when we clearly do not. It is perfectly acceptable in science to say that we don't yet know something. Religion, like the Divine Default says, begins with God, and because it does, the cause for everything is already known. God becomes a convenient excuse for things we don't understand and faith is the glue that binds that belief together.

The sad realization is that I am going to die and so are you. It is the most statistically probable event that one can think of. It tears me up inside to think that I will eventually be separated from everyone I love. My children will one day walk this planet without me. Depending on the timing of my own demise, I may never know my grandchildren or great-grandchildren. These are sobering thoughts. Christopher Hitchens once likened death to being tapped on the shoulder and told that you have to leave the party. The party will continue—just not with you. There is a profound sadness in this realization, but religion isn't the only anecdote. If my soul does not transcend this Earthly realm when I die, I can still find the majesty in my body being reduced to ash. My energy will not be lost but simply changed, and I will remain an everlasting part of our universe. The sobering truth is that everything must come to an end, and what provides me a measure of comfort is recognizing the fact that I am a child of the stars. My body shares the same makeup as the stars in the night sky. There is a certain amount of poetry in knowing that stars had to die so that I could live. Eventually even our own sun will burn out. It will grow bigger and hotter eventually engulfing our planet in one last warm embrace in which our currently lush planet will lose all of its water and much of its energy to space. The energy that was my body and the energy of those that I have loved will once again be reunited as particles sent out across a vast and awe-inspiring cosmos. We are and will forever be children of the stars. There is a beauty in stepping back and seeing the big picture. I wish more people could look at death from this perspective.

Perhaps faith is good because of the social component. There is certainly an inherent social aspect to most religious gatherings and it provides a common bond for its members. Religion has and continues to have an inclusive value in that it is good for those who are in the group. Unfortunately, this social inclusion rarely has a positive quality to those who are outside the group. For example, Christianity is good if you're a Christian. It's not so good if you are a Muslim and vice versa. Most Christians like to believe that Jesus' teachings were meant for everyone, however a critical look at his actual words would suggest otherwise. For example, Jesus refers to non-Jews as dogs, an insult that is just as biting today. In Matthew 10:5-6, we see a clear distinction being made between Jew and Gentile. Many of the Biblical references to the Gentiles (non-Jews) are of a derogatory nature.

A common belief is not always sufficient for social inclusion, however. Different sects of the same religion can be as far away from socially inclusive as a homeless man at a country club. From a historical macro level, religion has been one of the most dividing forces on the planet. How many people have died fighting over which invisible God was more real? As Walter P. Stacy, a former Chief Justice from the North Carolina Supreme Court, once said, "It would be almost unbelievable, if history did not record the tragic fact that men have gone to war and cut each other's throats because they could not agree as to what was to become of them after their throats were cut."

This reminds me of a story the comedian Emo Philips once told:

> Once I saw this guy on a bridge about to jump. I said, "Don't do it!"
> He said, "Nobody loves me."
> I said, "God loves you. Do you believe in God?"
> He said, "Yes."
> I said, "Are you a Christian or a Jew?"
> He said, "A Christian."
> I said, "Me, too! Protestant or Catholic?"
> He said, "Protestant."
> I said, "Me, too! What franchise?"
> He said, "Baptist."
> I said, "Me, too! Northern Baptist or Southern Baptist?"
> He said, "Northern Baptist."
> I said, "Me, too! Northern Conservative Baptist or Northern Liberal Baptist?"
> He said, "Northern Conservative Baptist."
> I said, "Me, too! Northern Conservative Baptist Great Lakes Region, or Northern Conservative Baptist Eastern Region?"
> He said, "Northern Conservative Baptist Great Lakes Region."
> I said, "Me, too! Northern Conservative Baptist Great Lakes Region Council of 1879, or Northern Conservative Baptist Great Lakes Region Council of 1912?"
> He said, "Northern Conservative Baptist Great Lakes Region

Council of 1912."

I said, "Die, heretic!" And I pushed him over.

Even when the inclusive social nature of religion is positive, is this aspect unique to religion? Can people get together socially for any other reason? Aren't there neighborhoods that we know, and neighborhoods we read about in foreign lands, where people of different religions respect and cooperate with each other? Shared supernatural beliefs are not necessary to bring people together. The social aspect isn't the exclusive domain of religion. Just like charities, the same effect can and is frequently achieved regardless of any faith in any God.

What is it about religion that makes it good? What is absolutely unique and quantifiable about religion that would be considered "good" and yet is not available to the nonreligious? I've heard people assert that it is good for your health, and it's a connection to something bigger than ourselves. Even though the Bible doesn't say it, a healthy diet is a quantifiable practice that is good for your health, yet I don't see people praying and claiming obedience to a grapefruit. Realizing that our bodies are made up of the same ingredients found in stars and that these stars gave us these initial building blocks of life most certainly gives us a connection to something bigger than ourselves, but we don't pray to Alpha Centauri.

If your mind is racing with examples of positive reasons to support religion, I hope you'll take a moment to ask yourself whether or not each reason 1) makes the religion true, 2) can be conducted without religion, and 3) comes at a cost we are comfortable with? When you're finished with this chapter, ask yourself what positive aspects of religion are enjoyed *solely* because of faith versus the cost that it and others have on our world. For myself, I have found that none of the claimed or perceived tangible benefits are exclusive to religion. Each benefit can still be achieved without religion. Conversely, there are clear detriments to religion and more often than not these detriments can be exclusively claimed by the faithful.

The cost of religion is far greater than someone devoting an hour of their time to sit in church on Sunday. Even those believers who only attend Sunday services don't get a free pass to be blind to the negative effects. Because religious moderates provide legitimacy and support for the core religious beliefs, they are complicit in the evils that are conducted under that banner of faith. In his book *The End of Faith*, Sam Harris correctly notes that "religious moderates are, in a large part, responsible for the religious conflict in our world, because their beliefs provide the context in which scriptural literalism and religious violence can never be adequately opposed." When a religious moderate gives legitimacy to faith-based belief in Jesus or Muhammad as being divinely inspired, it makes it more difficult for the rest of us to point out the rather obvious deficiencies that are inherent in these figures. Even dignifying the Bible or the Qur'an as informative sources makes it difficult to adequately oppose actions undertaken by those who are either inspired by or who believe, in good faith, that they are taking direct instruction from these sacred texts.

Who can forget the Protestant-led Ku Klux Klan and the terror that they inflicted upon thousands here in the United States? The KKK's religious foundation was built upon their interpretation of Christianity.[1] They didn't hide the fact that they wanted to "reestablish Protestant Christian values in America by any means possible," and they firmly believed that "Jesus was the first Klansman."[2] These attitudes haven't diminished over time. In July 2012, the KKK had a presence during the 3-day conference held by Christian Identity Ministries in Lamar County, Alabama, where the pastor welcomed only "white Christians." These men can and do find support for their beliefs and actions in the Bible. You and I may not like the outcomes of their interpretation of the Bible any more than they'd like the outcome of our interpretation, but we all have the same book. It should strike us as both odd and highly problematic that a divine being can't seem to dictate a book that doesn't lead to violent differences of view. If God is all-knowing and perfect, we should be able to expect a perfect text explaining in clear, unambiguous terms exactly what He wants and expects.

Simply stated, faith is gullibility personified. It is the excuse people give for believing in something without any credible reason for doing so. What can't be proven is often unreasonable and illogical. If something can only be taken on faith, then the honest truth is that the belief itself is simply unable to stand on its own merit.

Faith is not science, and by their very definitions, the two are incompatible. They differ both philosophically as well as practically. One works by assembling facts to form a conclusion. The other operates entirely in reverse. One is based greatly on the bedrock of logic and reason. The other is a complete surrender of logic and reason. Science is the unending desire to unlock the mysteries of the universe. Religion is the belief that we already have. Science and religion follow incompatible paths to knowing. We can see the differences when we apply the knowledge attained through each to explain or to make predictions about our physical world. Science for example can be used to predict when a particular comet will pass by our planet, when we may be in the path of severe weather, or when the next lunar eclipse will take place. Science allowed us to predict the very existence of the planet Neptune using mathematical modeling before we ever set eyes upon it. Pluto wasn't discovered until 1930, so we have never seen it actually complete a full orbit around the sun, but we know with mathematical certainty that it will take 248 years. We can use science to make predictions about many things with incredible accuracy.

Divine revelation, personal feelings, and indoctrination are appropriate in matters of faith but are profoundly useless in both matters of scientific dis-

---

1   Al-Khattar, Aref M. (2003). *Religion and terrorism: an interfaith perspective*. Westport, CT: Praeger. pp. 21, 30, 55, 91.

2   Michael, Robert, and Philip Rosen. *Dictionary of antisemitism from the earliest times to the present*. Lanham, Maryland, USA: Scarecrow Press, 1997 p. 267.

covery and dealing with the real problems of tomorrow. There is no beating around the burning bush here. Faith is a completely inadequate solution to the true dilemmas facing our species. With 7 billion people on the planet and growing, faith in a supernatural being will be of absolutely no help in finding new sources of food, energy, technology, or medicine. Religious people cannot pray away our ills nor can they provide for human advancement through prayer.. Historically speaking, the vast majority of our advances have come by the hands of science and there is no reason to believe that this trend won't continue. Our future economies will depend heavily on science—not faith!

We don't live in a world where we presently have to choose between faith and science exclusively, but if we stand to benefit more from science, by what logical reasoning would we allow faith to supersede it? There isn't a logical case to be made for the substitution, yet many will gladly support such things as the teaching of creationism over evolution in public school systems, thereby openly promoting faith over science. This type of religious encroachment on secular society has, does, and will continue to have negative consequences. Science builds knowledge through testable explanations, predictions, and critical assessments of evidence. Faith does not require evidence, and oddly enough, someone's faith is considered "stronger" when there's less evidence to support it. I fail to see how this is a virtue.

Elevating faith over science does more harm than simply encroaching on secular society. It devalues science and instills within us a complete disregard for the scientific method. For example, religious politicians in Louisiana tried to give thousands of students state voucher money so that they could have attended private religious schools using public school funding. The schools approved by Republican Governor Bobby Jindal's pushing of that bill introduced curriculum based on principles from the Bible. Portions of the curriculum involved the cohabitation of humans and dinosaurs, solar fusion portrayed as a myth, and evolution being "proven false" by suggesting that the Loch Ness Monster is actually a plesiosaur alive and well, having been tracked by a small submarine[1]. This type of curriculum elevates faith over science at every turn, without stringent burden of proof. The philosophy of Accelerated Christian Education (ACE) is that science is incapable of contradicting the Bible. If there is a conflict, then the scientific theory is wrong and will be ignored. This curriculum is completely scientifically-hostile. This cannot be a virtue.

Breeding a scientifically ignorant generation is detrimental to our entire nation, given a future that is so heavily dependent on science.

Whether the topic is education, morality, or human decency, religion presents itself as harmless, but the reality is that it has the power to be both divisive and harmful. As Steven Weinberg correctly points out, "With or without religion, good people can behave well and bad people can do evil; but for good people to do evil—that takes religion."

Religion provides convenient cover and justification for actions that range from merely irritating to criminal. Case in point: you may be surprised

---

1 Extract from *Biology 1099*, Accelerated Christian Education Inc.—1995

to learn that there are still witch burnings. In villages in Kenya, mobs literally drag suspected witches out of their homes and burn them. You can go online and watch these videos. This is what it looks like when Christians do exactly as God has commanded. Are these Christians interpreting the Bible wrong? The Bible is quite explicit in its condemnation of witches and witchcraft, even though there is no credible evidence to suggest that witches can manipulate the elements any differently than you or I. The Bible condemns witchcraft, thus providing justification for the act. If God commanded us to not let a witch live (as He clearly does in Exodus 22:18), who are we to say that burning those people alive is immoral? I assure you that the word *moral* is the last thing that comes to mind when watching the videos, but the clear fact remains that the Bible can be used to justify such actions.

Closer to home, we can simply pick up a newspaper in any major city and find evidence of the dangers that religion harbors. In Decatur, Georgia, Benjamin Edetanlen was sentenced to 18 years in prison after being found guilty of killing his 5-month-old child. The baby died from blunt force trauma and suffered brain injuries and a broken leg. In his own testimony, Edetanlen told the court that he was trying to discipline his children according to scripture. He pointed to several passages in Proverbs to support and justify his actions. Even after the child's death, Edetanlen maintained his faith and justification in Proverbs 13! If, as the religious are so fond of suggesting, absolute morality can be found with God, who are we to say that we shouldn't be beating our children? Deuteronomy 21:18–21 is quite explicit when it says that we should take stubborn and rebellious children unwilling to learn from parental discipline and stone them to death at the edge of town. Clearly God expects us to raise children in a way that would incur the wrath of any modern-day social services counselor.

The Catholic Church's irrational stance on contraception has led to millions of unwanted pregnancies and births. The Church's fear of losing papal authority has caused pain, heartache, financial difficulties, and broken homes for many people even though the vast majority of practicing Catholics in the developed world, at least, have both used and continue to support the use of contraception. This mandate against contraception is a relic that has very serious consequences in today's modern society. In 2012, the United Nations declared access to contraception a universal human right and that creating barriers, whether legal, financial, or cultural, would constitute an infringement upon that right. Unfortunately, the UN report was not binding, had no legal effect, and could not change the Catholic Church's mandate. Considering the source of the mandate, it would appear to be a bit hypocritical. As comedian Bill Maher once quipped, "Who would know better about women's reproductive parts than a bunch of 70-year-old men who wear dresses to work every day?"

The Catholic Church will likely one day apologize for its irrational stance on contraception—particularly in poverty stricken areas of the world. While they are quick to boast of their missionary/charity work in these areas, they remain blind to the devastating consequences that their immoral position causes. Throughout history, there has been one overwhelmingly positive and effective tactic to combat poverty and it's a rather simple one in concept— the empowerment of women. Give women a say in their reproductive role and the heavy weight of poverty can begin to be lifted. The Catholic Church continues to this day to oppose the only known panacea for poverty and they remain strident in their position. It shouldn't surprise us that an organization where women are still denied ordination (Can. 1024: A baptized male alone receives sacred ordination validly) considers this type of misogynistic viewpoint a virtue. It seems rather obvious that an unwanted pregnancy is the single biggest reason for abortion. The effects of unwanted pregnancies can be felt on multiple levels.

In a postindustrial society like the United States, unwanted pregnancies often lead to financial difficulties and single-parent homes. It's not uncommon for women facing unwanted pregnancy to neglect prenatal care, thus putting their babies at risk for such things as premature births and neurological disorders. The cognitive and behavioral issues arising from these situations have been well documented. As of 2007, unwanted pregnancies led to 1.3 million abortions. Study after study confirms the difficulties and negative consequences of unwanted pregnancies. In a third world country, these consequences are magnified many times over. When aid to these countries comes attached with strings of teaching abstinence and saying no to condoms, the pain and suffering that has been felt by millions of people over the span of generations is amazingly immoral. The Church is single-handedly responsible for much of this misery. It is my sincere hope that the Church one day recognizes the obscene nature of their position on contraception and apologizes for the unethical dogma that they've espoused to every corner of the world. They are responsible for the misery of millions.

There's no disputing that religion is the primary cause and justification for the persecution of gay people. God is very clear on this topic. Using the Bible as moral validation, an otherwise normally rational, intelligent individual will condemn a gay person. They'll condemn them not just for what they've done but more importantly for who they are. These same rational, intelligent people will proudly proclaim that man is made in the image of God, but fail to see gays and lesbians in the same light. It seems a rather simple question, but if Jesus never bothered to mention a topic, how can that topic be essential to his teachings? Jesus never says one direct word about gay people, but since Jesus and God are believed to be one entity (Holy Trinity), Christians have religious justification for their intolerance and hatred of homosexuals. For millions of people, the Bible is both the source and the justification for this hatred. A 2011 study published in the journal *Pediatrics* showed that teenagers who are gay are four times more likely to commit suicide than their heterosexual counterparts. Who says faith isn't dangerous when it is often the driver of justification for this persecution? It's not uncommon to see and hear about parents who will go so far as to disown their children upon learning of their sexual orientation. In fact, this has been a rather common theme among young gays and lesbians, and I continue to have difficulty reconciling these all too real scenarios to my own situation. If either of my children comes out as gay, abandoning them would be the last thought on my mind. Having a gay child doesn't mean that I've failed as a parent, however disowning them would be.

Dan Cathy, the CEO of the Chick-Fil-A restaurant chains and a devout Christian, made headlines in 2012 when he discussed his company's support for "the biblical definition of the family unit." His Christian beliefs directly influence the actions of the WinShape Foundation, the charitable group founded by S. Truett Cathy and his wife Jeanette. WinShape, heavily funded by Chick-Fil-A, has donated millions of dollars to anti-gay groups. In 2010 alone, the group donated nearly $2 million[1] to such groups as the Marriage & Family Foundation, Exodus International, Family Research Council, Georgia Family Council, and others. Not a single group views homosexuals in a positive light. "We are very much supportive of the family—the biblical definition of the family unit," Dan Cathy said. "We are a family-owned business, a family-led business, and we are married to our first wives. We give God thanks for that." Cathy invoked his religious beliefs on the equality of marriage by saying "I think we are inviting God's judgment on our nation when we shake our fist at Him and say 'we know better than you as to what constitutes a marriage' and I pray God's mercy on our generation that has such a prideful, arrogant attitude to think that we have the audacity to define what marriage is about." Cathy's religious beliefs spark actions. Those actions influence and support others. When Jesus taught his disciples against judging people, one can only assume he wasn't providing exemptions for folks like Dan Cathy.

By contrast, I was stunned to listen to the following comments from Dr. Reverend Phil Snider, a preacher from the Brentwood Christian Church in southwest Missouri, made in front of his local city council. The council was hearing public comments regarding a proposed amendment to an ordinance covering sexual orientation and gender identity protections. The transcript of his speech is below and is worth a read.

> My name is the Reverend Doctor Phil Snider. I was born and raised in Springfield, Missouri, and I stand before you this evening in support of this ordinance. I worry about the future of our city. Any accurate reading of the Bible should make it clear that gay rights goes against the plain truth of the Word of God. As one preacher warns, man, in overstepping the boundary lines that God has drawn by making special rights for gays and lesbians, has taken another step in the direction of inviting the Judgment of God upon our land.
>
> This step of gay rights is but another stepping stone toward the immorality and lawlessness that will be characteristic of the Last Days. This ordinance represents a denial of all that we believe in and no one should force it on us. It's not that we don't care about homosexuals. But it's that our rights would be taken away and un-Christian views will be forced upon us and

---

our children, for we would be forced to go against our personal morals. Outside government agents are endeavoring to disturb God's Established Order. It is not in line with the Bible. Do not let people lead you astray.

The liberals leading this movement do not believe the Bible any longer but every good, substantial, Bible believing, intelligent orthodox Christian can read the Word of God and know what is happening is not of God, When you run into conflict with God's Established Order you have trouble. You do not produce harmony. You produce destruction and trouble and our city is in the greatest danger it has ever been in its history. The reason is we have gotten away from the Bible of our forefathers.

The comments seemed completely in line with the kind of expectations one might have listening to a Southern preacher discussing the topic of gay rights. What happened next came as quite a surprise. Dr. Snider continued:

You see, the right of segregation... I'm sorry. Hold on. The right of segregation is clearly established by the Holy Scriptures both by precept and example.

I'm sorry. I've brought the wrong notes with me this evening. I've borrowed my argument from the wrong century. It turns out what I've been reading to you this whole time are direct quotes from White preachers from the 1950s and the 1960s all in support of racial segregation. All I have done is simply take out the words "racial integration" and substituted it with the phrase "gay rights".

I guess the arguments I've been hearing around Springfield lately sound so similar to these that I got them confused. I hope you will not make the same mistake. I hope you will stand on the right side of history.

In one swift movement, Dr. Snider cleverly frames the debate as a civil rights issue highlighting just how others have used the Bible in the past to condone the bigotry of segregation. I give him credit for being bold enough to confront the same type of rhetoric that was used during the struggles of racial segregation during the last century. Unfortunately, not every Christian is as liberal or tolerant as Dr. Snider.

If you've watched a national news show or picked up a newspaper anytime in the last decade, I'm sure you've seen the antics of the members of the Westboro Baptist Church. These are the same people that proudly proclaim "Thank God For Dead Soldiers" and "God Hates Fags." These fundamentalists use a literal interpretation of the Bible and often ignore the parts of the Bible that others might interpret as similes, parables, or metaphors. All of their actions are taken under the guise of Christianity. I'd go so far as to say that in the case of the Westboro Baptist Church, religion can be used to give people permission to behave in ways that even a lunatic might raise an eyebrow to. Whether you agree with their actions or their philosophies, there is no denying that they use religion to justify it all. They are extremely homophobic, and just like the witchcraft example from earlier in this chapter, there isn't anything positive to say about homosexuality in the Bible. When God refers to homosexuality as an abomination, as he does in Leviticus 18:22, He isn't mincing words. In the King James Version, Leviticus 20:13 tells us, *"If a man also lie with mankind, as he lieth with a woman, both of them have committed an abomination: they shall surely be put to death; their blood shall be upon them."* Again—no mincing of words. The appropriate punishment according to God is...death. If God condemns homosexuality and you're a Christian, who are you to call the members of the Westboro Baptist Church immoral? Your God has commanded it. This bigotry isn't the exclusive domain of the fundamentalist however. I know far too many people who are not outwardly expressive about denouncing homosexuality, but who harbor the same feelings and opinions quietly to themselves. They'll work with gays because they have to, but don't think for one second that a gay person will get the same type of consideration with these people that a heterosexual person will. They are a means to an end—something to be quietly tolerated.

No matter how someone slices it, gays and lesbians are human beings who deserve every bit of opportunity at a happy life as you and I do. To say that gays and lesbians can't get married because it is against my religion is like saying that someone else can't eat donuts because I'm on a diet. To say that gay marriage is a redefining of the word "marriage" is to conveniently ignore the fact that we no longer sell our daughters into marriage for five goats and a cow. Historically speaking, the word "marriage" has already been redefined. King David had many wives—many of which are named in 1 Chronicles 3:1-5. Jacob had two wives (sisters) and they were given to him by their father in exchange for working for seven years. God is apparently just fine with polygamy and also seems to be at ease with treating women as property. When we don't kill the bride at a wedding, in accordance with Deuteronomy 22:13-21, for the crime of not being a virgin on her wedding night, we've already redefined "Biblical marriage." For married couples caught committing adultery, God tells us in Deuteronomy 22:22 that we should kill both the man and the woman. There is something wildly hypocritical with Christians denouncing gay marriage while blatantly ignoring the specific commands given by their God in relation to heterosexual couples.

If we look at marriage the way it actually is and not how we want to view it, we'll see that it is a civil right and not a constitutionally-protected religious freedom. While people do get married in churches, they can also and frequently do get married in courthouses, backyards, country clubs, and even on beautiful, sandy beaches in foreign countries. A member of the clergy is not required to perform a marriage ceremony. Any justice of the peace, sitting judge, governor, mayor, county clerk, or ship captain (if you happen to be at sea) can and officiate at weddings, and they frequently do. While the religious often decorate the marriage ceremony with references to God, including the pretentious sacredness of commitment before God Himself, they often overlook some rather obvious facts like the marriage certificate which is issued by the government and not the church. A marriage is, after all, an agreement between two consenting adults and the government. When a marriage is dissolved, we don't require a priest, rabbi, or reverend to oversee the dissolution. More than clergy, we frequently find attorneys involved. Of course, who can forget the words uttered at the end of virtually every marriage ceremony: "by the power vested in me by the State of ..."? The power to officiate is derived from the State and thus from the people. This is the very essence behind what constitutes a civil right. To think of marriage solely in religious terms and bound by religious dogma is to remain completely ignorant of the reality of marriage.

Now, to go so far as to call someone an abomination because of their sexual orientation and to suggest that their punishment should be death is frankly disturbing. It would appear that God has no compassion or morality on this topic. The Christian god is a bigot by the very definition of the word. Even if a religious person does not personally believe in the persecution of homosexuals, that doesn't negate the fact that their religion surely does. If a social club held such intolerant views, how long would people remain members? Why should religion get a free pass?

Homosexuality isn't the only area of irrationality. If a particular irrational belief doesn't exist, it can be created. For centuries, the Roman Catholic Church told their faithful that unbaptized children would spend eternity in Limbo, a place without God. According to the church, baptism is necessary for salvation and infants would be punished for original sin even though they themselves had never committed any personal sins. It turns out that St. Augustine was wrong. Originally commissioned by Pope John Paul II and authorized for publication by Pope Benedict XVI, "The Hope of Salvation for Infants Who Die without Being Baptized" was released. It would appear that the Vatican had officially closed Limbo without ever officially endorsing it. Since the Middle Ages, Limbo had been a "real" place believed in by millions of people, but now we have the Vatican clearly going against the views of many previous popes including Pope Pius X who said, "Babies dead without baptism go to Limbo, where they do not enjoy God, but neither do they suffer, because, having original sin alone, they do not deserve paradise, but neither do they merit hell or purgatory." Try and imagine the kind of trauma that the concept of Limbo put millions of people through over hundreds of years. Can you imagine the millions and millions of tears shed by grieving parents thinking that their infants were in Limbo? That is the true power of religion. It can make people believe in anything...literally. What once was real is now imaginary. For centuries, people believed that Limbo was as real as Heaven and Hell. You couldn't convince them otherwise. Their faith was unshakeable. For some people, even the announcement from the Vatican can't convince them that Limbo isn't real. This situation bleeds delusion from every angle.

We can look through the pages of history to see more examples of this type of irrational behavior conducted under the banner of religion. As I have touched on before, the Crusades were responsible for the deaths of hundreds of thousands of people. Victims left in the wake were not always given death. Countless numbers of people were raped and tortured while towns were routinely pillaged. The Roman Catholic Church taught their soldiers that if they were killed defending their faith, they would bypass Purgatory and be taken directly to Heaven. This provided strong motivation for many soldiers and helped ease their fears of dying during battle. This was all done under the banner of Christianity and under the same papal office authority that both created and closed the fictitious Limbo. Interesting enough, this is precisely the tactics we see deployed on behalf of Islam by modern day clerics to ease the fears of those willing to put their lives on the line.

It's hard to pay attention to politics these days without seeing religion infused into it. The concept of religion has tangible, real-world consequences. It was revealing to watch the potential candidates for the 2012 Republican nomination for President of the United States debate the merits of the Obama administration's new mandate for contraceptive coverage in healthcare policies. Christian advocates, spearheaded by the Catholics, were up in arms that they would have to pay for something that violates their belief system. They would instead choose to make it more difficult for their flock to get coverage. Catholic leaders may fight this, but the inconvenient truth is that more than half of all American Catholics agree with the decision to have contraceptive coverage and an estimated 98% have used contraceptives in the past[1]. This is the very personification of "do as I say, not as I do."

Three of the Republican candidates that dropped out of the race for the 2012 Republican nomination have said that God told them to run for President. Herman Cain, Michelle Bachmann, and Rick Perry all had divine inspiration. Herman Cain even compared himself to Moses in hearing God's calling. With hindsight, we can say that if this were a baseball game, God would have struck out. The race, however, was telling as those folks, along with Newt Gingrich and Rick Santorum, played the religion card at every opportunity. We saw this later in the contest when Republican Vice-Presidential nominee Paul Ryan told thousands of Evangelical Christians listening to a call hosted by the Faith and Freedom Coalition that a vote for then-President Obama would compromise "Judeo-Christian" values, without actually explaining what specific "Judeo-Christian" values would be compromised by a Christian president. That type of accusation required no evidence for a crowd that can be inflamed and motivated on religious grounds alone. It's easy to sway the votes of those who have little to no knowledge of the issues, if one uses religion. The "evangelical vote" is an important part of the Christian-Conservative bloc. These people vote in great numbers so candidates tend to pander to them whenever they can. Rick Perry, Newt Gingrich, and Rick Santorum each suggested that they'd like to do away with the separation of church and state, when speaking to religious organizations, but later when asked about those comments by mainstream media, they try to backtrack and obscure their message.

The pandering is pathetic but it serves a purpose. Sadly and far too often, religious pandering is the reason why many voters cast their votes in favor

---

1 *Countering Conventional Wisdom: New Evidence on Religion and Contraceptive Use.* Guttmacher Institute. April 2011

of a particular candidate. It's getting nauseating. I'm not the only one who thinks religion and politics is a bad mix. The Pew Research Center released the results of a survey indicating that 38% of Americans believe that their political leaders are overdoing it with their prayer and faith. That's up from 12% in 2001. Today, 54% of Americans believe that churches should stay out of politics. That's up from 43% in 1996.

The biggest danger of faith in politics is that politicians may use faith in their decision making. I take issue with that because I would rather have our leaders use such tools as rationality, logic, evidence, and common sense over faith *every* time when making decisions that will impact me, my family, and my country. We saw this when Texas Governor Rick Perry suggested that we use prayer instead of changing our gun laws to address gun-related violence[1]. We saw this when Louisiana Senator Mike Walsworth grilled a high school teacher about evolution during a hearing, and asked the leading question of whether or not E. coli bacteria can evolve into a human being.

Lately it appears that we've taken several steps backward. We have somehow managed to elevate ignorance and punish elitism. In the political environment today, elitism has become a bad word. It has a negative connotation and is used to paint a candidate as out of touch with the normal American citizen. I can't think of another profession where elitism is so poorly regarded. Michael Jordan was an elite basketball player who lives a lifestyle that I (and 99% of America) wouldn't relate to. In no way does that mean that I would pass on the opportunity to have him on my team. Politicians have a tremendous influence on our daily lives and I think that because we place such a high emphasis on religion, we don't always get the elite. If a qualified person were running for president, how far could we expect that person to get if his/her answer to religious affiliation was: none? John F. Kennedy's Roman Catholicism was very tough to overcome on the campaign trail and that was a mere 50+ years ago. Imagine the difficulties for an atheist or agnostic candidate! The candidate could be absolutely brilliant with very sensible positions on issues of morality and fiscal responsibility, but that same candidate would be excluded from the race before it even began simply because he/she didn't profess belief in an invisible person in the sky. Considering that the vast majority of our scientific elite are either agnostics or atheists, that group is automatically ineligible. Religion is a barrier to getting the most capable of our society to even consider a run for public office. Religion is such a handicap in politics that a candidate can be religious but not agree with a specific religious doctrine, and find himself on the sidelines. When Jon Huntsman ran for the Republican nomination in 2011, he made the cardinal sin of telling people that he believed in evolution, which essentially eliminated his chances with the evangelical voters. His departure from the race could be clocked with an egg timer. The religious condition in politics forces us to dismiss many potentially elite candidates.

Barry Goldwater, the former 5-term Senator from Arizona and the 1964 Republican nominee for President, saw religion's ability to influence politics

---

1 Houston Chronicle. Perry pushes prayer, not legislation, to fight violence. January 16, 2013

and warned us of its dangers decades ago. The man known then as "Mr. Conservative" would be considered liberal by the Tea Party standards of today. Goldwater warned us of these dangers in a speech in the US Senate on September 16, 1981, by saying:

> "On religious issues there can be little or no compromise. There is no position on which people are so immovable as their religious beliefs. There is no more powerful ally one can claim in a debate than Jesus Christ, or God, or Allah, or whatever one calls this supreme being. But like any powerful weapon, the use of God's name on one's behalf should be used sparingly. The religious factions that are growing throughout our land are not using their religious clout with wisdom. They are trying to force government leaders into following their position 100 percent. If you disagree with these religious groups on a particular moral issue, they complain, they threaten you with a loss of money or votes or both."

> "I'm frankly sick and tired of the political preachers across this country telling me as a citizen that if I want to be a moral person, I must believe in 'A', 'B', 'C' and 'D'. Just who do they think they are? And from where do they presume to claim the right to dictate their moral beliefs to me?"

> "And I am even more angry as a legislator who must endure the threats of every religious group who thinks it has some God-granted right to control my vote on every roll call in the Senate. I am warning them today: I will fight them every step of the way if they try to dictate their moral convictions to all Americans in the name of 'conservatism'."

In 1994, Goldwater cautioned us about the dangers of mixing religion and politics, and nearly two decades later we've seen his words become reality.

> "Mark my word, if and when these preachers get control of the [Republican] party, and they're sure trying to do so, it's going to be a terrible damn problem. Frankly, these people frighten me. Politics and governing demand compromise. But these Christians believe they are acting in the name of God, so they can't and won't compromise. I know, I've tried to deal with them."

This is precisely what has happened to American politics. We have not heeded the warnings from folks like Barry Goldwater even though we've had ample time in which to do so. An August 2012 Gallup poll showed that a record low 10% of Americans approved of the job that Congress had been doing. When 90% of the population is sick and tired of the lack of civility and compromise by our political leaders, the infusing of religion into the political decision making process is not helping the situation. As Goldwater foresaw, many of these politicians were unwilling to compromise on positions where religion eliminates any middle ground. Religion is holding back progress and it is becoming imperative that we recognize this.

The retardation of progress by religion appears to know no bounds. Today we have politicians dismissing well-established scientific principles in favor of religious narratives. It becomes more than inconvenient when the politicians happen to be on the US House of Representatives Committee on Science, Space, and Technology. It becomes embarrassing and dangerous. Representative Paul Broun, a Republican from the great state of Georgia, delivered a speech in 2012 at the Liberty Baptist Church Sportsman's Banquet in which he referred to science as the work of the devil. Mr. Broun is a medical doctor with a B.S. in Chemistry, which makes his comments all the more troublesome and provides ample evidence to support the statement that religion has the ability to manipulate and warp even the most brilliant of minds.

> "God's word is true. I've come to understand that. All that stuff I was taught about evolution and embryology and the Big Bang Theory, all that is lies straight from the pit of Hell. And it's lies to try to keep me and all the folks who were taught that from understanding that they need a savior. You see, there are a lot of scientific data that I've found out as a scientist that actually show that this is really a young Earth. I don't believe that the Earth's but about 9,000 years old. I believe it was created in six days as we know them. That's what the Bible says.

> And what I've come to learn is that it's the manufacturer's handbook, is what I call it. It teaches us how to run our lives individually, how to run our families, how to run our churches. But it teaches us how to run all of public policy and everything in society. And that's the reason as your congressman I hold the Holy Bible as being the major directions to me of how I vote in Washington, D.C., and I'll continue to do that."

When a politician openly admits to allowing the Bible to be a major influence on how he votes, it is both inappropriate and problematic to have a man like that on such a scientific committee. Sitting next to him is Republican Todd Akin from Missouri who when talking about abortion and pregnancy as a result of rape famously said "If it's a legitimate rape, the female body has ways to try and shut that whole thing down." This is similar to comments made by another Republican Henry Aldridge who in 1995 told the state House appropriations committee that women who are truly raped can't get pregnant because "the juices don't flow, the body functions don't work." These are men who are not only influential in crafting laws that affect citizens on a daily basis but also on issues of great importance that are contradictory to science. Rep. Broun and Rep. Akin are members of an official government body whose purpose is to enhance "long-term economic competitiveness through investments in science and technology" and yet these same folks dismiss both scientific and medical conclusions. A man like Broun who dismisses overwhelming scientific consensus for abstract "scientific data" showing the Earth to be no more than 9,000 years old and created in 6 Biblical days does not belong on a government committee charged with keeping scientific advancement at the forefront. It's no different than asking a pedophile priest to run a daycare—it's inappropriate and wrong.

Politics isn't the only arena in which we as a country seem to be elevating faith over substance. Religion has the ability to infect the very fabric of our society. A significant percentage of the American population literally believes in the talking snake from Genesis. They readily believe the creation of the first woman from the rib of her partner while he himself was created from a combination of dirt and divine breath. Among the world's developed, industrial nations, the United States ranks at the very bottom, just above Turkey, in the percentage of the population that believes in evolution. This ignorance of scientific facts breeds scientific ignorance in other areas. Denying scientific facts in favor of supernatural explanations leaves us stupid. The combination of stupid, complacent, and powerful is dangerous.

The simple lightning rod is a fantastic case in point. In 1749, the lightning rod was introduced to America by Benjamin Franklin. In the event that you are unaware of how a lightning rod works, the electricity from a lightning strike is attracted to a metal rod, follows the attached wire, and discharges the electricity into the ground eliminating the danger of electrocution or fire to the building and its inhabitants. The lightning rod became ubiquitous in our society precisely because of its life and property-saving benefit, and yet religious leaders at the time denounced Benjamin Franklin for circumventing God's will. Lightning was considered an act of god, and how dare Franklin show such arrogance in denying His will!

This exact same line of defense is still being used today in poorer, less literate parts of the world where vaccinations are seen as a circumvention of God's will. If God's plan was for millions of people to die each year from such illnesses as malaria, polio, and measles, by what right do we as His flock have to prevent such illnesses? Even today there are groups around the world who object to vaccination on religious grounds. This endangers them as well as the people around them. Only a religiously-warped mentality can find the moral justification here. In each of these cases, religion serves as an intellectual slaveholder to progress and those actions have consequences.

It may be hard to believe, but in the years 800–1100, the intellectual base of the world was in the Middle East. Forgive the pun, but it truly was the Mecca of intellectual advancement. To this day, we have the Arabs to thank for things like algebra (al-Khwarizmi) and the recognition that fever is actually part of the body's natural defenses (Abu Bakr Zakariya al-Razi). Two thirds of all the named stars in our skies have Arabic names. If you deal with money at all, you're doing so using Arabic numerals. The world saw amazing advances in mathematics, natural sciences, and astronomy during this 300-year period.

To give you an idea of the American equivalent, Baghdad back then would have been to multiple disciplines of science what Silicon Valley is to information technology today. All of the latest advancements, both philosophical and physical, came from this part of the world and Baghdad was open to ideas from people of all religions. For those folks who have only contemporary knowledge of this part of the world, they may be forgiven for not knowing some of its historical contributions. What happened? It's as simple an explanation as it is tragic. Imam Hamid al-Ghazali was a Muslim theologian, philosopher, and mystic who changed the course of Islam and Islamic scientific progress. He denounced math, science, and philosophy as completely inadequate in solving any sort of spiritual concerns. In *The Confessions of Al Ghazzali*, we see that he believed strongly in these disciplines only for studying earthly matters. Anything that could not be found in the Qur'an was essentially the work of the devil. Under al-Ghazzali, often considered the second most important Muslim after the prophet Muhammad, this region of the world began elevating faith over logic. Revelation became more important than reason. The entire intellectual foundation built up over centuries crumbled and it has never recovered. A thousand years later the Middle East is considered "backward" and a relic in comparison to the rest of the world. Can you seriously imagine Baghdad today being what it was back then? The Islamic clerics would never allow such a thing. The clerics back then put faith above all else and the region continues to reap what they've sowed.

There is a lesson to be learned here. As George Santayana once said, "Those who cannot remember the past are condemned to repeat it." I can't help but look around my country and see similarities. Looking ahead, I believe our future and our economy depend on reasoning, logic, and scientific advancement. Faith has the ability to kill this progress as it has done in the past. I'm literally watching this happen with every new political season. My country has become complacent and religiously motivated which does not bode well for future progress.

For example, from an economic and medical perspective, we have allowed faith to prevent us from furthering our research with embryonic stem cells. President George W. Bush famously cut federal funding for this research and the faithful in our society cheered him for it. China, on the other hand, has significantly increased its efforts in this field over the past decade. They have devoted considerable research on bone marrow and embryonic stem cells and have clinical applications of stem cells in cases of acute heart failure and acute liver failure. China has created the most favorable environment for this type of research. They have leapfrogged us in this area and we have nobody to blame but ourselves. This type of tissue engineering holds tremendous potential, both medically and economically, precisely because the new tissue won't invite the same type of attack from the patient's immune system as is commonly found in donor tissue. We as a society applied religious reasoning to this situation and are losing out on this advancement because some believe that these embryonic cells are...babies. The problem is that they are not babies. Human embryos are smaller than the period at the end of this sentence. Blastocysts are made up of just 100 cells. They do not have a central nervous system and cannot feel pain. Because they do not have a brain, they are not conscious beings. We will allow someone's life to be ended when there is no more brain activity, but stem cells without brains are somehow off limits. We treat the potential of life as more important than the potential betterment of existing life. Religious belief has stopped that process. Imagine if history one day references us in the same breath as the Middle East from 1,000 years ago. In retrospect, the Middle East paid a terribly high price for their faith. It saddens me to think that my country could pay a similar price for our faith.

Faith is the name that we give to the practice of believing something without rational justification and it is the excuse we give each other for allowing the belief to perpetuate. In fact, the very definition of faith should give us pause for concern: a firm belief in something for which there is no proof.[1] Once given critical consideration, it becomes obvious that religious faith is not a virtue. Voluntary ignorance is not something to be proud of and yet we can find great numbers of people doing this on a daily basis. These same people will use reason and logic in virtually every facet of their lives, but when it comes to the big questions, they readily abandon all reason and logic particularly if it conflicts with their faith. Why should we choose faith over reason for the most important truths?

Faith can make us do things that others might question but that we can morally justify purely on the basis of our faith. For example, a dear friend of mine that I have known for more than a decade has a terrible marriage. She has suffered through physical and verbal abuse. She has considered divorce and has even gone so far as to consider legal proceedings. When asked why she didn't go through with it, she responded "because it would be wrong in God's eyes." Faith in God is preventing her from leaving a bad situation. She truly believes that being in that marriage is better than disappointing God. That seems, to me at least, to be utterly ridiculous, however she can morally justify it. Her vows to God on their wedding day transcend the physical and verbal abuse that she has endured and will continue to do so. She is religiously faithful, so it begs the question: how is faith good in this situation? In the tragic event that her husband takes it too far one day, what will be said about the virtues of that vow to God? In the event that her God does not exist, who was that sacred vow given to?

There is no doubting that faith influences our actions. In December 2012, a 25-year-old woman entered the emergency room of a medical facility in Cologne, Germany. As a point of reference before we begin, it is worth noting that the Catholic Church is the second-largest employer in Germany and more than 90% of the funding for the Church's social facilities comes from the government. This gives the Church incredible latitude in the standards of morality that employers and patients must adhere to. Upon arrival, the young woman notified the attending physician, Dr. Irmgard Maiworm, that she had been raped[2]. The police were notified and Dr. Maiworm prescribed the morning-after pill—emergency contraception that can be used to prevent pregnancy up to five days after unprotected sex. When Dr. Maiworm tried to transfer the woman to the nearby St. Vincent Hospital for evidence-gathering purposes, the hospital refused to accept the victim because acceptance could breach their ethical guidelines and put nuns and doctors in a position where a possible abortion could take place. The mere mention of the morning-after pill prevented the Catholic-run St. Vincent's as well as the Hospital of the Holy Spirit from assisting the victim. The practices and

---

1 Merriam-Webster dictionary
2 *Church and State: Where Catholic Beliefs and Public Needs Collide.* Frank Hornig, Barbara Schmid, Fidelius Schmid and Peter Wensierski. SPIEGELnet GmbH. January 24, 2013.

preachments of the Catholic Church were more important than helping a woman who had been raped. Whether it's refusing to help rape victims or a woman staying in a dangerous marriage out of fear of God, I just can't picture Jesus Christ endorsing these actions.

Faith can make us take other kinds of irrational actions as well. Harold Camping, the president of Family Radio, whose mission is to send the Christian Gospel into the world, has on multiple occasions predicted the Rapture—Jesus' second coming. Each of his predictions came and went without Jesus coming back. Many scholars believe that when Jesus spoke to his disciples about his return, the timeline was more immediate. Matthew 24:34 says *"Truly I tell you, this generation will certainly not pass away until all these things have happened."* Obviously, Jesus did not come back. Nor did Jesus come back in 1844 when William Miller predicted it. Jesus failed to return during the many predictions in the 1900's from Jehovah's Witnesses, Chuck Smith, Edgar C. Whisenant, or Harold Camping. Other than the failed predictions themselves, what remains common through each of these moments is the utter disappointment along with the emotional and financial difficulties heaved upon the gullible believers. Each of these days came and went without anyone being magically whisked away up to Heaven. These failed predictions are a great example of cognitive dissonance, which refers to the difficulties that one experiences by having conflicting understandings. They believe in Jesus and they believed that Jesus was coming. When he didn't come, these people were left to try and reconcile the reasons why. They'll do as Harold Camping did by revising their predictions or simply abandoning the prediction all together. Surely it couldn't be because Jesus isn't coming back, right?

Many people laugh off the absurdity of these prognosticators, but the consequences are not nearly as funny. During the run up to Camping's first 2011 prediction of May 21, 2012, I was surprised at how much money was being spent to "save" everyone. Billboards went up all around the country warning us of the impending date. Believers spent their life savings, left their jobs, and traveled around the country warning others. What took years to acquire was lost quickly, and there's little humor in that. Sadly, the belief of an impending return by Jesus is not relegated to the margins of society. According to a recent Pew Research survey, 4 out of every 10 Americans believe that Jesus is coming back during their lifetime. That number approaches 6 out of 10 among Evangelicals (of which more than half live in the South). Should this not strike us as egotistical? Why else would 41% of Americans believe that they're going to meet Jesus soon in the Rapture? I'm not sure that it would be a good idea for the religious to start dumping their life savings just yet. I'm fairly certain that Jesus is not coming back during our lifetime any more than Elvis is living quietly incognito somewhere. Jesus didn't come back to destroy the Roman Empire as his followers believed he would. He didn't come back during the next generation, or the next generation, or any of the generations that followed. There is no reason to believe that Jesus is coming back anytime soon and certainly not during our lifetime. If someone really believes that Jesus is coming back, what is their incentive to make the world a better place? What motivation exists to improve the lives of others, if 41% of Americans believe that everything is coming to an end in the very near future? That type of thinking can and does influence our actions.

At every step of the process, faith is entirely about irrational thinking. If, for example, the Abrahamic faiths were founded today and made the same type of irrational claims, they would be largely ignored. To have made a cosmological claim two or three thousand years ago about the creation of the universe is one thing. It would be entirely different to try and make that initial claim today. The claim that someone was born of a virgin was plausible two thousand years ago, but that type of claim wouldn't find much traction today, because in addition to being a theological claim, it would also be a biological claim that could be accurately evaluated. Every faith can be painted with the broad brush of irrationality and this irrationality warps our ability to think critically. For example, if we were to give the Israelis the state of Florida in exchange for giving up Israel, would they take this offer? It would mean no more rockets being lobbed over their border, no more suicide bombings, and no more living in fear. God's chosen people would finally have peace. The Jewish people would never accept this, however, and the reason they wouldn't ever accept a proposition like this is because they believe that they were given rights to a specific area of land by God himself. This kind of thinking puts not only the Israelis in danger but their allies as well. Believing that God, in his role as a divine real estate broker, gave certain primates exclusive domain over a piece of land is the very essence of religious irrationality.

Religious irrationality becomes plainly evident any time we encounter religious fundamentalists. To read and interpret the Bible or the Qur'an as it was written gives us people who do derive their morals from these texts; however, these are not universally-accepted morals. Our mainstream society in the United States generally frowns upon fundamentalists and the messages they spread. It seems like a rather obvious question, but if we as a society find fundamentalists deplorable, why don't we extend that same deplorability to the religion to which they adhere so strictly? We can't logically argue that their interpretation of the text is wrong per se. Frankly, fundamentalists are generally much more knowledgeable about their holy book than their moderate counterparts. If we could bring a first century Christian or a seventh century Muslim into the 21st century, we would likely find their religious knowledge to be as comprehensive as that of any fundamentalist today, but their world knowledge would embarrass any grade school teacher. At one time it would have been deemed both rational and moral to stone someone for working on the Sabbath, yet most Christians and Jews wouldn't consider such a thing today. Modernity continues to chip away at religious irrationality, but there is still work ahead of us.

Perhaps one day modernity will finally eliminate the differences between non-religious and religious people. A nonreligious person believes that man is born good and is made bad through his actions. A religious person believes that man is born incurably bad and can only hope to become well through faith. The nonreligious person believes that our time on Earth is all that we have and it should be treated with care while we're alive. The religious person believes that the show doesn't end with death. There is a better place to go once they die. The problem is that every religion has a different place to go. Sadly, religious zealots would like to get us there quickly, and that's a dangerous problem.

CHAPTER 5: THE OMNI PARADOX

> "Take the risk of thinking for yourself, much
> more happiness, truth, beauty, and wisdom will
> come to you that way."—Christopher Hitchens

The Omni Paradox is a continuation of the Epicurean Paradox put forth by the ancient Greek philosopher Epicurus and deals with the problem of evil in the world. Let's quickly define the words above so that we have a common understanding of what the Omni Paradox is. The word "omni" comes from the Latin word "omnis" which means "all" or "universally." Something that is omnipresent means that it is literally "present in all places at all times." Paradox refers to contradictory conclusions based upon accepted logic and reasoning. God is frequently described in "omni-like" terms. For most religious people, they never give any meaningful thought as to what this means, so let's examine this concept.

1. God is All-Powerful (omnipotent)
2. God is All-Knowing (omniscient)
3. God is All-Good (omnibenevolent)

If we were to try and define "God," we would likely use these three characteristics to describe Him. Does God fit all three of those statements? Is He perfect? Does He have any limitations? If we could show that God is not all-powerful, would that change our minds as to what He can accomplish? If God was not all-knowing, would that wash away the perception of God having a plan for each of us? If God was not all-good, would the admiration and love heaped upon Him seem misplaced? If God couldn't fulfill these 3 concepts, would you still consider Him God? Let's apply a few real-world scenarios to these statements and see how this impacts our perception of God and His capabilities. Once we've looked at these cases, we'll review some of the common arguments against them.

~ Haiti ~

If we look at the devastating earthquake that ravaged the people of Haiti in January of 2010, 3.5 million people were affected of which an estimated 316,000 people died[1] and 300,000+ were injured. The 7.0 magnitude left nearly one million people homeless[2] and rendered much of the surrounding infrastructure destroyed or severely limited. Hospitals along with emergency and communication services in the capital city of Port-au-Prince were decimated. The quake spared neither the rich nor the poor. 80% of the population is estimated to be Roman Catholic so the faithful suffered the same as everyone else. Morgue facilities in the city were so overwhelmed that government workers had to solemnly load thousands of bodies into trucks for deposit into mass graves. In the settlement of Titanyen, dump trucks carried the dead to impersonal and undignified mass burials. The stench of death hung in the air amid Haiti's normal heat and humidity while bodies literally piled up outside the morgues.

- If God is All-Powerful and All-Knowing but not All-Good, then we could justify the suffering because He simply doesn't care.

- If God is All-Knowing and All-Good but not All-Powerful, then we could justify the suffering because He was powerless to stop it.

- If God is All-Good and All-Powerful but not All-Knowing, then we could justify the suffering because He was clueless and had no idea that it was going to happen.

Regardless of how we choose to explain God's involvement in the earthquake, or lack thereof, the end result is still the same. A large number of people died and suffered and God did nothing to prevent it.

~ Elisabeth Fritzl ~

In April 2008, Elisabeth Fritzl reported to police that she had been held captive for 24 years by her father Josef Fritzl. Josef built a chamber and concealed it in the basement of the family home. One day he held an ether-soaked towel to his daughter's face until she was rendered unconscious. He then confined her to this area where he raped and physically assaulted her repeatedly over the course of those 24 years. Elisabeth gave birth to seven children, who were often forced to bear witness to the subsequent sexual abuse, and she had one miscarriage during her incestuous time in the "dungeon."

After she was finally uncovered, Elisabeth recounted to authorities her first days in the dungeon. She screamed for help. Blood dripped down her arms as she tore her fingernails, clawing away at the 5'6" ceiling and banging on the walls for help that never came.

If God is All-Knowing, He was certainly aware that she was down there every single day of those 24 years. Why didn't He act? If God is All-Powerful,

1 Haiti raises quake death toll on anniversary. CBC News, 12 January 2011
2 "Haiti will not die, President Rene Preval insists." BBC News. 12 February 2010

why was He unable to intervene? If God is All-Good, why didn't He show His love to her or her children by stopping the abuse? To Elisabeth and any reasonable person, God displayed none of those traits.

~ Catholic Sex Abuse Cases ~

This is a pretty well-known story having received much publicity over the past few years. Catholic priests from around the world have been accused of committing sexual abuse with children. The stories of abuse are not one-time incidents as many go back literally decades. Members of the Catholic Church are still under investigation for ignoring the allegations, not reporting them to authorities, and for intentionally reassigning those that committed these crimes to other parishes.

Lest you think this is merely a few bad apples, the John Jay report in 2004 concluded that there were a total of 4,392 priests and deacons whom more than 10,000 allegations have been made[1]. In 2009, the Pope indicated that these numbers were in line and comparable to those found within other groups and denominations.

The Catholic Church has never been accused of being "current with the times." Their often draconian interpretation of the world has historically led to conflicts between the church and various cultures. Just prior to his death, Cardinal Carlo Maria Martini, the former papal candidate and archbishop of Milan, said "The Church must admit its mistakes and begin a radical change, starting from the pope and the bishops. The pedophilia scandals oblige us to take a journey of transformation." He said the Catholic Church was "200 years out of date." Today we see 60% of Catholics in the United States voicing their concern that the Church is still out of touch with the views of its flock[2]. In an interview with George Stephanopoulos, Archbishop of New York Cardinal Timothy Dolan said that "Sometimes by nature, the Church has got to be out of touch with concerns, because we're always supposed to be thinking of the beyond, the eternal, the changeless. Our major challenge is to continue in a credible way to present the eternal concerns to people in a timeless, attractive way. And sometimes there is a disconnect—between what they're going through and what Jesus and his Church is teaching. And that's a challenge for us."

Perhaps part of that cultural divide stems from the Catholic bishops who chose to view pedophilia as a spiritual problem requiring a spiritual solution. Instead of seeking criminal charges for the priests who committed the sexual abuse, many were recommended for psychiatric and psychological treatment. These bishops believed that those who could successfully complete the treatment, similar to alcoholics, could safely be returned to religious service. In fact, many centers like the Saint Luke Institute in Maryland were used to do just this. This is yet another example, repeated over the course of

---

1 John Jay College of Criminal Justice (2004), "Executive Summary," *The Nature and Scope of Sexual Abuse of Minors by Catholic Priests and Deacons in the United States 1950–2002*, United States Conference of Catholic Bishops, ISBN 1-57455-627-4, retrieved February 7, 2012

2 ABC News/Washington Post poll. March 2013

decades, illustrating the ability of religion to warp minds into thinking some very bizarre, irrational, and immoral things.

Decades later we're still learning about just how corrupt and deep the cover-ups were. Personnel files from Los Angeles showed how retired Cardinal Roger Mahony and other Roman Catholic Archdiocese leaders shielded pedophile priests while keeping details secret from parishioners. When Mahony learned of allegations that Reverend Lynn Caffoe was locking young boys in his room, videotaping their crotches, and participating in phone sex, he wrote, "This is all intolerable and unacceptable to me." Clearly his moral compass was having difficulty with the situation, but Mahony didn't attempt to defrock Caffoe until more than a decade later. The lawsuit against the archdiocese includes the personnel files of thirteen other Catholic officials showing internal decisions on how best to shuffle problematic priests from parish to parish. In one case, a memo to Mahony suggested that the offending clergyman be sent to a specific therapist because that therapist was also an attorney. Any information from those sessions would be legally protected by the attorney-client privilege. In another case, an exiled priest sent to the Philippines was paid a secret salary after information arose about a teen that became pregnant by either this priest or any of six other priests who were illegally having intercourse with the minor. In every one of these instances, the church leadership explicitly showed a greater interest in the church than they did for the welfare of more than 500 victims of the abuse. This wasn't a momentary lapse in judgment. This was a concerted effort to protect the church, and what's worse is that these types of examples can be found in every major city across the country.

The Reverend Benedict Groeschel is a well-known Catholic priest who hosts a weekly show on EWTN, the Catholic television network. The 79-year-old host found himself in hot water during an interview with the National Catholic Register when he said that child sex abusers are often seduced by the victims and do not deserve jail time for first-time indiscretions. "People have this picture in their minds of a person planning to...a psychopath. But that's not the case. Suppose you have a man having a nervous breakdown, and a youngster comes after him. A lot of the cases, the youngster, 14, 16, 18, is the seducer." Groeschel used convicted pedophile Jerry Sandusky as an example, saying, "Here's this poor guy Sandusky. It went on for years. Interesting. Why didn't anyone say anything? Apparently, a number of kids knew about it and didn't break the ice. Well, you know, until recent years, people did not register in their minds that it was a crime. It was a moral failure. Scandalous—but they didn't think of it in terms of legal things." This kind of thinking from a Catholic priest should strike us as both disturbing and dangerous.

What makes the Catholic sex abuse cases different from the rape and abuse that happens daily in our world is that these atrocities were committed by the very people who have the most knowledge and strongest devotion to Jesus Christ. These are the people who preach to us the morals of the Bible and then turn around and do the opposite. These are our spiritual leaders. To blame the Vatican's slow response to an issue that has been known internally to them for decades on cultural differences is both naive and dangerous—indicative of poor leadership, a serious lack of morality, and a draconian interpretation of the modern world.

If we apply this situation to the Omni Paradox, we can conclude that God either allowed this to happen because He couldn't prevent it, had no clue that it was happening, or He stood by and watched it happen with complete indifference for the safety of those children. God is often described as being all-powerful, all-knowing, and all-loving, but it seems rather obvious that those three attributes are completely unearned in each of these stories as well as millions of other daily examples.

~ In God's Defense ~

One of my favorite responses from Christians as to why God allows this to happen is that we, as human beings, are not meant to understand His powers or His way. We have a mere human understanding of God so we shouldn't attempt to question His motives or His capabilities. I've been told on more than one occasion that His logic is so far beyond anything that we can possibly hope to comprehend. If that's the case, then I should be forgiven for asking the rather self-evident question of why we should pay attention to the priests, rabbis, clerics, reverends, and all of the other religious leaders who have written down His words and have done such a fantastic job of interpreting those words for us. After all, it is this same merely human understanding of God that is used to give Him the attributes of all-powerful, all-knowing, and all-loving in the first place.

Mankind's inability to comprehend a deity may be my favorite defense offered up, but the most common defense given for the Omni Paradox is that of free will. God put man on Earth and gave him the ability to make choices. God didn't do those things. Man did those things. Man has the ability to choose between good and evil. If you really think about free will and how it plays into this defense, I hope you'll follow it through to its logical conclusion. All it takes is one—JUST ONE—act of suffering or evil that is NOT caused by man to validate the Omni Paradox and discredit the "free will" defense. Surely we can't blame 2005's Hurricane Katrina or the massive 2011 flooding in Thailand on free will, can we?

Believers can choose to ignore the floods, droughts, genocide, and mass starvation that we see every day on our planet and God's role in it all, but that doesn't mean that those things aren't happening. For those who are standing pat on the "free will" defense, I have to ask whether or not free will circumvents God's abilities? Does free will render God useless? Does the Christian belief that man is a sinner alleviate God of any responsibility to act? Does free will turn God into something no more useful than an impotent bystander—powerless to stop our choices? If free will does not transcend God, then logically God must be powerful enough to override free will. If God is more powerful than free will, He has chosen not to intervene during any of these atrocities or perhaps He wanted them to happen for a reason only known to Him, in which case He falls tragically short of the All-Good (loving) trait.

Regardless of how one chooses to interpret His abilities, the end result is the same and it cannot be argued. Those events happened. God was completely impotent to affect real change. If He could stop it, He didn't. If He loved them, He didn't show it. If He knew it was happening, He looked the other way. At some point, the Omni Paradox should be become self-evident to any rational human being.

I've even heard the argument from Christians that it was Satan who did those things. It was Satan who entered the hearts of those priests. It was Satan who brought the devastation. For those who believe that, I encourage them to read the previous paragraph again and substitute the words "free will" with "Satan." You can achieve the same result. It also seems a rather obvious question, but why can't an omnipotent God defeat Satan or render him powerless? Comedian Bill Maher once asked this same question and rhetorically answered, "...it's the same reason the comic-book character can't get rid of his nemesis. Then there's no story. If God gets rid of the devil—and he could, he's all powerful—well, then there's no fear."

-- Reflection --

Why do bad things happen? People have been asking this question for thousands of years and no religious authority has ever been able to answer that question with any sort of confidence. This should strike us as odd particularly because these same religious authorities claim to personally know not just the creator of the universe, but this creator's mind as well. In fact, they claim to speak on behalf of Him.

In today's constant stream of 24-hour news and information overload, it's easy to gloss over stories like these so please indulge me for just a moment. I'd like you to close this book and think about each of these stories. Seriously—really give them some thought. Try to put yourself into those places. Imagine what it would be like to have the buildings around you suddenly shake and crumble. Imagine hearing your family members scream through the rubble of an earthquake only to hear their voices trail off into silence. Imagine Elisabeth screaming for help. Imagine the confusion and sheer terror she must have felt as she tried to claw her way out of a room built to hold her. Imagine the tears that she shed as her father violated her over and over again, often in front of her own children. Now put yourself into the church and imagine those young boys and girls unable to defend themselves and the shame they felt being abused by someone they had trusted. Imagine the physical act itself of a priest inserting himself into a young child. What if that child were your child? Imagine the pain that this caused, not only physically but emotionally. Finally, imagine each of these situations and the people crying out for God's help. They're crying for a God that isn't going to come—a God that did not come.

The real takeaway here is that the Omni Paradox provides ample evidence to support the common cliché that life is not fair. Every day we can find examples of bad things happening to good people and good things happening to bad people. If a personal god were real and indeed had a plan for each and every one of us, then that would mean that we deserved the bad things that happened to us. The corollary here is that the good things happening to bad people are somehow deserved as well. The purpose behind the Omni Paradox is to show us that God is either imaginary or completely indifferent. When we apply the Omni Paradox to any of hundreds of daily or historical examples (consider the Holocaust for example), we see that life is absolutely not fair and we can reasonably conclude that there is likely no moral arbiter dishing out positive and negative actions. There is just reality and when we finally realize this, the rewarding of good behavior and the punishing of bad behavior takes on new meaning. We become more accepting and understanding of reality without resorting to a naïve, cosmic security blanket telling us that good will always be rewarded and evil will somehow always be punished. Life doesn't work that way.

The next time there is a school shooting, an earthquake, flood, or any other newsworthy event take a moment to apply the Omni Paradox to the situation. Look at the situation and ask yourself whether God could have known about it in advance, cared enough to intervene in it, or was powerful enough to prevent it. You may find your own conclusions to be illuminating.

CHAPTER 6. THE CHRISTIAN REWARD SYSTEM

> "When I was a kid I used to pray every
> night for a new bicycle. Then I realized that the
> Lord does not work that way so I stole one and
> asked Him to forgive me."—Emo Philips

John 1:29 famously tells us, "Behold the Lamb of God who takes away the sin of the world." With more than a billion adherents worldwide, Christianity is the world's largest religion. Nearly one out of every three people walking this planet professes belief in Jesus Christ. With such a large and devoted following, one might be surprised to learn that Christianity is truly one of the most morally-bankrupt belief systems ever created by man. As a former Christian, I can attest to how easily and quickly a Christian either overlooks or through the process of indoctrination simply doesn't realize the implications of vicarious redemption. In fact, this concept is at the very core of the religion. Christianity, a religion built entirely upon a single human sacrifice, would completely be altered if we took away the concept of vicarious redemption, yet it's this immoral belief that is responsible for the faith's complete lack of accountability. This lack of accountability is an unspoken yet desirable quality of a concept that I refer to as the Christian Reward System. As I did with the Omni Paradox, I want to lay out a certain set of conditions—conditions in which we all agree to be true—and then apply them to real life situations to determine their validity.

I refer to the concept of Heaven in Christianity as the reward that all Christians aspire to achieve in the afterlife. If we were to ask a random Christian what it takes to get into heaven, we're likely to hear such answers as "live a good life," "follow the commandments," "believe in God," "go to church," and "don't kill." The Bible can be, and very often is, interpreted in whatever way the interpreter wants it to be. This is evident among the many different denominations of Christianity. It's a telling fact that Christians cannot even agree among themselves on the "correct" interpretations. The Christian Reward System is one thing that is essentially universal to all of these denominations however it remains a concept that often escapes the moral considerations of the common Christian. To get into heaven and enjoy eternal bliss, we need only repent our sins and accept Jesus Christ as our savior. Yes—that's it. We could look at some of the different ways that the various denominations try to interpret the requirements to get the reward, but the acceptance of Jesus Christ as savior is the only true constant.

> "For God so loved the world, that he gave his only Son, that whoever believes in him should not perish but have eternal life." (John 3:16)

> "For by grace you have been saved through faith. And this is not your own doing; it is the gift of God, not a result of works, so that no one may boast." (Ephesians 2:8-9)

> "I am the way and the truth and the life. No one comes to the Father except through me." (John 14:6)

> "For my Father's will is that everyone who looks to the Son and believes in him shall have eternal life, and I will raise them up at the last day." (John 14:6)

> "to open their eyes and turn them from darkness to light, and from the power of Satan to God, so that they may receive forgiveness of sins and a place among those who are sanctified by faith in me." (Acts 26:18)

> "For the wages of sin is death, but the free gift of God is eternal life in Christ Jesus our Lord." (Romans 6:23)

The only way to attain the Christian Reward is through belief. No matter how heroic your deeds as a mortal, you will not be eligible to set foot in Heaven without belief in Jesus. The Christian faith tells us that we are born into sin and are therefore guilty before we've even had the opportunity to take our first breath. No amount of good deeds alone can eliminate the magical curse that was placed upon us. Reread the previous passages and you'll see that the only way to achieve the reward of eternal life is to become a sycophant. Any individual, who believes that Jesus was crucified, buried, and rose again will receive forgiveness for all of their sins. They will receive His gift of eternal salvation through faith in Him.

In our modern world, how do we then reconcile this belief with the reward for it? When I laid out my case for the burden of proof, I demonstrated that belief alone isn't sufficient to make something true. The mere fact that I believe in the invisible pink unicorn living in my backyard doesn't make it so. How can the simple belief in Jesus trump the totality of a person's life and why should a rational person consider that concept virtuous? What about people who have committed actions that are deemed criminal not only by society, but deemed immoral by the Bible itself? If a man has murdered or raped in the past, do those actions prevent him from being able to lay claim to the Christian Reward? Even if they can't name them all, every Christian is familiar with the Ten Commandments, so let's look at this question through the commandments that God considered so profound as to write Himself.

The simplest Commandment from the King James Bible says *"Thou shalt not kill."* Seems pretty straightforward, doesn't it? I think we would all agree that it doesn't leave much room for misinterpretation. Does violating this or any of the other Commandments mean that someone is destined to spend eternity in hell? If a Christian murders someone, will that person go to Hell? Considering the fact that the Bible never clearly states what the eternal, non-negotiable, long-term consequences are for violating any of the Commandments, it's difficult to make that case. We can find more immediate penalties for these crimes throughout Leviticus and Exodus, but in every case, that immediate penalty is death. For example, blasphemy is punishable by death (Leviticus 24:16) and working on the Sabbath day is punishable by death (Exodus 31:15). Death sentences commanded as punishment by a "loving god" for minor things like uttered words or work conducted on a particular day of the week might seem extreme to modern, rational people, but at least the immediate penalty is clearly spelled out for those offenses. In order to find out what the *eternal* penalties are, we have to look further into scripture.

To highlight a Biblical example of murder and its implications on the Christian Reward System, we do not need to look any further than the apostle Paul. Paul was one of the most influential early church missionaries and one of the most powerful influences on the books of the New Testament. In fact, much of the content from the New Testament is attributed to him. Before Paul became a Christian, he was known as Saul of Tarsus. As Saul, he was responsible for the deaths of many Christians. He was involved in the murder of Stephen (Acts 7 & 8) and he actively persecuted early Christians. He doesn't deny any of this as evident from 1 Corinthians 15:9: (*"For I am the least of the apostles and do not even deserve to be called an apostle, because I persecuted the church of God"*) and Galatians 1:13 (*"For you have heard of my previous way of life in Judaism, how intensely I persecuted the church of God and tried to destroy it"*).

In the Bible, Paul is courted by Jesus and goes on to become a pivotal figure in the spread of Christianity. This isn't just amazing by my standards; it's amazing by Paul's as well (1 Timothy 1:12-15). There are many more stories of murder in the Bible, but this one is particularly relevant to our discussion. If Paul, self-admittedly one of the worst sinners, is able to repent, accept Jesus Christ as his savior, and get into heaven, this doesn't preclude others from committing atrocities and still being able to enjoy the Christian Reward System. A murderer can be saved by Jesus; so the Ten Commandments ultimately become irrelevant as it relates to murderers and Heaven. Consider the fact that most (if not all) people, Christians included, have lied, cheated, coveted, or stolen during their lives in direct violation of the Ten Commandments. Reading just the first three Commandments should give us cause for worry if these are the most moral lessons God could impart to us. If the Ten Commandments were truly unbreakable moral "rules" by which we had to live our lives, Heaven would be an awfully empty place. Most Christians would disagree with the concept of an empty heaven, so let's call the Ten Commandments what they really are: the Ten Suggested Guidelines.

Let's just start with the story in Exodus chapter 32, where Moses comes down from Mount Sinai with the commandments in stone. Moses discovers the golden calf created by the people as a false idol. To punish them, God tells Moses to have the men go through town with their swords and kill their brother, friend, and neighbor. The Levites did as they were told and 3,000 people died that day. Then the Lord "struck the people with a plague because of what they did with the calf Aaron had made." It didn't take God long to deviate from "Thou shalt not kill," lending Biblical evidence to the notion that "guidelines" are perhaps more appropriate than "commandments".

While taking the Lord's name in vain cannot be forgiven (Mark 3:28-29), murder is apparently no big deal when it comes to getting into heaven. Under the basic tenets of Christianity, a murderer need only come to Jesus, ask forgiveness, and find himself ushered into Heaven. If a righteous man who has contributed a great deal of good to those around him so much as utters a disapproving word about the Holy Spirit, that kind of transgression is considered unforgiveable. Now I ask you, what is reasonable, equitable, and moral about a belief like this? Acts with life-and-death consequences are forgivable, but negative words uttered about an invisible spirit are somehow unforgivable and punishable by eternal damnation? If this belief holds even a kernel of truth, we must question the morality of a god whose priorities are arguably both arbitrary and psychotic.

To return to our initial question, it becomes clear that murder does not ultimately prevent someone from entering the gates of Heaven as long as they have taken Jesus Christ as their Savior and have asked for forgiveness.

The other half of the question dealt with rapists. While the Ten Guidelines mention murder, God didn't find rape important enough to include in the Ten Guidelines. Fortunately, we can find many examples of rape within the good book. For example, when God commanded Moses to attack Midian (Numbers 31:7-18), all the men were killed, including the five kings of Midian. The Israelites then burned the towns and villages and rounded up all of the women, children, animals, and valuables. They then took all the people, animals, and valuables to Moses and Eleazar. Moses was furious that his military had allowed the women to live. He yelled to his commanders, *"Now kill all the boys and all the women who have slept with a man. Only the young girls who are virgins may live; you may keep them for yourselves."* Here we have Moses, commanded by God, instructing his men to have their way with any young virgin girl. This would appear to be an approval of rape. God will not intervene.

In Judges 21 we are treated to the bizarre story of 12,000 warriors sent to Jabesh-Gilead to kill everyone. They are told to "completely destroy all the males and every woman who is not a virgin." There were several hundred young virgins (how they ascertained this is questionable), so the warriors took them and were allowed to make them their "wives." Sadly, there weren't enough women to go around for all of the men, so the rest of the people felt sorry for them. The leaders instructed the remaining men to visit Shiloh during the annual festival of the Lord. The men were instructed to hide in the vineyards, and when the women came out for their dances, they were to kidnap the woman of their choosing. They did this and returned home with their new "wives." These men not only destroyed a town, they took virgin girls as their own. We have to be certifiably insane to think that these women would give in to the desires of their new "husbands" willingly. No, these women were raped. What's worse is that the warriors didn't get enough, so they had to go to another town to kidnap and rape more women. All of this was done under God's watchful eye. This too would appear to be a tacit approval of kidnap and rape. God again will not intervene.

Deuteronomy 20:10-15 gives us explicit instructions on what to do when attacking a city and offering peace to the citizens. If they accept the offer of peace, every citizen will live but will be forced to become a slave. If they refuse an offer of peace, God commands that we lay siege to the city. Every man should be put to death, but the women, children, and livestock (notice how they are all neatly grouped together) may be taken as plunder. This is how we are to treat any city that does not belong to a nearby nation. This essentially gave the men a license to take what they wanted by force (plunder). Take anything, including women and children. Here God is endorsing the enslavement, murder, and raping of anyone who chooses to stand and fight these advances. Again, this would appear to be another example where God approves of rape done in His name.

Deuteronomy 21:10-14 appears to show God's restraint in this area. If we are to find ourselves attracted to a beautiful woman that we have taken captive in war, we may take her as our "wife." Before we can do this in the eyes of the Lord, we must first take her to our home, shave her head, trim her nails, and give her a change of clothing. God commands that we give her a month to mourn the passing of her parents. Once that time has passed, she can be our "wife." Somehow I can't imagine many of these women falling in love with their captors, and perhaps God agrees with me because He commands us to release her if we are not pleased with the woman. Notice that God doesn't say if the woman is displeased with us—only in the event that we are displeased with the woman. If that happens, we are not to sell her or treat her as a slave. While He doesn't discourage the practice of rape, it would appear that God felt it necessary to wrap some arbitrary moral rules around it.

In 2 Samuel 12, we learn that David has killed Uriah the Hittite and taken his wife. This did not please the Lord, who takes David's wives and allows someone close to sleep with the wives (2 Samuel 12:11-14). As additional punishment, the child that David has with his new "wife" is dead seven days later. Because David sinned, his wives are raped in broad daylight. It would appear that God not only approved of rape yet again but actually commands that it be done!

We mustn't overlook the story of Sodom and Gomorrah. Abraham's nephew Lot offers up his virgin daughters for rape as appeasement to a crowd that wants to rape male angels. In Judges 19, a similar story is told of a Levite (priest) traveling with his concubine who is given shelter by an old man. The other men of the city knock on his door, demanding the male guest be turned over to them for rape by the crowd. The man pleads to leave the male guest alone and urges the crowd to take not only the man's concubine, but the homeowner's virgin daughter as well. The crowd gang-rapes the two women all night long and doesn't stop until the sun rises the following day. The poor concubine stumbles to the doorstep after a vicious night and crumples to the ground. In the morning, the Levite sees her there and patronizingly said, "Get up; let's go." There is no answer because the woman has died (Judges 19:25-29). God did not intervene. In fact, it would appear that God watched with complete indifference.

In all of these instances, God is either unconcerned with or explicitly rewarding men with rape, but that doesn't mean that there isn't punishment for "immoral" sex. Deuteronomy 22:23-24 tells us that if a man meets a virgin who is pledged to be married and sleeps with her, both he and the woman should be stoned to death. It is somehow assumed that if the woman doesn't manage to escape, she must be a willing participant and therefore guilty of not being faithful to the man she's expecting to marry.

Deuteronomy 22:28-29 actually provides instructions in the event that a virgin girl who is not engaged to be married is raped. If the act is discovered, the rapist must pay the girl's father 50 shekels of silver, marry her, and he can never divorce her. I couldn't make this up if I tried. Not only does the girl get violated, but now she has to wed the very man responsible for raping her. While this presumably means he is also responsible now for her upkeep, there is no specification as to how well he has to treat her. There is not much positive in this scenario for the woman. Now, many religious people will make the case that this passage, along with every other uncomfortable passage in the Bible, is simply taken out of context and that the Bible doesn't actually mean to say any of this. Even if it were possible to explain away the immorality of these passages, the fact that there is dollar value attached to the girl highlights a common misogynistic theme of the Bible. As we have seen, women are held in such low regard that it wouldn't be out of place to have such bizarre rules in the event that such a rape occurred.

Search high and low, but there is absolutely nothing in the Bible to suggest that the despicable act of rape would prevent someone from entering Heaven as long as they accepted Jesus Christ and asked for forgiveness. God is willing to forgive people of their sins (Ezekiel 18:27-28). Based on this information, it's fair to conclude, that according to the Bible, neither murder nor rape is an automatic gate closer for Heaven.

At the beginning of this chapter, I likened the Christian Reward System to the Omni Paradox. If we lay out a certain set of conditions, conditions in which we all agree to be true, and then apply them to real life situations, the conditions seem to either contradict themselves or become senseless and moronic. Unlike the Omni Paradox, we only have one condition for the Christian Reward System: accept Jesus Christ as your savior and you will get into heaven. As we did with the Omni Paradox, let's apply this condition to some real world examples.

Joshua Milton Blahyi is a name that most of us in the United States have never heard of. We may not have even heard of his nickname, "General Butt Naked," but people living in the West African country of Liberia still fear him. As a former warlord, Blahyi was responsible for the deaths of more than 20,000 people. That's not a typo. Twenty thousand people are dead because of him. He has admitted to regular human sacrifice as part of his pre-battle preparations, saying, "Usually it was a small child, someone whose fresh blood would satisfy the devil." He admitted to "the killing of an innocent child and plucking out the heart, which was divided into pieces for us to eat." He told the *Seattle Post-Intelligencer*, "Sometimes I would enter under the water where children were playing. I would dive under the water, grab one, carry him under and break his neck. Sometimes I'd cause accidents. Sometimes I'd just slaughter them." He earned his nickname by going into battle wearing only his shoes and a gun, believing that his nakedness would protect him. He believed that he had magical powers that could make him invisible, which allowed him to be so successful when capturing towns.

In 1996, Blahyi claimed that Jesus Christ appeared to him as a blinding light during a difficult battle, similar to the Apostle Paul's conversion on the road to Damascus. Jesus apparently told Blahyi that he would die unless he converted and asked forgiveness for his sins. The story continues that Blahyi put down his weapon and converted to Christianity. Later he founded and currently serves as the president of End Time Train Evangelistic Ministries in Ghana where he preaches the Gospel. He is also the subject of a documentary entitled "The Redemption of General Butt Naked," produced by *The Economist* and PBS "NewsHour", where he travels the nation preaching the word of God and asking forgiveness from those that he has hurt. "It's the toughest moment in my life to see somebody who I hurt in the past," he says during the film. "There are thousands of people that can stand up here and say, this is what he did to me, this is what he did to my brother. I'm guilty. I'm 100 percent guilty for all the things I did in the past."

Watching the documentary, it is important to see for yourself how Blahyi is being held up by some Christians as the ideal example of what redemption looks like. Just like the apostle Paul, Blahyi was responsible for many deaths but was saved by his repentance and conversion to Christianity. This is not a hypothetical situation. This takes the very idea of redemption and puts a face on it! Do you think Joshua Blahyi should go to Heaven? Do you think he should be rewarded with everlasting life? What do you think the families of the 20,000 murdered victims might say? Your opinion doesn't matter. My opinion doesn't matter. God doesn't care about our opinions. According to Christian doctrine, we have absolutely no influence in whether or not this mass-murderer gets to spend eternity in Heaven.

As we did with the Omni Paradox, when we apply the Christian Reward System to this situation, Blahyi is clearly able to have eternal bliss in Heaven on the basis of belief alone. To be a Christian is to believe that Blahyi has been forgiven of his sins and will not face punishment for them. Just as the apostle Paul before him, Blahyi was responsible for the deaths of his fellow man but found redemption in Jesus Christ. Blahyi himself says, "I know that my sins are forgiven if I accept Jesus, because he's already died for my sins."

Here in the United States, Warren Buffett will be remembered as one of the most successful businessmen and investors of our time. In 2011, the "Oracle of Omaha" was ranked 3rd among the richest people on the planet by Forbes magazine. He has pledged to give away more than 99% of his wealth to philanthropy. Worth a 2011 estimate of $39 billion (that's billion with a "B"); Buffett will leave behind a legacy as one of the greatest philanthropists to ever exist. His money has been pledged to the Bill & Melinda Gates Foundation, which is the largest transparently operated private foundation in the world. He didn't leave any of his money directly to any church or religious foundation. Like me, Warren Buffett is an agnostic who "did not subscribe to his family's religion. Even at a young age he was too mathematical, too logical, to make the leap of faith. He adopted his father's ethical underpinnings, but not his belief in an unseen divinity."[1]

Millions of peoples' lives will be positively impacted by what Mr. Buffett has done. Lives will be saved and families strengthened. His positive impact will be felt long after he has left this world. According to the Bible, though, Mr. Buffett will spend eternity burning in Hell. His crime: he didn't believe in Jesus Christ as personal savior.

Mentioning the Bill & Melinda Gates Foundation leads us to Bill Gates himself. Bill Gates is the former CEO and current chairman of software titan Microsoft. He, along with Paul Allen, delivered the Windows operating system to the world. In 2011, Forbes listed Bill Gates one spot ahead of Warren Buffett at #2 among the world's richest people and #1 among those in the United States. In 2007, the Foundation's founders were ranked as the second most generous philanthropists in the United States. Today, Gates spends much of his time on the Bill & Melinda Gates Foundation, whose purpose is to enhance healthcare, reduce extreme poverty globally, and to expand education in America.

Because of the time, efforts, and financial contributions made by Bill & Melinda Gates and Warren Buffett, children around the world are being vaccinated where vaccinations weren't available before. Hundreds of millions of dollars have been spent on HIV research. Hundreds of millions of dollars have been spent on tuberculosis research. Millions of dollars have been provided for micro-financing networks in impoverished countries around the world to help lift people up and out of poverty. Millions of dollars have been spent on rice research to help keep up with world demand for a food staple. Donations are made to charities every year ranging from CARE International

---

1 Roger Lowenstein. *Buffett: the making of an American capitalist.* New York: Doubleday, 1995 (ISBN 0385484917), p. 13.

to Save the Children. Thousands of students benefit each year through the diversified network of scholarships.

Move over Mr. Buffett, because according to the Bible, Bill Gates will burn in Hell for eternity alongside you. Bill has not accepted Jesus Christ as his personal Savior, and according to Christianity, that is grounds for eternal punishment. Gates was interviewed in 1995 by David Frost for PBS and said, "I'm not somebody who goes to church on a regular basis. The specific elements of Christianity are not something I'm a huge believer in." He continued, "In terms of doing things, I take a fairly scientific approach to why things happen and how they happen. I don't know if there's a god or not, but I think religious principles are quite valid." When asked whether there was something special, perhaps even divine, about the human soul, he responded, "I don't have any evidence on that. I don't have any evidence of that." He later comments, "Just in terms of allocation of time resources, religion is not very efficient. There's a lot more I could be doing on a Sunday morning."

Conversely, on most Sunday mornings you'll find Pat Robertson, a well-known televangelist and ex-Baptist minister, preaching the virtues of Jesus Christ. You may know Pat Robertson from such ventures as the Christian Broadcasting Network and The 700 Club. He believes in Christian dominionism, which means that he believes that Christians have a right to rule the world. If you are not a regular viewer of The 700 Club, you may have missed some of his more controversial statements regarding the terrorist attacks of September 11, 2011, or his many failed predictions. After Hurricane Katrina claimed the lives of 1,836 people, Robertson told his audience on The 700 Club that this hurricane was likely a response from God as punishment for our country's stance on abortion. After the 2010 Haiti earthquake, Robertson attributed the devastation to the Haitian founders and their "pact to the Devil." Of course, he has never offered up so much as a shred of evidence to support any of his theories, but the dumbest of the dumb and the most gullible of the gullible believe him. This is the same man responsible for uttering the following statements:

> "Just like what Nazi Germany did to the Jews, so liberal America is now doing to the evangelical Christians. It's no different. It is the same thing. It is happening all over again. It is the Democratic Congress, the liberal-based media and the homosexuals who want to destroy the Christians. Wholesale abuse and discrimination and the worst bigotry directed toward any group in America today. More terrible than anything suffered by any minority in history."

> "The feminist agenda is not about equal rights for women. It is about a socialist, anti-family political movement that encourages women to leave their husbands, kill their children, practice witchcraft, destroy capitalism and become lesbians."

> "I know this is painful for the ladies to hear, but if you get married, you have accepted the headship of a man, your husband. Christ is the head of

the household and the husband is the head of the wife, and that's the way it is, period."

"There is no such thing as separation of church and state in the Constitution. It is a lie of the Left."

Robertson has used his extensive religious knowledge and apparent "spiritual connections" to make a number of predictions. Pat apparently has a direct line to God which he has used to predict the end of the world. In fact, he used his TV show to say, "I guarantee you by the end of 1982 there is going to be a judgment on the world"—a prediction that Russia would invade Israel. In 2004, Robertson claimed that God Himself told him that President George W. Bush would win re-election in a "blowout." In 2006, he predicted that the Pacific Northwest would be hit by a tsunami. "If I heard the Lord right, about 2006, the coasts of America will be lashed by storms." In 2007, he heard from God again who told him that a terrorist attack on the U.S. would bring about "mass killings." "The Lord didn't say nuclear, but I do believe it will be something like that." In 2008, he predicted that if the U.S. opposed Russia's expansion and future desire to enter the Middle East, nuclear strikes could hit our coastal cities. When he made this prediction, he added that "In conclusion, it is my opinion that we have between 75 and 120 days before the Middle East starts spinning out of control." Demonstrating his superior financial acuity in 2009, he heard from God yet again, "If I'm hearing [God] right, gold will go to about $1900 an ounce and oil to $300 a barrel."

For a man who claims to personally hear from God so frequently, he sure has difficulty understanding Him. The end days promised in 1982 came and went. We're still here. The landslide that George W. Bush was to win by in 2004 ended up being one of the closest large elections in history. A tsunami never came to destroy the coasts of our Pacific Northwest. There was no major terrorist attack on America in 2007, let alone a nuclear attack. The Middle East has always been a political mess, but they didn't spin out of control and our coastal cities didn't experience a nuclear attack. Gold never hit $1,900 an ounce and oil never reached $300/barrel in 2009. In fact, gold opened at $874.50 in 2009[1] and peaked briefly at $1,212.50 on December 9th. Oil never went above $82/barrel all year. This shouldn't surprise us as this is the same man who went on television, squints his eyes straining to understand what God was telling him, and told his viewers that God was going to provide one million dollars to the lucky 700 Club viewer who was praying at that exact moment for one million dollars. If it were that easy, we'd all be millionaires.

At the risk of offending the estimated 1 million people who tune into this mountebank each day, at what point should a rational person cease giving this man our time and money? It is a far greater likelihood that he is either delusional or lying about God speaking to him than the assertion that he maintains a direct line to the creator of the universe. In any event, enough people believe what this man says to make him one of the wealthiest televangelists in the world. He is a classic example of what makes religion danger-

---

1 http://www.usagold.com/reference/prices/2009.html Retrieved 11/18/2011

ous. Religion allows us to disregard logic and reasoning in favor of faith. Even with apparent direct knowledge provided by God Himself, Robertson has been completely wrong so many times, and unlike science, he has absolutely no burden of proof to bear. When no nuclear terrorist attack happened in 2007, he remarked in January 2008 "All I can think is that somehow the people of God prayed and God in his mercy spared us." This, my friends, is a good example of the Divine Default—the attribution of God where no evidence exists. Robertson could have attributed it to the flying spaghetti monster and the validity of the attribution would be the same.

Charles Taylor, the former President of Liberia, gave Pat Robertson mining rights in Liberia. Robertson used The 700 Club program to show support for Taylor during the Second Liberian Civil War and criticize the United States' role in 2003. As Taylor was being indicted by the United Nations for war crimes, Robertson's investment in the mine had reached a value of $8 million. During all of his public support for President Taylor, Robertson never mentioned his interest in keeping Taylor in power. When Congress passed a bill offering $2 million for the capture of Charles Taylor, Robertson accused then-President George W. Bush of "undermining a Christian, Baptist president to bring in Muslim rebels to take over the country." While Robertson was publicly supporting Charles Taylor, Taylor was providing safe haven for the Al Qaeda members responsible for the 1998 bombings of U.S. embassies in Kenya and Tanzania. The stench of hypocrisy should choke his followers, but it doesn't. He may say one thing, but his actions time and time again are 180 degrees different.

Robertson's tax-exempt organization, Operation Blessing, was useful in furthering his interests. Most Americans will understand the concept of a "blood diamond." Perhaps you've seen it referenced in movies or books. It involves the practice of wealthy, powerful people who use slave or near slave labor to extract diamonds from the mines. It is a brutal situation for those who are forced to work in those mines. While Robertson was telling his viewers the planes were taking relief supplies to genocide victims in Rwanda, his planes from Operation Blessing were being used to haul diamond-mining equipment to his mines. Robertson's company African Development Corporation (ADC) was a major beneficiary. ADC is a private venture that involved both Robertson and the cruel dictator of Zaire, Mobutu Sese Seko.

A former pilot of Operation Blessing admitted during an interview in 1996 that perhaps 2 of the 40 flights to Zaire were actually used for the humanitarian work that Operation Blessing was telling its donors that it was doing. The rest of the flights were related to the business of mining diamonds. For an individual who claims to be a moral man of God, Robertson's actions over the course of decades are at odds with the image that he tries to project.

The point behind these stories is to highlight the lives of 4 men and how they ultimately relate to the Christian Reward System. If we apply the Biblical criteria for admittance into Heaven, a mass murderer like Joshua Blahyi and a deceitful, bigoted, homophobic, charlatan like Pat Robertson get rewarded with eternal life in the kingdom of Heaven, while billionaire philanthropists like Bill Gates and Warren Buffett will burn in Hell for eternity. Ask yourself honestly: which of these types of men would you rather have more of on our planet?

It seems to me that morality can't exist without accountability. If there is no accountability in the Christian faith, the Christian faith simply cannot be considered moral. When a belief system like this will allow a man who literally cut out the hearts of children to enter the gates of Heaven, but the men responsible for vaccinating children in poverty-stricken parts of the world will face "eternal punishment" in a "lake of fire." To believe in Christianity is to believe that men like Blahyi will never be forced to account for their actions while on Earth. A Christian can preach the virtues of divine forgiveness all day, but it doesn't negate the fact that personal accountability is completely absent in the Christian faith. Is it ethical to believe that the wrongs that you are responsible for could be paid for by someone else? Justice does not prevail over evil in these scenarios because mercy is the suspension of justice. Perfect justice and perfect mercy are contradictory. This critical fact shatters the perception of a religion promoted as moral and honorable. Atonement in Christianity is an illusion.

Atonement was important to the Jewish people. During Yom Kippur, for example, we would find goats being sacrificed for this reason. It was common during Jesus' time for Jews to symbolically pass sins onto one of the goats to relieve the people of their sins. One goat would be used as a blood sacrifice. Another would be sent away never to be seen again. This is the very definition of the term "scapegoat." Christianity is a scapegoat religion. It might sound nice if we could take all of our sins and put them onto something or someone else, but by engaging in this primitive practice, we are saying that it's acceptable for another person to be punished for what we do. The totality of one's life becomes completely irrelevant. It doesn't matter whether we are good or bad people. It doesn't matter if we kill people or save lives. Our legacies on Earth do not factor into the Christian Reward System. Jesus is the scapegoat upon which we cast our sins and alleviate any responsibility for them. To refuse this offer of scapegoating is to welcome upon ourselves an eternity of pain and suffering. This is the most basic and central tenet to Christianity...and the most immoral.

Bill Gates and Warren Buffett will leave a far greater and more positive legacy than Joshua Blahyi and Pat Robertson ever will, and yet according to the Bible, these men are destined for an eternity of pain solely because they haven't accepted Jesus Christ. The moral implications are unavoidable. If I commit murder, our legal system will hold me accountable for my actions. If our legal system were like Christianity however, I could commit murder and let you go to prison for my crime instead of me. Vicarious redemption is appalling because there is absolutely no correlation between being a good, moral person and heavenly reward. It's sad really. Other than taking the Lord's name in vain, our actions during our few decades here on Earth ultimately have no effect on our eligibility into Heaven for eternity. Believe and we'll be saved. This type of thinking can (and does) have disastrous consequences. Think about it—Christianity gives us a license to do whatever we want as long as we repent and believe in Jesus. The ultimate importance of our time on Earth is diluted by this faith which is a shame because our time on Earth is the only time of which we can be certain to have.

The Christian Reward System is a morally-bankrupt belief system with no place in today's modern society. To view it any other way is naïve, dangerous, and insulting.

CHAPTER 7. CHRISTIANITY AS A MORAL FRAMEWORK

> "To be fair, much of the Bible is not systematically evil but just plain weird, as you would expect of a chaotically cobbled-together anthology of disjointed documents, composed, revised, translated, distorted and 'improved' by hundreds of anonymous authors, editors and copyists, unknown to us and mostly unknown to each other, spanning nine centuries"—Richard Dawkins

Morality is quite simply the belief that certain behaviors are either "good" or "bad." Christians frequently make the claim that their religion forms the framework for their moral behaviors and without it we wouldn't be able to tell right from wrong. For all monotheists, actions commanded by God are deemed inherently good—a concept frequently referred to as Divine Command Theory. We are going to apply this concept to some real world cases to determine just how well the perceived belief holds up to the scrutiny of common examples. On a side note, this topic is not the exclusive domain of Christianity. The same end result can be achieved by replacing the word Bible with the Qur'an, Torah, the Book of Mormon, or the Bhagavad Gita. While the examples I give are from the Bible, I'm confident that we can find equivalent examples from any holy scripture.

Before we can even begin to discuss morality, we must admit that the capacity to care for others is the most basic prerequisite for this type of discussion. If any sentient being has the capability to feel, then that being also has the potential to experience pain and suffering as well as joy and happiness. Any statement of morality can eventually be reduced to this kind of experiential claim where we can ask the very simple question: how do our actions impact not only our own well-being but the well-being of those around us in either a positive or negative manner? This is important because if we can agree that actions contributing to a healthy and happy state of well-being are better than actions resulting in suffering and misery, then we can look at specific actions against the backdrop of what we'll call our Moral Ladder. At the lowest rung of the ladder we'll find the Moral Void —a place where the worst possible situation for everyone can be found. Conversely, the top rung of the ladder is where the best possible situation for everyone can be found. I refer to this as the Pinnacle of Morality. The moment we acknowledge that right and wrong has something to do with the well-being of another sentient being, then every choice we make can be assigned somewhere between those two rungs on our ladder. Some actions are worthy of being placed higher on the Moral Ladder than others. For example, would it be a good idea for a community to remove the eyeballs of every first-born child? Besides the obvious pain and suffering felt by the child, there would be a significant negative social impact to this type of decision. Any potential parent would be seriously worried about the well-being of the future child he/she planned to introduce to the world. Because this doctrine would affect the first-born child, no parent would be immune to this decision. A reasonable person can see how this type of decision would likely be detrimental to the community. It wouldn't do a very good job of maximizing the happiness of the community. If we are measuring happiness and well-being and we can agree on this basic concept, then the doctrine of removing every first-born child's eyeballs would likely warrant placement closer to the Moral Void. The Moral Ladder is a simple, yet objective way of determining the morality of a particular action or decision by allowing us to rank actions according to their effect on a community.

Here's where religion has had and continues to have the ability to warp our sense of right and wrong. What if the community's decision to remove the eyeballs of every first-born child was the result of interpreting ancient scripture that explicitly stated every first-born child is incapable of truly seeing God without first having the light of the material world removed from his/her sight? How would this affect our original placement on the Moral Ladder? Before his death in 399 BC, the Greek Athenian philosopher Socrates posed the question, "Does God command a particular action because it is morally right, or is it morally right because God commands it?" Once we introduce religious dogma into our equation, we have the ability to take what was once objectively considered immoral and make it moral. Based upon the same amount of pain and suffering, our objective placement of this act near the Moral Void really hasn't changed. Every first-born child still has his/her eyeballs removed and future parents will still have to contend with this, but the religiously dogmatic would have us believe that this act warrants higher placement on the Moral Ladder simply because it was divinely mandated.

Where religion still finds safe haven is in the perception that without it we wouldn't know right from wrong. We have been led to believe that without religion, we wouldn't be able to determine what our values should be. Without its dogma we are somehow helpless in formulating our own moral compass and thus would be more apt to make decisions closer to the Moral Void. As I intend to show, this type of claim (a claim being made on behalf of virtually every religion incidentally) is simply an illusion. In fact, when we consider the actual contents of our religious texts, it seems profoundly troubling that millions consider books like the Bible to be perfect guides to morality. As Sam Harris points out, most of the arguments made on behalf of religion and its exclusive claims on morality are generally conducted under the auspices of one of three positions: 1) a specific religion is true, 2) a specific religion is useful, or 3) atheism/agnosticism is morally corrosive. Rarely does a religious person argue for the truth of their religion. Rarely does someone come forth with confirmation of Biblical prophecies or overwhelming evidence of miracles for example. They more often than not take the second position and argue for the beneficial, social utility of the faith. Every religious person will tout the generosity of their charity work, the comfort delivered to the sick and dying, and the personal fulfillment they find in their faith. The usefulness of something has no bearing whatsoever on the truthfulness of it however. A medical patient given a placebo can achieve recovery even though the placebo had no medicinal value. The usefulness of religion doesn't mean that any of its metaphysical claims are true including any that relate to issues of morality. Throughout history, religion has falsely presented itself as the arbiter of absolute moral truths under the banner of the Divine Command Theory.

If we are being intellectually honest, Divine Command Theory should cause us some grief. A reasonable person should find more than a few issues to warrant a pause in this line of thinking. The first is with the very existence of God. As I am fond of saying ad nauseam, there has not been persuasive enough evidence put forth on behalf of any religion to anoint one as true. To use unsubstantiated faith as the bedrock for belief is a rather fragile and flawed approach. The burden of proof has simply not been met. If the very existence of God cannot be proven, it begs the question as to where "His" commands came from. Here is where religious dogma takes over. The moment you accept that there has been some type of divine revelation to some human being somewhere on our planet, you will then be forced to surrender to the compulsory position of being told what you can think, what you can feel, and how you should act by another human being who is no better a primate than you are. If God cannot be proven, how can we prove that any of the divine instructions that are routinely placed upon us are in fact divine?

Even if we grant the concession that God does in fact exist, why do we rush to believe that God is good? Why do we assume that this being is incapable of bad conduct? What evidence exists to suggest that any command given by God is moral and thus worth following? In virtually every religion, we can find examples of truly barbaric acts being attributed to God. The God of the Old Testament is a sadistic, misogynistic, and homophobic figure guilty of acts that if conducted by a mortal would be immediately considered psychotic and reprehensible. This double standard begs the question of whether "good" means something different for humans than it does for God.

If so, it becomes highly illogical to base our morality on such a double standard. Additionally, what does this say about human beings if we can't figure out right from wrong without Big Brother telling us which is which? Faith robs us of an innate ability.

If morality is truly dependent upon a religious framework like Christianity, it could be logically concluded that someone like me, who no longer believes in the divinity of Jesus Christ and is by all accounts no longer a Christian, has no basis for morality. Does this mean that I, along with millions of other agnostics and atheists, don't have a sense of what's right or wrong? There is no reason to believe such a thing. Let's just for a moment imagine that a group of archaeologists have uncovered the tomb of Jesus Christ. They rolled back the stone at the entrance to the tomb and his bodily remains were found inside. DNA evidence confirmed it. With his divinity proven false, Christianity completely unravels. Are we to believe that two billion Christians around the world would suddenly start murdering each other? Would their moral compass suddenly vanish? A dash of common sense should tell us that this scenario would be highly unlikely. If Christianity faded away today, there is no reason to believe that our sense of morality would fade away with it.

As Richard Dawkins correctly points out in *The God Delusion*, there are two ways to derive morality from the Bible. The first is through direct instruction. God does this through the Ten Commandments and other various instructions that He gives throughout the Bible. The second is through examples, similar to a role model. The cliché "actions speak louder than words" comes to mind. I think everyone, religious and nonreligious alike would agree that if morality comes from God or the Bible, these would be the two methods by which we would retrieve it and this should give us cause for concern.

For a case in point, we need only look at the Book of Genesis and the story of Abraham's nephew Lot to see this Biblical morality in action. The cities of Sodom and Gomorrah, the historical existence of which is still in dispute by modern-day archaeologists, were cities of wicked sin that God saw fit to destroy with fire and brimstone. In an unbelievable exchange, Abraham negotiates with an all-powerful God (Genesis 18:22-33) to spare the city if fifty righteous people can be found within it. God, being an atrociously awful negotiator, gets whittled down to ten. If just 10 righteous people can be found within the city, God agreed to spare them. Like the story of Noah, there lived a righteous man whom God also saw fit to spare. God sent male angels to warn Abraham's nephew Lot. One can only assume angels were sent because a personal visit from God would be less believable. Regardless, Lot invited the angels into his home, but the wicked townspeople gathered around the house. The townspeople demanded that Lot turn the male angels over to them so that they may be raped by the masses (Genesis 19:5). Lot, not wanting to see his angel guests sexually assaulted, comes up with an idea to appease the crowd. He offers to them his two virgin daughters so that they may be raped in place of the angels. Fortunately it doesn't come to that as the angels strike the crowd with blindness and instruct Lot to gather his family and leave immediately. The destruction of Sodom and Gomorrah is at hand, and as Lot's family is leaving the city, they are commanded not to look back at the city. Lot's wife makes the mistake of looking back and God turns her into a pillar of salt for committing such an apparently heinous crime. With the family's matriarch nothing more than sodium chloride, Lot and his daughters escape. Keep in mind that the all-knowing God deemed Lot and his family to be righteous. This makes the next part of the story and the moral lessons derived from it all the more concerning. Lot and his daughters found a cave to stay in. The girls get their father drunk on wine and the older daughter has sex with him. The next night the girls do the same, but this time the younger daughter has sex with her father. Both girls end up pregnant and Lot was apparently none the wiser. What are the moral takeaways from this story? What's righteous about turning a mother and wife into salt for something so petty? What type of respect is placed upon women when offering up virgin daughters to a crowd is deemed moral? Where should we place each of these acts on our Moral Ladder? If the Bible establishes a moral framework, how do stories like these contribute to it in a positive manner and what are we to make of the absolutely immoral portions? Are we to ignore those parts, and if so who decides what should be morally ignored? What is the real moral lesson supposed to be?

I think it's appropriate to classify the people who hold the Bible up as their moral compass into two groups: Biblical moralists and modern moralists. As I will show through this chapter, and really throughout this book, there are plenty of distinctions that separate these two groups. A Biblical moralist uses the Bible, warts and all, to set the guidelines for morality. Most Biblical moralists are known by their more common name: "fundamentalists." To these people, the burning of witches, the persecution of homosexuals, and the suppression of women are not only "right", and beyond question or debate; they are actually dictated by God. 1) God has provided explicit instructions in these matters, and 2) God has provided examples of actions taken either by Him or under His direction that support these moral guidelines. A Biblical moralist uses the whole Bible. Conversely, modern moralists pick the parts of the Bible that they believe are moral and reject the parts that they don't.

I'd wager that a great deal of modern moralists can be found in the pews on Sunday mornings. A modern moralist uses only those parts of the Bible that fit his/her personal notion of what is right and wrong. They would never consider burning someone alive or stoning someone to death. They would almost certainly consider those actions to be immoral, regardless of any command reported to have been given by God or any example in which He is said to have directly or indirectly supported such actions. Modern moralists do not get their morality from the Bible, and this premise can be highlighted by the simple fact that if actions like adultery were actually punishable by stoning and death, we would likely face a shortage of politicians.

If some people consider themselves to be modern moralists, I would like to ask how they determine which parts of the Bible are right and which parts are not? How do they know which of God's commands or actions to reject as immoral and which ones should be followed? What prevents them from stoning unruly children? What prevents someone from killing a person who has committed blasphemy or apostasy? God has given us explicit instructions in these matters and clearly expects us to follow through with them. If God and the Bible are supposed to be the basis of morality, where does this "extra" source of morality come from that is being used to negate the parts of the Bible that someone doesn't morally agree with?

When the obvious contradictions are considered, it should readily become apparent that morality is not based upon the Bible, nor is it derived from a supernatural being. God does not create moral truths—we do; and these truths exist independent of any claimed divine knowledge. Morality is based upon a rational understanding of reality and not upon any assertion of invisible authority. Morality can be found within us irrespective of our religious beliefs, including no religious belief. I would suggest that this extra source of morality comes not from any divine scripture but instead has its roots in biology. Charles Darwin makes a compelling case in *The Descent of Man* for the development of a moral sense from a naturalistic frame of reference. Our innate sense of morality is a natural result of both the biological and social characteristics of human beings. This is why an understanding of God has no bearing whatsoever on whether or not we would instinctively dive into a pool to save a drowning child or throw ourselves in harm's way to prevent our own children from danger.

Incidentally, this altruism is not the sole domain of the human condition which is why it is safe to say that it is biological in nature. We have watched chimpanzees help humans and conspecifics without any sense of reward in return[1]. We have watched vampire bats regurgitate blood for sick bats unable to feast for themselves.[2] At great danger to themselves, velvet monkeys are known to loudly warn other monkeys about a nearby predator[3]. Dolphins have been seen banding together as a raft to help keep an injured dolphin breathing above water[4]. Frans de Waal, an expert on primate social behavior and the Charles Howard Candler professor of Primate Behavior at Emory University, makes a very persuasive case for associating morality to evolution when he says "... conscience is not some disembodied concept that can be understood only on the basis of culture and religion. Morality is as firmly grounded in neurobiology as anything else we do or are. Once thought of as purely spiritual matters, honesty, guilt, and the weighing of ethical dilemmas are traceable to specific areas of the brain. It should not surprise us, therefore, to find animal parallels. The human brain is a product of evolution.

1 *Science Daily: Human-Like Altruism Shown In Chimpanzees.* June 25, 2007
2 F rans de Waal, *Good Natured: The Origins of Right and Wrong in Humans and Other Animals* (Cambridge, Mass.: Harvard University Press, 1996), pp. 20-21.
3 Cheney, D. L. & Seyfarth, R. M. (1990). *How monkeys see the world: Inside the mind of another species.* University of Chicago Press. ISBN 978-0-226-10246-7.
4 New Scientist. *Dolphins form life raft to help dying friend.* Michael Marshall. January 25, 2013

Despite its larger volume and greater complexity, it is fundamentally similar to the central nervous system of other mammals."[1]

Human beings cannot lay exclusive claims to issues of altruism, empathy, or even basic instinctual emotions derived through evolutionary means and molded by societal customs. We can find examples of sexual jealousy for example in apes. The fact that we can find a similar human emotion in an evolutionary cousin shouldn't surprise us, but it is interesting to see where we humans have taken this emotion. As we have progressed morally over time, we have placed cultural restrictions upon each other. Like apes we feel sexual jealousy, but unlike apes that don't possess sophisticated forms of customs like humans, we modify that behavior with cultural practices such as formal marriage ceremonies. There are great benefits to be had by evolving our moral compass. While we can find examples of sympathy-related traits and internalization of rules among the animal kingdom, no species has perfected it as well as our own. Evolution has served us well in this respect. The intellectual superiority of our species has given rise to an umbrella of philosophies and ethical perspectives known as Humanism. Its focus on reason, ethics, and justice allows us to reject the divine as the source for things like morality. Morality is the natural evolutionary product of reason and logic. I would be remiss if I didn't highlight one of the more obvious delineations between humanistic altruism and religious altruism. If the religious argument is true that God is necessary for people to act against their own self-interest (giving alms to the poor for example), then there is either divine reward or divine retribution as a result. If religious people are acting altruistically only because God has commanded it and they want to either enjoy the reward or avoid the punishment in the next life, the irony is that the reward/punishment is actually motive enough for them to act in their own self-interest. If I give to the poor, I'll be rewarded in Heaven. If I don't give to the poor, I'll be punished by disobeying God. This type of thinking robs us of our humanistic compassion and fraudulently takes our natural sense of morality and undeservedly gives it to God. Even though many in our society may not consciously embrace it, their full sense of morality doesn't come from the Bible or any religious text. If it did, the population of fundamentalists in our country and world would be far greater than what we see today.

Within our population, there will always be some who claim that there are absolute moral truths to be had by embracing religion. If killing is wrong and this is a moral absolute, then any killing would be immoral. If lying is wrong and this is a moral absolute, then any lie would be immoral. If you can think of a single instance where either killing or lying would or could be considered moral, then by definition neither is a moral absolute. Chances are that you have already thought of at least one example for each. It's not difficult to find an example where killing or lying can be done in the name of the greater good, and yet we are led to believe that absolute morality not only exists but that it can only be found within a religious framework like

---

1 Frans de Waal, *Good Natured: The Origins of Right and Wrong in Humans and Other Animals* (Cambridge, Mass.: Harvard University Press, 1996), pp. 217-218.

Christianity. Is it reasonable to suppose that the Jews would not have understood that killing other people was wrong before they reached Mount Sinai, where God first commanded them not to kill? Do we really need God to tell us this? Are we to believe that the Jews wandered the deserts for years happily and indiscriminately murdering their fellow humans, oblivious to the consequences of such actions? Common sense should tell us that this is highly unlikely. Morality is innate in us as human beings. To say otherwise is to imply that humans would be incapable of distinguishing right from wrong without a divine big brother.

Our holy texts are not always the best sources of moral lessons. I'm supremely confident that we can find more moral inspiration and moral agreement in such works as Aesop's Fables than we can in the Bible. A great deal of morality can be found in *The Tortoise and the Hare, The Lion and the Mouse, and The Fox and the Grapes*, more than we can find in many of the stories of the Bible. The best part is that we can accept these moral lessons without having to directly reject any specific commands or divinely-inspired actions. For example, we won't find any mass killings of innocent children and women through a global flood in any of Aesop's Fables nor will we find abuse of any kind endorsed. None of the characters in Aesop's Fables kills everyone just to punish a few.

This is not to say that practical life lessons cannot be learned from the Bible or any other religious text, but rather to emphasize the readily apparent and easily digestible wisdom of the parables is also offered through alternatives like Aesop's Fables. Can you imagine the neighbor in *The Honest Woodman* being punished not by losing his own ax but instead by having scores of people killed by an intentional plague? It's terribly difficult to hold up a volume like the Bible as an instrument of absolute morality when that volume includes the story of how God indiscriminately kills

- 500,000 people in 2 Chronicles (13:15-18)

- 14,700 people for complaining about the LORD killing people in Numbers (16:41-49)[1]

- 50,700 people for the petty crime of looking into the Ark of the Covenant in 1 Samuel (6:19)

- 3,000 men and women when God helps Samson destroy the temple in Judges (16:26-30)

- 51 men who were burned to death with fire sent from Heaven in 2 Kings (1:9-10)

- 70,000 people when David takes a census (2 Samuel 24:1-17)

---

1 Some scholars suggest that God only killed 70 people in 1 Samuel 6:19 suggesting an error in an earlier translation. This would certainly be more believable as there likely weren't enough people in the Beth Shemesh village or area. Regardless of the number, does it make God's killing of people for simply peeking into the Ark of the Covenant more moral or honorable?

- And of course the largest genocide ever, when God drowns the entire world, sparing only a single family (Genesis 7:21-23).

If one is able to come to the conclusion that genocide is wrong, we would be best served to ignore Joshua 6:20-21, Numbers 31:6-18, Deuteronomy 2:32-35, Deuteronomy 3:1-7, and 1 Samuel 15:1-9 where God either directly assists or divinely commands the Israelites to destroy Jericho, eradicate the Midianites (except for their virgins, which may be raped), kill everyone including children in Heshbon and Bashan, and exterminate the Amalekites. A normal person would find infanticide and child sacrifice to be morally reprehensible and yet the Bible gives us a God who was responsible for the slaughter of all Egyptian firstborn children (Exodus 12:29), accepted the virgin daughter of Jephthah as a sacrificial offering (Judges 11:30-39), and threatened His followers with forced cannibalism (Leviticus 26:27-29).

Every one of these examples can be verified in the Bible. If the Bible is true, then God has personally intervened in our world and performed actions that a normal person would deem to be immoral. Would these actions be considered moral if they had been committed by an ordinary man? Where should we place each of these actions on the Moral Ladder? God has been responsible for so much death and suffering that His murder tally would make even the most determined serial killer blush with embarrassment. When faced with the astoundingly clear evidence of God's immorality, Christians will inevitably default to the position that God is not human and therefore not bound by human laws. We are not supposed to judge God because we are not qualified to judge Him. Under the Divine Command Theory, the actions of both God and those who follow His commands are always moral even if the absence of God would otherwise place those actions near the Moral Void. This seems an absurd proposition. When we critically evaluate religious claims to moral superiority, we can see that the Bible is no more useful as a guide to morality than a map of Chicago is to guiding us around New York City.

If many of the stories from the Bible have questionable moral value, how should we view the core beliefs of the faith? The central tenet of Christianity is vicarious redemption. To be a Christian is to believe that we inherit the sins of Adam, and yet I find it interesting that many people believe the story of Adam and Eve was not meant to be taken literally. Even the Catholic Church itself questions whether to take the story literally or figuratively. Cardinal George Pell described the Adam and Eve story as mythical, saying, "It's a very sophisticated mythology to try to explain the evil and the suffering in the world." To anyone who doubts the literal creation of Adam and Eve, I wonder how they reconcile a parable to original sin. If Adam didn't literally exist, how can we associate the sin of an imaginary person to Jesus and everyone who came after? Conversely, for those who believe in the literal interpretation of Adam and Eve, does this policy not strike you as asinine? The act of Adam eating the fruit seems to be a rather petty crime worthy of a mere reprimand, certainly not eternal hereditary damnation. This would be no different than you being responsible for the one-time, petty action of your great, great, great, great grandfather. What kind of accountability system is this? As Matt Dillahunty once said, "Anyone who advocates infinite punishment or infinite reward for finite crimes and deeds is morally inferior."

In the end, what is the moral of the Adam and Eve story? Disobey me and your entire hereditary line will be cursed? That doesn't sound very "loving"... but it is close to the real lesson. The moral of the story is a subconscious lesson. According to the talking snake, the fruit is "good for becoming wise." Their eyes were "opened" after eating the fruit and they suddenly became aware of their nakedness. God would punish each of them (including the talking snake) for disobedience. The subconscious moral lesson here is to always obey God and do not ever question Him. In politically incorrect terms, the lesson here is to "shut your mouth, do as you are told, and don't ask any questions."

But if we never seek to "become wise," we become the equivalent of sheep. Oddly enough, Christians tend to make this a virtue. They are happy to be part of the "flock" blindly following their shepherd. Considering the fact that lambs were ritualistically offered as daily sacrifices in Jerusalem (Exodus 29:38-42), what's virtuous about being compared to livestock? To this day I question my own past desire to be part of that livestock. There is no morality in the Genesis story of original sin. It is the house of cards upon which we are convicted of wrong doing without even knowing it. If God is all-knowing, He would have certainly known that Adam and Eve would disobey Him, correct? What's moral about creating man from soil and breath (such an absurd notion in and of itself that I feel the need to repeat it whenever possible), knowing that he's going to disobey you and then passing judgment on every soul ever born thereafter for a decision that you knew he would make in the first place? The concept of original sin is simply bizarre, and just like Alice in Wonderland, it becomes more bizarre the further down the rabbit hole we go.

Atonement means to be "at one" with someone. Christians use the crucifixion of Jesus Christ as the atonement between them and God. I'll never understand how this can be rationalized. In order to reconcile the world to Himself, He needs to send Himself to Earth as Jesus so that He can be murdered (Christians call it a sacrifice) so that God (who is also Jesus) will be at one with the creation that He knew would disobey Him in the first place. Really?

If God didn't know that man would sin, then God is an imbecile who falls tragically short of the all-knowing moniker. If He did know that man was going to sin and went through this whole process anyway, He did it to please Himself. What kind of God is this that builds something faulty, blames His mistakes on the faulty creation, and then requires Himself to sacrifice Himself to Himself for the redemption of His faulty creation? Can you follow the thread on this? To further confuse the situation, when Jesus is apparently raised from the dead, what do we make of the "sacrifice" itself? If the Son and the Father are one, the sacrifice would be purely cosmetic, hardly worthy of the term "sacrifice." Nothing of value was lost.

The moral laws that God apparently established are ones that none of us would ever be able to live up to. Paul makes that pretty clear in Romans. If God had a profession, He would have been an attorney, and a brilliant one at that. He built a loophole into this set of laws. That loophole is Jesus. We are essentially presented with a system that we won't be able to adhere to, but that's OK. It's OK because ultimately it doesn't matter. As long as we believe in Jesus, the laws become suggested guidelines with no real everlasting consequences. In the modern interpretation of Christianity, a violation of one of these laws is irrelevant as long as we believe in the vicarious "sacrifice" of Jesus and his resurrection. This is the most basic tenet of Christianity.

This concept was covered in greater detail in the previous chapter, but it bears repeating because it directly relates to our topic of using Christianity as a moral framework. I would argue that the belief in Jesus as a savior is immoral and therefore cannot be used as the framework for a system of morality. I need only use common sense to back up my assertion. When I reference the "vicarious sacrifice" of Jesus, this means that a Christian is being saved through Jesus' actions, not his/her own. By that definition, our sins and bad deeds can be "paid" for by someone else. Here's the real takeaway on this. This simple belief relieves us of any personal responsibility. If there is nothing else that you take away from this book, I hope you'll remember this concept. Belief in Jesus relieves us of having to take any responsibility whatsoever for our actions, and there is nothing moral, honorable, or virtuous about this. When we really stop to think about it, Christianity is entirely based upon the immoral practice of human sacrifice. It celebrates a single human sacrifice and it portrays it as something that absolves us of any future or previous wrongdoing. If I murder someone, would it be moral for you to go to prison instead of me? Do I not need to be held accountable for my actions? Where do Christians find the morality in this? How can we have morality without accountability, and if we can't, then how can Christianity serve as a framework for morality?

Allow me a quick digression. There is one question about Jesus and his sacrifice that is frequently raised by Christians that I talk to: Doesn't the notion that Jesus went through so much pain and suffering convince you that what he said was real? The corollary question is, why would someone put himself through all of that suffering if it wasn't real? Now, ultimately these questions are both naive and irrelevant. Replace "Jesus" with "Heaven's Gate" and you'll achieve the same result. Is belief alone enough to make something true? When 39 members of the Heaven's Gate cult committed suicide so that they could hitch a ride on the space craft that was supposedly following the Comet Hale-Bopp, did their undeniable belief and inner conviction mean that an alien space craft was actually following the comet? What religious people fall victim to, and fail to understand, is that the level of one's conviction has absolutely no bearing whatsoever on whether or not something is actually true. The fact that people are willing to die for something only means that they believe strongly in it.

I would propose and will provide evidence to support the following statement: Morality changes. Unlike the Bible, morality changes over the course of time. To say that we must have the Bible to have morals would be like saying that a new Ford F150 pickup truck still needs a buggy whip to drive forward. The Bible has essentially remained the same for centuries but acts that Christians deem moral has and continues to change. The Catholic Church is a great example. On March 12, 2000, Vatican official Bishop Piero Marini said, "Given the number of sins committed in the course of 20 centuries, [reference to them] must necessarily be rather summary." In layman's terms, the Church said that they acknowledge the sins that they have committed in the past and that the number of sins is so great that they are not going to take the time to discuss them individually. This was part of a bigger *mea culpa* offered up by Pope John Paul II. Even the Catholic Church can admit that what they've done may have been considered moral at the time but would not be considered moral today. Otherwise, why bother apologizing?

One of those sins was the burning of witches. Between 40,000 and 100,000 women have been killed by Christians using the Bible (Exodus 22:18, Deuteronomy 18:10) as the moral foundation for deciding whether or not someone deemed a witch should be executed. The people who imprisoned, tortured, and murdered those women probably thought they were morally right in doing so. Yet today there an estimated 800,000 adherents to Wicca. Why haven't modern-day Christians, who outnumber Wiccans by a factor of 20,000 to 1, followed God's will and killed them all? If a Christian's co-worker practices Wicca, should the Christian feel morally obligated to execute her? Most Christians would say no, to which I would ask, why not? Exodus hasn't changed. The fact that the practice was once deemed immoral and it no longer is shows that morality changes with time.

There are many passages in the Christian Bible that condone and encourage slavery. In fact, nowhere in either the Old Testament or the New Testament will you find the Bible condemning slavery. It would appear that even Jesus was in favor of slavery. He never once criticizes the institution of slavery and can be found using analogies about the practice. For those who simply ignore the Old Testament, where slavery was quite common, I'd ask you to consider Ephesians 6:5-9 in the New Testament:

> "Slaves, obey your earthly masters with respect and fear, and with sincerity of heart, just as you would obey Christ. Obey them not only to win their favor when their eye is on you, but as slaves of Christ, doing the will of God from your heart. Serve wholeheartedly, as if you were serving the Lord, not people, because you know that the Lord will reward each one for whatever good they do, whether they are slave or free. And masters, treat your slaves in the same way. Do not threaten them, since you know that he who is both their Master and yours is in heaven, and there is no favoritism with him."

Lest you think that I'm cherry picking passages and that reference to slavery in the New Testament is seldom, I offer up another in I Timothy 6:

> "All who are under the yoke of slavery should consider their masters worthy of full respect, so that God's name and our teaching may not be slandered. Those who have believing masters should not show them disrespect just because they are fellow believers. Instead, they should serve them even better because their masters are dear to them as fellow believers and are devoted to the welfare of their slaves."

The Bible actually provides guidelines for the acquisition of slaves as property. Leviticus 25:44-46 educates us on how we can morally pass the ownership of slaves down to our children.

> "Your male and female slaves are to come from the nations around you; from them you may buy slaves. You may also buy some of the temporary residents living among you and members of their clans born in your country, and they will become your property. You can bequeath them to your children as inherited property and can make them slaves for life, but you must not rule over your fellow Israelites ruthlessly."

The practice of slavery in the United States continued until January 1, 1863, when President Abraham Lincoln, using his war powers, issued the famous Emancipation Proclamation. This freed many slaves but did not make them citizens. Slavery wouldn't be officially abolished until the Thirteenth Amendment to the Constitution took effect in December 1865. For the overwhelming majority of human history, slavery was accepted. Using the Bible as a moral framework, slavery was often encouraged. It was big business and slave owners from Biblical times to the founding of our nation certainly considered it moral. Even though there were certainly elements of Christian abolitionists fighting to end slavery, we mustn't forget the historical fact that the banning of slavery was being vehemently opposed by the Catholic Church and other Christian organizations as our government considered outlawing the practice.

If the Bible is dictated by the creator of the universe, He clearly expects us to keep slaves as long as we don't beat them too much. Again—Jesus never says that slavery is bad or that it should be outlawed. This should strike us as somewhat hypocritical if we apply Jesus' most well known and most universal moral teaching—the Golden Rule (Matthew 7:12 & Luke 6:31). The Golden Rule "Do unto others as you would have done unto you" was clearly not followed by any slave-owning Christian, for if it was, it would mean that a Christian was willing to be owned or indentured to another person. Jesus clearly saw no evil in the practice of slavery, nor did Paul, who tells slaves to treat their masters, particularly their Christian masters, well. Until it can be demonstrated that a reasonable person would actually desire slavery for himself, slavery and the attitudes of Jesus and Paul are completely incompatible with the concept of the Golden Rule.

When confronted with the issue of slavery, Christians inevitably fall victim to thinking that the slavery of the Bible is not the same slavery that many of us instantly picture in our minds. If the definition of slavery is "the state of one bound in servitude as the property of a slaveholder or household" or "a civil relationship whereby one person has absolute power over another and controls his life, liberty, and fortune"[1], then any attempt to cleanse the definition in an effort to make it more agreeable is both inappropriate and obscene. We can find examples and instructions in both the Old Testament as well as the New Testament regarding various forms of enslavement ranging from debt slavery to sexual and conjugal slavery along with time frames ranging from manumission to permanent enslavement. No matter how hard a Christian might try and redefine the term "slavery," it is nearly impossible to make it nicer or more palatable. Slavery cannot simply be erased because of the uncomfortable and immoral implications that it springs forth any more than the condoning of these actions can be wiped from the Bible. Let's fast forward to modern days in which religion has finally caught up to morality. How many Christians do you know who own slaves? Most Christians would say zero, to which I would ask why not? Ephesians and I Timothy haven't changed. The fact that the practice of slavery was once deemed moral, and today it no longer is, means that morality changes.

For early Jews and Christians as well as modern-day, devout, fundamentalists, it is considered immoral to work on the Sabbath. Like many consequences spelled out in the Bible, death is the penalty for working on the Sabbath. Surely an act worthy of the consequence of death must be considered wrong by God. We find evidence for this in Numbers 15:32-36:

> "While the Israelites were in the wilderness, a man was found gathering wood on the Sabbath day. Those who found him gathering wood brought him to Moses and Aaron and the whole assembly, and they kept him in custody, because it was not clear what should be done to him. Then the LORD said to Moses, 'The man must die. The whole assembly must stone him outside the camp.' So the assembly took him outside the camp and stoned him to death, as the LORD commanded Moses."

When the punishment is death, it's fair to say that early believers took the Ten Commandments seriously. There have been cases made, even plausible ones, that the Sabbath commandment was annulled with Jesus and rendered obsolete. Mark 3:1-6; Luke 13:10-17; 14:1-6 are often picked as evidence that only nine of the Old Testament commandments should stand. Even if someone considers this commandment obsolete, that doesn't mean that people didn't practice this for many years. Many Jews along with the Christian denominations Seventh-day Adventist Church, the Seventh Day Baptists, and the True Jesus Church still observe the Sabbath. For quite some time in the history of the Judeo–Christian religion, people would have considered working on the Sabbath to be morally offensive. Today we have stores that are open 24 hours each day and 7 days per week staffed by people of all faiths. Is it wrong to work on the Sabbath today? Most Christians and Jews would say no. Why not? The Commandments haven't changed and early followers adhered to them. The fact that the practice was once deemed immoral, and it no longer is, means that morality changes.

1 Farlex Dictionary

If what we deem to be moral can change with time, while the framework that we try to house it under does not, what does that say about the strength of the framework? There are real consequences attached to using a rigid, morally-questionable framework. We can look through the pages of time to see the pendulum swing on issues of morality. Every example that I have provided highlights changes in moral attitudes over a certain period of time. What was considered moral one day is not considered moral the next. As I asked earlier in this chapter, if Christianity were proven to be a hoax, would that suddenly mean that the two billion Christians living on our planet would lose their sense of right and wrong? Would they start lying, robbing and killing uncontrollably? Of course not! That would be absurd, which is why trying to tie morality to religion is absurd.

Morality can (and does) exist without religion. To find a moral compass, a person needs empathy, not religion. Consider the following:

1. Can you find an ethical statement made or a moral action performed by a believer that could not have been made or performed by a non-believer?

2. Can you find a wicked statement or immoral action that could be or has been performed by someone who believed they were doing it in the name of God?

If you give this a few moments of thought, you'll find that the second statement is much easier to answer and plenty of examples readily come to mind, but answers to the first question remain elusive. That should speak volumes about morality and religion.

This is, of course, the Hitchens Challenge, conceived by the late Christopher Hitchens. While many have tried to provide an answer to the first statement, the statement itself is a bit of a paradox with the only right answer being one that the asker would agree morally with. Still, it merits ample thought.

Another important question posed by Christopher Hitchens can be found in the following scenario. Somewhere tonight, there will be a child born to a Wahhabi Muslim couple. Wahhabi Muslims are some of the most conservative fundamentalists practicing Islam. Would a Christian or Jew prefer that child to be born and bred to be a Wahhabi or an atheist/agnostic? If religion and belief in a god is truly a good moral guiding force, they should have a preference for the fundamentalist Muslim. If not, then it's worth asking ourselves why there's a distinction, and whether the belief that religion forms the basis of morality needs to be dismissed.

-- Atheism as a Moral Framework --

Many of us were raised in a religious community where a perception of moral dependency was fraudulently inculcated in us. If Christianity (or any religion) is deemed unable to provide an adequate framework for morality, the inevitable follow-up question becomes, "should we replace that void with atheism?" I've always found this question to be a bit misleading as it depends wholly on the presumption that religion forms the basis for morality in the first place. As I've demonstrated using nothing more than common sense and common examples, it doesn't. Morality can exist without a celestial big brother watching our every move and listening to our every thought. God is irrelevant in this equation. I wouldn't advocate for atheism as a moral framework any more than I would advocate for the lack of belief in pixies, Bigfoot, or leprechauns in determining morality. From a practical perspective, empathy is a bigger contributor to morality than God could ever hope to be. Reason, logic, discussion, and consensus all make more significant contributions to morality than God. None of these characteristics are the exclusive domain of atheism and agnosticism however because the potential for each already exists in us irrespective of religious belief.

For some reason, I have found that in such discussions as these, someone will eventually bring up Joseph Stalin and Adolf Hitler. It happens that Stalin was an atheist, but it wasn't atheism that made him what he was. Atheism is the absence of religious belief—it has absolutely no divine objects or methods of worship, no special rituals, and no sacred texts. At the same time, Hitler was born and raised Catholic. He never formally renounced his Catholicism and interestingly enough the Catholic Church has never excommunicated Hitler nor any other leader of the Third Reich.

The problem with trying to associate atheism to the horrors and atrocities committed by people like Stalin and Hitler is that they did not commit these horrors and atrocities because of their religious beliefs or lack of religious beliefs. Never has unbelief in a divine being led to genocide. Unlike such events as the Inquisition conducted by the Roman Catholic Church, Stalin and Hitler didn't commit their atrocities "because" they were atheists in the same way that they didn't commit their atrocities "because" they both had mustaches. There is no atheistic doctrine justifying genocide and mass murder; there is no atheistic doctrine in the first place. The Holocaust was not a result of the German people or its leadership not believing in God.

History has shown us that religion is not a moral barrier to immoral actions and virtually every religion has blood on its hands. In fact, many egregious atrocities have been committed by those who believed that they had God on their side. Many crimes throughout history have been religiously motivated and even religiously justified. The same can't be said about atheism. If we were to look at the history of the 1920s and 30s for example and replace the word "fascism" with "Catholic right wing," we wouldn't need to rewrite a single page of history.

CHAPTER 8. INDOCTRINATION

> "...it is a telling fact that, the world over, the vast majori-
> ty of children follow the religion of their parents rather than
> any of the other available religions."—Richard Dawkins

Babies are not religious. Babies do not leave the womb with a belief in God. When we're brought into this world, we do not know who Jesus, Allah, Xenu, or Shiva is. We are introduced to one of these characters at some point, usually during our formative years. Rarely are we introduced to anything beyond our parents' religion, yet we will readily and proudly proclaim our religion to be true to anyone who will listen. On what basis can religious persons claim to know the truth when they frequently don't even know the basic tenets of any other religion? This feels disingenuous.

One of the reasons why religion continues to permeate society is because it gets indoctrinated into a large percentage of children from a very early age. Of course, no religion uses the word "indoctrinate" because of the negative connotation, but the definition certainly fits. When a parent introduces his/her religious opinions to a child, what reasonable outcome can one expect to see? If a young child will readily believe that a jolly fat man in a red suit delivers presents once a year to all the good children because Mom and Dad say so, is Jesus really such a stretch? Santa is as real a person to a child as Jesus is to an adult. Interestingly enough, both figures require belief in them as the most basic prerequisite before you're eligible to receive a gift.

Many religions force young children into commitment ceremonies like Confirmations and Bar Mitzvahs. Most even have infant ceremonies. For example, Christians baptize infants as a means of washing away ancestral sin. Jewish male infants are ritualistically circumcised. Even though it is explicitly outlawed in many Islamic countries, Muslim girls as young as 8 in

Somalia undergo genital mutilation called infibulations. Many of these girls actually want to be cut, as it is considered to be a rite of passage. And who says that religion doesn't have the ability to warp our minds?

The problem with indoctrinating children into a specific faith is the fact that children are not intellectually mature enough to make such distinctions. They are not intellectually mature enough to make the commitment, either. Children do not have adequate background knowledge to critically think through what's being presented to them, and as such are more vulnerable to wild beliefs than educated adults. When scary monsters, tooth fairies, and Santa Claus are legitimate phenomena, making the case that children are intellectually mature enough to be able to adequately think through religious stories and comprehend the potential for truth becomes a fool's errand.

Philosopher Arthur Schopenhauer once said, "And as the capacity for believing is strongest in childhood, special care is taken to make sure of this tender age. This has much more to do with the doctrines of belief taking root than threats and reports of miracles. If, in early childhood, certain fundamental views and doctrines are paraded with unusual solemnity, and an air of the greatest earnestness never before visible in anything else; if, at the same time, the possibility of a doubt about them be completely passed over, or touched upon only to indicate that doubt is the first step to eternal perdition, the resulting impression will be so deep that, as a rule, that is, in almost every case, doubt about them will be almost as impossible as doubt about one's own existence."

The brain of a child can absorb so much information with such little effort. Children frequently establish permanent neural pathways as they learn, which helps explain why those who are religiously indoctrinated as children can hold onto those beliefs throughout their adult lives. It becomes much more difficult to indoctrinate an adult into a new religion. It happens, but it takes much more effort to convince an adult than a child. An adult never exposed to Christianity would likely question the talking snake or transubstantiation in a critical manner, but a young child can be convinced of such things with relative ease.

Every religion targets children, just as tobacco companies tactically did for years, and they do it for the same reason. Both tobacco companies and the church benefit greatly when they can attract young people to their product. The tactic of targeting young children isn't even a "dirty little secret." In fact, April 14th is celebrated as 4/14 Day. It's openly accepted and Christian strategists like Luis Bush preach it loudly for all to hear. Christian leaders are well aware that about 85% of all Christians make their commitment to Jesus between the ages of 4 and 14. The Barna Research Group surveys indicate that once children get past age 14, there is only a 4% chance of them becoming a Christian before becoming an adult. Once they reach adulthood, it increases slightly to 6%. The statistics are overwhelming and clearly make a case for targeting this age group. From the church's perspective, it is easy to understand why commitment ceremonies are so important. The child might not be "saved" if we wait!

Luis Bush, the author of *The 4–14 Window: Raising Up a New Generation to Transform the World*, has written extensively about this topic and how Christians need to take this fight directly to the "enemy." Who, you might ask, is the enemy? "While universal primary and secondary education may be considered a worthy goal, its ultimate effect can sometimes be negative," Bush wrote. "Unless the teachers and administrators are Christ followers, the world view that is taught will not transform the minds of the 4/14ers." He continues by saying "Secular education does not enlighten; rather it dims one's grasp of the 'real reality' rooted in the truth of scripture."

When we have people like this working so hard to elevate Christianity over secular education for the "real reality," is it any wonder why the United States is losing its grip as a scientific leader in our world? What is it exactly that our educators are doing wrong? Are they teaching non-Christian versions of math, history, and science? According to Bush and too many others like him, everything that we need to know about our world and our place in it was given to us 2,000 years ago. Bush proclaims in the same vein as Martin Luther that only Christian educators can enlighten us.

No parent or clergy ever encourages a child to gain a greater understanding of all religions. That would be counterproductive. The goal after all is sustainability. If children aren't indoctrinated early, the religion will eventually become statistically unsustainable. Once the child reaches an age where he/she has enough background knowledge to critically use reason and logic, the odds of converting to Christianity become next to nil. Think about that for a moment. If a child is allowed to reach maturity without religious indoctrination, the potential for belief in talking snakes and walking giants is reduced greatly. The key is to convince them of these things while young so the belief doesn't seem so strange when they become older.

Lutherans and Protestants are certainly familiar with the life and work of Martin Luther. Perhaps they are also familiar with the following quotes: "Reason is the greatest enemy that faith has: it never comes to the aid of spiritual things, but—more frequently than not—struggles against the divine Word, treating with contempt all that emanates from God." and "But since the devil's bride, Reason, that pretty whore, comes in and thinks she's wise, and what she says, what she thinks, is from the Holy Spirit, who can help us, then? Not judges, not doctors, no king or emperor, because [reason] is the Devil's greatest whore." Luther found it both convenient and virtuous to elevate faith over reason. If there was ever a conflict between the two, faith should always supersede reason.

Luther was well aware that reason and logic are the enemies of faith, except "when enlightened" as he once said "so it is with human reason, which strives not against faith, when enlightened, but rather furthers and advances it." This means that when someone says that it is neither reasonable nor logical to believe in talking snakes, they are being openly contemptuous towards God. Conversely, someone who believes that talking snakes are both reasonable and logical is using "enlightened reasoning." This premise is both moronic and dangerous. It allows a religious person to say with conviction that "his" logic is correct even when that logic is completely uncoupled from reality. Only religion can make secular concepts like reason and logic seem detrimental and out of place. If reason and logic are viewed in a bad light, believers will be less inclined to use either in their faith. The plain and simple truth is that when a child, who has not been indoctrinated, reaches a stage where they become mature enough to be able to adequately apply reason and logic to religion, they are much less likely to become a Christian, Muslim, or Jew.

This becomes painfully evident when we witness the tactics of groups like the Child Evangelism Fellowship (CEF) which proudly boasts on their website, "God has allowed us to reach over 387,000 people (70% of that number children) in more than 130 countries!" They reach these children through multiple programs including the "Good News Club" and its primary setting: public schools. I read with interest how Ray Paulson, a CEF worker for the past thirty-plus years, managed to achieve this[1]. He uses balloons to get the children's attention. Apparently the process of turning balloons into animals while teaching children about Jesus is called "ballooning" and Mr. Paulson is an expert at it. He's been targeting public schools as of late and says, "You have to be sneaky about it." He continues, "You can't say to a kid, 'If you come to the group, I'll give you a balloon,' because that's considered a bribe and can get you in trouble. But you can stand outside the school doing balloons, or have kids tell other kids about it." Is it just me or does Ray Paulson's tactic seem creepy? He's proud when he says, "I've been in trouble in just about every kind of every which way! But you have to be very careful. We have an enemy. And he is real. And he is effective."

To me, this kind of tactic is appalling. I cannot fully express in print how angry I would be if someone tried to entice my children with balloons in exchange for listening to someone preach about Jesus. Does the end justify the means? Does it make a difference if this same creepy guy is handing out balloon animals to your child in exchange for listening to him preach about Jesus or Muhammad?—would it be OK if the topic was Scientology or Mormonism?

When asked about whether the message or methods might upset people, Jan Akam, the director of a CEF chapter in Washington, answers, "The Bible tells us we don't have to worry about anything!" This answer might suffice for Bible-thumping believers, but to a non-Christian it's indicative of a narrow, parochial view of the world. These tactics are deceitful and disgraceful. I know that not every Christian parent would do as CEF does, but the length that some will go to is representative of the worth of the prize. The fact that they're targeting public schools causes me additional frustration. We don't force Christians to teach science in their churches, so it would be appreciated if they didn't bring their faith into our public schools.

I have no intention of telling parents how to raise their children and I am under no illusion that highlighting the reasoning behind indoctrination

---

1 *The Good News Club: The Christian Right's Stealth Assault on America's Children.* Katherine Stewart. (ISBN 1610390504) pp 137-139.

will sway anyone. I'd venture a guess that most Christian parents have never given it more than a passing thought. It's commonplace in many Christian households to take kids to catechism or place them in parochial schools. I'm not questioning the motives of Christian parents as I believe they have, to a great extent, honorable intentions. As honorable as their intentions might be, though, the fact is that they are ultimately taking advantage of the child's intellectual vulnerabilities by forcing their beliefs onto the child. I would challenge any Christian parent with this: if you really believe that your religion is true, then your child will eventually find it on his/her own. Don't force it upon them. Have faith in your faith.

Even though religious indoctrination is biased and doesn't promote critical thinking, there is a fine line between it and religious freedom. Parents have the right to preach any religion that they deem appropriate even if a young child is not mature enough to fully understand the decisions that are being made for him/her. They may have the right, but that doesn't make it right. It is much more important and valuable to teach a child how to think... not what to think.

CHAPTER 9. INCONVENIENT CHRISTIAN TRUTHS

> "If I were not an atheist, I would believe in a God
> who would choose to save people on the basis of the to-
> tality of their lives and not the pattern of their words. I
> think he would prefer an honest and righteous atheist to
> a TV preacher whose every word is God, God, God, and
> whose every deed is foul, foul, foul."—Isaac Asimov

People who call themselves Christians are often unaware of many inconvenient truths about the Bible and their chosen religion. For years, I counted
myself among them. Here are some of the odd facts that I wish more Christians knew.

~ Authorship of the Gospels ~

The stories of Jesus reside in the gospels, and these gospels form the basis
for the Christian faith. Who couldn't be forgiven for thinking that the Gospel of Luke was written by Luke or that the Gospel of John was written by
John? However, it is a well-established fact that nobody knows who wrote
the Gospels of Mark (c. AD 65–70), Matthew (c. 80–85), Luke (c.80–85), or
John (c. 90–110). The authors of these works are anonymous. None of the
authors had any first-hand accounts. None of the actual authors who put
ink to papyrus ever actually met Jesus. Each of these texts was written many
decades after Jesus died. Everything was originally passed down verbally and
original manuscripts of the Gospels do not exist. As we will discover, we
are instead left with thousands of fragments of copies of copies—many with
clear signs of later interpolations.

A 2011 *USA Today/Gallup* poll showed that nearly 80% of Americans believe the Bible to be either the actual word of God or at least divinely-inspired
by God. Nearly 1 out of every 3 Americans thinks the Bible should be inter-

preted literally. While more than three quarters of our neighbors believe that the creator of the universe authored a perfect book of wisdom and morality, few understand how the book they hold in their hands on Sunday came into existence. Ask the average Christian about the creation of the Bible, and you'll find many holding the assumption that it was created exactly as it appears sometime within the last 19 centuries. The truth is that there are over 25,000[1] complete or fragmented manuscripts of the New Testament, with the vast majority being fragments. Most date to between the 10th and 15th centuries, but some go as far back as 125 AD[2]. The preeminent New Testament scholar Bart Ehrman states, "It is true, of course, that the New Testament is abundantly attested in the manuscripts produced through the ages, but most of these manuscripts are many centuries removed from the originals, and none of them perfectly accurate. They all contain mistakes—altogether many thousands of mistakes. It is not an easy task to reconstruct the original words of the New Testament."[3] While some differences between manuscripts were likely due to legitimate errors in translation or understanding, biblical scholars are reasonably certain that many were the result of explicit interpolations (insertions made into the text by new authors oftentimes many years after the original).

The King James Bible is only 400 years old, and if we look at just the Gospel of Mark, we'll find that it ends at Chapter 16 Verse 20. This is a problem, because the earliest fragments of manuscripts end at Verse 8. Verses 9 through 20 do not exist in any of the earliest manuscripts or other ancient texts, yet these verses claim that Jesus visited Mary Magdalene as well as others after he had risen. Pentecostal preachers embrace Verses 17 and 18 in particular, because that is where it says that they can drink anything deadly and handle snakes without harm as well as heal the sick with a simple laying on of their hands. The Gospel of Mark ends with Jesus' resurrection to stand at the right hand of God. Again, this is problematic because the earliest known Gospel of Mark doesn't end that way. These were enhancements added centuries later.

The story in John 7:53-8:11 about the adulterous woman whom the scribes and Pharisees wanted to have stoned to death gives us the famous phrase, "Let the one who is without sin be the first to cast a stone at her." The problem here is that the earliest manuscripts of John do not contain this pericope. The first time we see it like this is in the late 4th or early 5th century, which begs the question of who wrote it?

Biblical scholars will confirm all of this. You can read the entire King James Bible and never know for sure what verses were actually in the original manuscripts. It just seems highly illogical that the creator of the universe, the being we credit for creating the laws of physics, couldn't have the

---

1 ~5,800 Greek, ~10,000 Latin, and ~9,300 manuscripts in other languages including Ethiopic, Coptic, Armenian, Slavic, Gothic, and Syriac
2 Rylands Library Papyrus P52
3 *The New Testament: An Historical Introduction To The Early Christian Writings*, Bart Ehrman p. 449

original manuscripts preserved. God can simply will every complex creature into existence, including mankind, but is somehow unable to create papyrus that would survive more than a few years. While these deficiencies in the Bible have been known to scholars for centuries, this isn't the type of thing that gets mentioned during Sunday service, is it? This seems to be a rather precarious foundation upon which to build and sustain a belief in Jesus as the son of God.

-- It's Time to Intervene --

The late author Christopher Hitchens was fond of highlighting the absurdity of the timeline for the Christian faith with a short story. The scientific consensus is that our species (Homo sapiens) has been on the planet for between 100,000 and 200,000 years[1]. If we use just the lower end of that estimate, this means that for the first 98,000 years of mankind's existence, our species struggled mightily with famine, war, and suffering. Many women and children died during childbirth and most people never saw life beyond 25 years of age. With all of this going on, Heaven does not deem it necessary to intervene but rather watches all of this misery with complete indifference. To be Christian is to believe that God then thinks to Himself, "Well, that's enough of that. It's time to intervene and have a revelation." So God decides that the best place to have this revelation is in the desert. He doesn't appear to the Chinese, for example, who have a more intellectually robust civilization but instead determines that the best way to deliver instructions for all of mankind is to appeal to men living in one of the less literate and most barbaric parts of the world. As Hitchens says, "This is nonsense. It can't be believed by a thinking person."

There is more that we can take away from Hitchens' story. Even if we go further back in time beyond Jesus to the revelation between God and Moses, we are still left with thousands of years of the Judeo–Christian God not finding it terribly worthwhile to deliver instructions to mankind on how to live righteously and attain eternal peace. Think for a moment how many generations of people lived and died without ever having had this kind of divine knowledge revealed to them. How many people had to die before God felt it important enough to reveal himself? An even bigger question lies with the people in which this god chose to reveal his message. If we are all God's children, why did He decide to only speak to one capricious and superstitious group of humans living in one of the most backward, desolate areas on the planet? Imagine the overwhelming religious case to be made about the plausibility of this god if He had appeared to every civilization at the same time and delivered identical instructions! It seems like a rather trivial thing for an omnipotent being to accomplish and yet a mere mortal like me can produce a more believable way to convince a planet of God's existence than God himself.

The coddling of the Jews and the later elevating of Christians and Muslims seems to be in stark contrast to the portrait of God as a loving father.

---

1 Fossil Reanalysis Pushes Back Origin of Homo sapiens, February 17, 2005, *Scientific American*.

No other civilization outside the desert was made aware of the Judeo–Christian god. Christianity, for example, wouldn't be known across the world for many centuries and was often spread by the sword. If the purpose of Christianity is to safeguard the souls of man, what loving father is willing to condemn the rest of his children to an eternity in Hell for the simplistic crime of disbelief—a disbelief they didn't even know they had! The morality of a God who would let his children perish under parameters He Himself established should rightly be called into question and yet this is the very essence of the Judeo–Christian god. Hitchens was absolutely correct. This is nonsense.

~ Historical Accuracy ~

There are no unbiased, extra-Biblical, historical accounts of Jesus' miracles written while he was alive. Written accounts were not put down on paper until decades or even centuries later. For someone who performed miracles, walked on water, and rose from the dead, the basic expectation is that at least a few historians from that time would have noticed these amazing events and written about them. Perhaps it has something to do with the fact that miracles like resurrection were fairly common up to this point in history. Osiris, Horus, Asclepius, Achilles, Lazarus, and the daughter of Jairus were all resurrected and they were not all divinely-conceived. As human knowledge has advanced, resurrections have declined. Infer what you like from that fact.

There have been many debates on the historical accuracy of Jesus' resurrection. Sufficient evidence does not exist to persuade everyone of the event's historicity; however it is safe to say that without the resurrection, the religion we know as Christianity would cease to exist. The resurrection of Jesus hinges completely on eyewitness testimony, but unfortunately eyewitness testimony is not as reliable as some may commonly believe. In fact, from a neuroscience perspective, it is incredibly unreliable. As we now know, human memory is malleable and prone to mistakes. As it relates to the resurrection, there was far less "eye" witness testimony and more "ear" witness testimony. The Gospels are our only source of "evidence" for the resurrection, with particular attention paid to Mark's Gospel as it was the earliest of the four gospels. If I reference Thomas and Peter being visited by Jesus, this account is not coming from an unbiased source. Everything is coming from the Bible, so frankly it doesn't matter if one person said he saw Jesus or 500 people did. The number of witnesses becomes irrelevant if it can't be corroborated. The Bible could make the claim that every person on Earth was personally visited by Jesus and the same problem remains. This is all being reported according to a single source: the Bible—hardly an unbiased source of historical accuracy.

Not only is the Bible biased, it's contradictory. The Gospels cannot even agree with each other on details surrounding such a monumental event. For example, John tells us that Jesus died the day before the Passover meal was eaten but Mark explicitly says that he died after. John says he died at 9:00 in the morning. Mark says it was noon. After his resurrection, did the women rush out to tell everyone what happened? Matthew, Luke, and John say "yes," however Mark says "no" (16:8). Could the faithful physically touch the resurrected Jesus? John says no (John 20:17), yet in Luke we have Jesus appearing to the disciples and saying, "*Look at my hands and my feet. It is I myself! Touch me and see; a ghost does not have flesh and bones, as you see I have*" (Luke 24:39). Did Simon of Cyrene carry Jesus' cross or did Jesus carry it the whole way? What did Mary, or Mary and the group of other women, see in the empty tomb? Was it one man, two men, or an angel? Where were the disciples supposed to go see Jesus: Jerusalem or Galilee? The answer to each of these questions depends entirely upon the Gospel that is being read. The Bible purports to describe a historical event, however the contradictions within it are real and they are undeniable. If we give historical weight to Jesus' resurrection simply because it is written in the Bible, we must also give historical weight to Matthew 27:52-53, which tells us that the moment Jesus died, the tombs of all the dead saints broke open and the inhabitants rose alive and physically walked around town where people could see them. Surely this event would have been worthy of a sentence or two by any one of the Jews who allegedly witnessed it, yet unbiased third party accounts of this event do not exist. We can find non-Biblical sources that make reference to Jesus, his baptism, and his death, but we have to rely on the Bible for the resurrection. Resurrections and dead people walking around town are far more impressive events and yet authentic, contemporary, non-Biblical texts corroborating these events remain elusive. To highlight the contradictions, I would challenge any Christian to give me an accurate description of the events that occurred between the resurrection and the ascension of Jesus. Using just the Gospels, any believer should be able to give me a plausible, coherent account of events surrounding what is arguably the most important moments of Christianity. The only caveat is that the believer must use *all* of the details from the Gospels. This seems like a relatively easy task for a text purported to be the inerrant and infallible word of God, and yet it is impossible. Try it for yourself. Read the Gospels as they are written and in context. It's an interesting exercise. The many contradictions make it impossible to deliver a coherent, plausible narrative of the resurrection without ignoring parts of each Gospel.

The determination of whether or not Jesus was resurrected is not the point behind highlighting the contradictions. The contradictions themselves do not disprove the resurrection, but they should cast serious doubt upon the available evidence. In what is an already biased and interpolated collection of ancient texts, the unsubstantiated and uncorroborated assertions are more than just troublesome particularly because of the extreme significance of the resurrection portion of the narrative. Nobody makes this clearer than Paul (I Corinthians 15:14-15) when he says that if Christ was not raised, then Christians are false witnesses. Their preaching and, more importantly, their faith are useless. With such a monumental event as the resurrection and ascension of Jesus into Heaven, we should be inundated with contemporary sources vanquishing any possible doubt of the event's historicity and yet doubt and skepticism are far more intellectually honest than blind faith in this matter.

The resurrection isn't the only topic upon which to cast doubt. There isn't a viable historical account outside of the Bible claiming that Herod ordered the slaughter of all the infant boys in Bethlehem because he was afraid of losing his throne to the newborn King of Jews. No conclusive evidence exists of this infanticide. Jesus' triumphal entry into Jerusalem where he is welcomed by crowds of people laying their clothes on the ground never warranted a mention by non-Biblical contemporary sources. When the veil separating the Holy of Holies was torn from top to bottom at the moment that Jesus gave up his spirit, surely a contemporary Jewish historian would have found the spontaneous tearing of a 60-foot, 4-inch think veil in such a significant Jewish location to be worthy of mention. It's one thing to make a theological claim. It's something entirely different to make a historical claim. The latter has a higher threshold of proof.

Scholars have looked for unbiased, contemporaneous sources to support the gospels, but nothing worthy or authentic exists. Philo of Alexandria was a Jewish philosopher who lived during the time of Jesus. He was responsible for dozens of writings and never once does he mention Jesus. If there was any Jew who would have taken a profound interest in the Son of God, Philo was it, and yet Jesus (and all of his miracles) never even became a blip on his proverbial radar. The Jewish historian Justus of Tiberias lived in the decades immediately following the crucifixion and never once mentions anything about Jesus or the influence of his followers. In the following decades, we find scarce mentions of Jesus from Roman historians Suetonius and Cornelius Tacitus, and neither historian makes any sort of divine reference. The only somewhat contemporary source we find divine reference to Jesus is in the "Antiquities of the Jews", written by Flavius Josephus sixty years after the death of Jesus. In it, Josephus makes reference to James (the brother of Jesus), John the Baptist, and the resurrection of Jesus. The *Testimonium Flavianum* describes the story of Pontius Pilate condemning Jesus to the cross, Jesus rising on the third day, and the continuation of the tribe of Christians. There is broad consensus that the references to James and John were authentic, however the consensus among *both* Christian as well as secular scholars is that the *Testimonium Flavianum* may only be partially authentic. As has happened many times throughout history, later Christian interpolations "enhanced" the authentic nucleus of the story. Most scholars believe that Josephus tried to write a historical account and the original work was likely neutral until its modification sometime between Origen and Eusebius. Minus the forged Josephus account, there does not exist a single unbiased, contemporaneous source to corroborate the resurrection.

~ Original Languages ~

The Bible was originally written in Hebrew, Greek, and Aramaic. It has since been translated into hundreds of different languages over the years. When this happens, original meanings/intent can get lost in translation. Many of the stories contain idioms that are not easily translated. Scholars still debate today whether there is more merit in translating these stories word for word or providing a parallel idiom using the target language. Etymology, wishful theological thinking, and misinterpreted metaphors have influenced many of these translations.

For example, when the original Hebrew word "almah" was used to describe Jesus' mother Mary, most translations refer to a virgin; however, most scholars today believe that it more accurately translates to "maiden" or "young woman," not necessarily "unmarried" or virgin. In fact many scholars believe that Mary was not meant to be portrayed as a virgin at all but rather a young woman. The gospels of Mark and John never mention Mary as a virgin nor do they portray her as a virgin.

It has always struck me as odd that a significant detail like the virgin birth wasn't deemed important enough to appear in all four gospels. Perhaps this is due to either the virgin birth being a mistranslation or the fact that it didn't really break new ground. Just as resurrections were apparently no big deal, virgin births were no big deal either. In fact, divine conception has been asserted historically numerous times with Alexander the Great being the son of Zeus, Krishna being the divine offspring of Vishnu and Devaki, Kabir born unto a virgin, Houji born of the virgin Jiang Yuan, and many of the Egyptian kings claimed lineal descent from Ra. The problem is not just the fact that two of the gospels omit the virgin birth portion of the Jesus narrative, but that Mary is largely absent in all four of the gospels. This would be much more understandable if the translated word of "virgin" was supposed to be the more plausible maiden or young woman.

When we look at the tenth commandment which tells us "thou shalt not covet," we are made to think that the act of wanting something that our neighbor has is somehow immoral. If Biblical scholar Dr. Joel Hoffman is correct, this was a mistranslation. He believes that translators misunderstood the word "desirable" and "take" because they use the same Hebrew root— similar to the way "host" and "hostile" have a similar root but vastly different meanings. Thou shalt not covet might have actually meant thou shalt not take.

In any event, it's worth recognizing the fact that the Bible we take literal meaning from may not mean what we literally think it does.

~ Moses as Original Author ~

The religious faithful believe that Moses wrote the five books of the Torah. The only exception for this would be the last eight verses of Deuteronomy which describe the death and burial of Moses—an event that would have obviously been difficult for Moses to write up himself. Many scholars today believe that the Pentateuch may have been written by many people over the course of hundreds of years.

Most universities now teach the composite nature of the Pentateuch. Over the course of centuries, scholars have identified four potentially different authors and identify their work with the letters J, E, D, and P. The "J" portions are thought to have been written around 900 BC by people who referred to God as Jahweh or Jehovah. The "E" portions are thought to have been written around 750 BC by people (likely from the region of the Northern Kingdom) who referred to God as Elohim. The "D" portions refer to Deuteronomy and are thought to have been written between 650–620 BC. The "P" portions refer to spots like Leviticus that are thought to have been written by priests in exile after the destruction of Israel in 586 BC. The final Pentateuch is believed to have been combined and edited approximately 400 BC.

~ There Is No One Bible ~

There is no common version of the Bible. Depending on the denomination and translation, the contents and order of the individual books can vary. For example, there are 39 books in the Protestant Old Testament, 46 books in the Catholic Old Testament, and 51 books in the Eastern Orthodox Old Testament. Theological issues have influenced a number of translations.

~ Rejected Gospels ~

Several gospels exist outside of the canonized ones Christians are most familiar with. The Gospel of Judas portrays a different relationship between Jesus and Judas than the one Christians are routinely taught. The Gospel of Peter places the responsibility of Jesus' crucifixion on Herod Antipas instead of Pontius Pilate. The pseudepigraphical Gospel of James (c. ~145) asserts the perpetuity of Mary's virginity not only prior to, but during and after Jesus' birth. My favorite however is the Infancy Gospel of Thomas, rejected by religious authorities, which tells remarkable stories about Jesus as a child. No texts exist to tell us anything about Jesus as a child, which makes this particularly interesting. Apparently Jesus made some clay birds one day and then brought them to life. He forced another child's body to become a corpse by cursing him. Another child accidentally bumped into Jesus so Jesus cursed him and he fell dead. When the neighbors complained, Jesus blinded them. Some of his miracles included creating a huge meal from just a single grain, resurrecting various people, and stretching a beam of wood to help his father finish a construction project. Jesus seemed to be a very interesting little boy!

~ Happy Birthday Baby Jesus ~

Christians celebrate the birth of Jesus on December 25th; however Jesus wasn't likely born on December 25th. There is no historical evidence for the exact day or month of Jesus' birth (most likely in the year 4 BC), but even religious scholars will concur that December 25th isn't likely the correct date. That's right. There's no need to take an agnostic's word for it. This consensus can be quickly verified on many of the most popular Christian websites. If you are a Christian, please don't sing Happy Birthday to baby Jesus on Christmas. It's not his birthday.

~ Fulfilling Prophecies Requires Effort ~

Joseph was descended from the house and family of David. To fulfill the prophecy, Jesus had to be born in Bethlehem. The problem is that Jesus of Nazareth was from...Nazareth. The Gospels have to go to great lengths to get him to Bethlehem. The Gospel of Luke (Luke 2:1–7) tells us that Joseph and Mary were residents of Nazareth and that Caesar Augustus ordered a census for taxation purposes while Quirinius was governor of Syria. People of the region were apparently required to go back to their ancestral hometowns to be registered. To fulfill the Jewish prophecy, the savior would be "of the house and lineage of David." The problem is that we have quite good documentation about the reign of Caesar Augustus and no such census ever took place under those circumstances. Compounding the problem is the bizarre claim that everyone had to register in their ancestral hometown. What census have you ever heard of that requires people to go to their ancestral homes? King David, if he existed, lived a thousand years earlier! Would you even know who your ancestors were from 1,000 years ago and where they lived? If not, why would it be more plausible for an ancient people to know this? It was not common for a Roman census to force people back to their ancestral hometowns, nor is there any historical evidence that a Roman-controlled census would cover anyone beyond Roman citizens. Try and imagine the sheer chaos that would result with this type of mass migration and at the same time recognize the fact that not a single historian thought it significant enough to jot down a few words about it.

In fact, there is no reason to believe in any of the story of the nativity particularly because none of the Gospels agree with each other. For example, the Gospel of Matthew says that the birth occurred just after the reign of Herod the Great, who died in 4 BC. There's a decade difference between Herod and the census from 6/7! If we read the Gospels as they are written, we can't dismiss the conflicts. At no point did the authors of Luke or Matthew ever make the claim that the Nativity of Jesus was told to anyone directly by either Mary or Joseph themselves. These aren't direct accounts and the conflicts make it awfully hard to believe that the story of the nativity has any hint of truth to it.

A rather obvious yet frequently overlooked question is: what is the relevance of Joseph's lineage, anyway? In neither Luke's nor Matthew's Gospel is Joseph a blood relative of Jesus. The genealogical accounts of Joseph provided by Luke and Matthew are quite different and the discrepancies and contradictions are just as easily verifiable as they are troublesome. This leads many of the faithful to assume that one of the accounts "must have" been about Mary's lineage instead. Anyone who gives weight to that theory must abandon the fact that both Gospels are rather explicit that they are talking about Joseph's lineage. Another rather obvious yet overlooked portion of the narrative deals with the Star of Bethlehem, which in Matthew's account guides the Magi (wise men) the rather short distance from Jerusalem to Bethlehem. Mark's Gospel, the earliest one, never seems to mention this guiding star, nor does any other Gospel. When the Magi visit Jesus sometime after his presentation in the Temple of Jerusalem, they visit him in a house. Unlike popular portrayals, Jesus would likely have been around the age of two when the wise men visited. Whether born in a manger, cave, barn, stable, or inn, why is Jesus still in Bethlehem, living in a house? If you recall, they are only in Bethlehem for the census. Whose house is this that he's living in? The Bible never says.

In the interest of calling a spade a spade, the infancy narrative is likely an outright fabrication. At no point does it appear to be based upon historical facts. This is not just problematic; it is corrosive to the Christian faith because the promised Messiah had to be a descendant of King David and would have to fulfill all of the prophecies. If Jesus fails in fulfilling the prophecies, he would then be a false Messiah. This is why pious accounts like Matthew and modern-day Christian scholars have to go to great lengths to explain away such obvious contradictions.

-- The Importance of Baptism --

Depending on the Christian denomination, baptism can be a very important ritual. While some denominations dismiss the practice as having no sacramental (saving) power, others believe baptism is a literal supernatural transformation. For many, baptism is an essential step to becoming "saved." As an ordained minister, baptism is one of my expected duties. Oddly enough, a religious authority is not required to perform the baptism. In fact, no witnesses are even required. Anyone can baptize anyone else. There are no formal requirements to perform something so religiously significant.

-- Jesus: Gentle and Loving --

Most Christians portray Jesus from the New Testament as loving and peaceful. In fact, most Christians would hold Jesus Christ up as the ultimate model and innovator of love and peace. A very persuasive argument can be made that the teachings of Jesus were often beautifully moral; however Jesus was not as loving and peaceful as modern day Christians would like us to believe. For example, those who do not believe in Jesus' divinity will be "*cast forth as a branch, and is withered; and men gather them, and cast them into the fire, and they are burned.*" (John 15:6 KJV) In Luke 19, Jesus is explicit in his parable about killing those who do not want to be ruled over by him. The Book of Revelation is anything but loving and peaceful. In Matthew 10:34-37, I fail to find the morality in Jesus telling his disciples that he did not come to bring peace, but rather a sword. He came to turn family members against each other (also mentioned in Luke 12:51-53). Anyone who dares to love their parents or children more than Jesus is not worthy of him. This is again drilled into us in Luke 14:26 when Jesus says "If anyone comes to me and does not hate his own father and mother and wife and children and brothers and sisters, yes, and even his own life, he cannot be my disciple." There is and always has been a religiously-twisted perception among Christians that it is of utmost importance to place Jesus before our own family. To be forced to love and yet fear a figure like Jesus Christ is the essence of sadomasochism. While compulsory love is not a virtue, none of this compares to the ultimate evil.

The concept of Hell, which is responsible for the wicked installation of fear into billions of children throughout history, is introduced to us by the gentle, peace-loving Jesus in the New Testament. Hell is never mentioned throughout the Old Testament. In fact, the afterlife is a topic that is barely broached in Judaism and a single, consensus view of the afterlife is unobtainable even today. The closest the Old Testament/Hebrew Bible comes is through the use of the word "sheol" which simply means "grave." In Judaism, everyone goes there when they die. Conversely, the afterlife has been expanded upon greatly in both Christianity and Islam. This begs the question of whether or not Hell was important enough for God to tell Moses about or whether Hell is even real to begin with. If it isn't real, the pain, suffering, and fear that this concept has inflicted upon billions of people are unforgiveable, making this the single most immoral thing ever preached in the last two millennia. Is a reasonable person supposed to believe that God never felt Hell was an important enough concept to mention until the gentle Nazarene arrived on the scene?

Additionally, many of Jesus' teachings were not original concepts or even consistent. For example, the teachings about love and forgiveness could be found well before Jesus in Judaism, Hinduism, Buddhism, and Jainism. Confucius, Plato, and the Jewish sage Hillel all preached the "golden rule" centuries before Jesus. The only difference between the previous "golden rules" and Jesus' version is semantic in nature. Jesus simply reworded it in a more positive manner which doesn't negate the fact that as a Jew, Jesus would have already been exposed to these concepts. In most cases, Jesus plagiarized existing concepts. Even though Christians regularly attribute the concepts of love and forgiveness to Jesus, neither of these concepts was unique or original. In fact, of the original concepts attributed to Jesus, many are downright immoral and detestable. Jesus, on more than one occasion, teaches and encourages the abandonment of family (Luke 14:26-27 and Matthew 19:29) and renounces his closest relatives (Matthew 12:46-50). Jesus tells his followers to "take no thought for the morrow" (Matthew 6:24-34) which I've always believed had both a benign message (don't let daily worries overwhelm you) mixed with more short-sighted, immoral messages (God will always provide tangible things and don't waste your time planning for the future as the end is very near). Christians believe that Christ was unique in that he fulfilled Jewish prophecy. It seems like a rather obvious question, but if Jews do not believe that Christ fulfilled their prophecies, why should anyone else? After all, these are their prophecies. The Jewish religious leaders at that time thought Jesus was a fraud and imposter. At no point did they believe Jesus to be the Messiah, and unlike the folks who eventually wrote the gospels many decades later, these leaders were much closer to being eyewitnesses to Jesus.

For a silly, yet morally-questionable example, a good chuckle can be found in the story of Jesus and the fig tree (Matthew 21:18-22). It becomes apparent that Jesus was not as nice and benevolent as his followers might suggest when we read about him acting like an immature child who didn't get his way—juvenile actions hardly worthy of the distinctive title of Lord.

> "Early in the morning, as Jesus was on his way back to the city, he was hungry. Seeing a fig tree by the road, he went up to it but found nothing on it except leaves. Then he said to it, 'May you never bear fruit again!' Immediately the tree withered."

If Jesus was the ultimate model of love and peace, why not simply give the tree the ability to bear an abundance of fruit? Why was his first instinct something negative? It would have displayed to his followers a more moral example of his power by magically enabling it to bear fruit. There are more examples like this throughout the New Testament where Jesus shows both tolerance and intolerance through his actions and teachings.

Jesus of the New Testament had many positive messages, and it is not my intention to dismiss, disparage, or belittle the moral teachings themselves. I believe that many of the stories, when separated from their divine claims, can still find some relevance today. The problem lies with the very common perception of Jesus as a moral innovator and the ultimate teacher delivering the most perfect words of peace, love, compassion, and forgiveness. The inconvenient truth is that this perception isn't as true or rosy as Christians would have us believe. If Christianity, one of the world's most powerful and far-reaching religions, is truly a religion that preaches love, respect, forgiveness, and peace, one should be able to expect a commensurate influence on love, respect, forgiveness, and peace in our world. At a minimum, we should at least be able to expect a commensurate influence on peace among believers of Jesus and yet we don't see that. Christianity portrays itself as peaceful, yet the inconvenient truth is that after more than two thousand years, it has not lived up to that billing. For centuries, it was deemed not only appropriate but imperative that heretics be tortured and killed. St. Augustine, St. Thomas Aquinas, Martin Luther, John Calvin, and countless popes advocated this among many other contemptible acts. Christians today are certainly able to interpret the Bible and Jesus' message any way they deem appropriate, but it should not go unnoticed that their interpretation is often vastly different than those of the most influential and venerated patriarchs of their faith.

CHAPTER 10. THE ORIGINAL FISH STORY

> "Don't wonder at those who are good without god.
> Pity those who need God to be good."—Anonymous

There is no better story from the Bible to highlight the principle of the Divine Default than that of Jonah. The story appears in Christianity, Judaism, and Islam and it essentially deals with a man named Jonah who is ordered by God to go to the city of Nineveh and tell them to repent for their sins. Apparently Nineveh was a "wicked" place. Jonah refused by fleeing to Jaffa and sailing to Tarshish. I assume that God wasn't paying attention during the whole time Jonah was fleeing towards the ship and setting out to sea or else He probably wouldn't have let him board the ship. In any event, God realized that Jonah had disobeyed Him and He brought about a massive storm. This massive storm terrified the sailors who tried to figure out why it was happening. They eventually learned that Jonah was the one to blame for the storm and if they threw him overboard, the storm would stop. Once Jonah was thrown overboard, God settled the seas and the storm went away.

Here's where the story gets really interesting. A great fish came along and swallowed Jonah. This was not a metaphorical fish. A large fish literally swallowed Jonah and he remained in there for 3 days and 3 nights. While inside the fish, Jonah prayed for the first time. God then commanded the large fish to vomit Jonah out on the beach outside of Nineveh. Jonah then did as God originally commanded and warned the people of Nineveh to repent (which of course they did) and the city was saved from God's wrath.

Believers are left with wonderful morals from the story such as God's compassion in giving Jonah a second chance, the futility in disobeying God, and a reminder of God's omnipotence. Skeptics are left trying to reconcile how a man could survive in a fish for 72 hours. The problem is that the story wasn't written as a parable. It was written as a historical event, and for centuries, people of all three Abrahamic faiths believed it to be literally true. In the Gospel of Matthew, Jesus makes reference to Jonah when pressed by the Pharisees for a miracle. Muhammad speaks highly of Jonah and even says "One should not say that I am better than Jonah" (Sahih al-Bukhari, 4:55:608), which implies that they are equal as prophets. If the story wasn't deemed true, what point would there be for Muhammad to make such a comparison? If early adherents to the Abrahamic faiths believed Jonah's story to be true and it was written as a historical event, then it speaks volumes about the historical authenticity of our religious scriptures. To believe the story as true and accurate requires one to willfully ignore the logistics involved with making this happen. If the story is false, then why should we believe any of the other "historical" events that these ancient texts purport to be true? Let's explore the plausibility of this story.

I will gladly concede the fact that it could be possible for a large fish to have swallowed a man whole. There have been circumstances where we've found whole men inside great white sharks, for example. The men weren't in there for 72 hours and found alive, but a whole man could fit. It could also have been a whale. Depending on the type of whale, the size of the esophagus might make it difficult to swallow a man whole. For example, it couldn't have been a whale shark, as its throat is at most only 4 inches wide, with a sharp bend behind the opening. I doubt that it was a baleen whale either, but a sperm whale with a 20-inch esophageal opening could be a likely candidate. In 1955, a 405-pound squid was removed from the stomach of a sperm whale. It wasn't alive, but it was intact. If it was a shark, we'd have to assume that he was swallowed without the shark's many razor-sharp teeth injuring him somehow. If it was a sperm whale, again—the most likely candidate, we'd have to assume the same thing. Using a sperm whale as the most likely type of "fish," the safe swallowing of a man is still not likely, but it's possible, so we'll assume that this was the species in the story.

So here we have Jonah, the reluctant prophet, sitting in the belly of a great fish. It's in here that he begins to pray to God. Considering his options, I'm sure there wasn't much else to do. I have a few logistical problems with this story that I can't seem to overlook. The first is the lack of oxygen for Jonah. Even if the great fish made frequent trips to the surface to swallow oxygen, he is in the fish's belly. A suitable amount of oxygen could be available if he stayed in the constantly-surfacing mouth of the great fish, but the difficulty in keeping oxygen flowing down to the stomach makes this scenario less plausible. Unfortunately, the Bible fights us on this and never says that he stays in the whale's mouth, but is rather explicit on where Jonah is: *"For as Jonah was three days and three nights in the belly of a huge fish, so the Son of Man will be three days and three nights in the heart of the earth"* (Matthew 12:40). Read your favorite translation of the Bible and you'll see that they will all refer to it as a belly or stomach.

We've identified the most likely "fish" to be that of a large sperm whale, and if you're not familiar with the digestive system of a whale, it's important to note that the stomach is made up of multiple chambers. The first chamber is called the forestomach. The second chamber is where the chemical digestion takes place. The chemicals that a person would encounter in this chamber are certainly not going to help him survive, so let's assume that Jonah was in the first chamber. We still have to get regular oxygen to him for 72 hours in a part of the whale that wouldn't normally be expected to hold oxygen. We also need to accomplish this by using the mouth to get that air, which would be unnatural. Whales pull in oxygen through blow holes.

The next problem I have relates to Jonah 2:6: "*To the roots of the mountains I sank down; the earth beneath barred me in forever. But you brought my life up from the pit, O LORD my God.*" This tells me that Jonah went down to the bottom of the sea bed. If they reference mountains and not hills, I would assume that the rocky formation at the bottom of the sea was quite tall. Just how far down did he go? The Bible doesn't say he went to the peaks of the mountains, he went to the roots. The deepest recorded point in the Mediterranean Sea is 17,280 feet (Calypso Deep) and the average depth is 4,900 feet.[1] The Bible also never says where in the Mediterranean Sea Jonah was thrown in, so let's use the average depth of the sea for the "roots of the mountains" instead of the deeper depths. With this "gimme," it means that Jonah sank an estimated 4,900 feet.

In April 2010, a 29-year-old man from New Zealand, William Trubridge, broke the world record for the deepest free immersion dive at 380 feet in the Atlantic Ocean. The "no limits" free dive record is an amazing 702 feet. In no limits free diving, divers descend on a weighted sled to their target depth. Once they want to go back up, they open a pressurized tank which fills a large inflatable balloon that helps them ascend to the surface. Keep in mind that this is 1/7th the distance that Jonah had to go and Jonah never had any inflatable balloons or tanks—all he had was a great fish!

While religious people relish the analogy in Jonah going as far away from God as he can, the real implications are quite inconvenient. Consider the conditions that Jonah would have to endure. At 4,900 feet, Jonah would have had to withstand approximately 2,192 psi. The water temperature is 36 degrees Fahrenheit so hypothermia becomes a legitimate concern. Assuming Jonah was as trained as today's world record holders, he could have found his heart rate slowing to as low as 14 beats per minute as he descended. Considering the depth he was going down to, oxygen would have been the least of his concerns. His lungs would have collapsed and he would have blacked out well before he even got close to that depth. You could take our estimate based upon the average depth of the Mediterranean Sea and cut it in half and then cut it in half again and Jonah still wouldn't survive.

The *only* way for the story of Jonah to be plausible would be to invoke the Divine Default. Once we place God in all of the scientifically inaccurate parts of the story, the story of Jonah becomes much more believable doesn't it? God got Jonah safely into the whale's first stomach chamber. God gave Jonah oxygen while he was under water or magically eliminated his need for oxy-

---

1 http://en.wikipedia.org/wiki/Mediterranean_Sea Retrieved 2/2/2012

gen. God provided a warm cocoon for Jonah that was impervious to the cold temperatures of the deep sea. God must have suspended all natural laws and changed the rate at which water pressure accumulates as Jonah descended into the water. Do you see where I'm going with this? None of this could have happened without God's divine intervention, thus the Divine Default must be invoked. This story is realistically and scientifically impossible.

The trouble with the story of Jonah is that it speaks directly to the historical accuracy of these texts. There are a great many things that I do not agree with religious fundamentalists on, but I do tend to concede their assertion that whenever the Bible writers, for example, used parables or allegories, they generally made that evident in the context of the story. Reading the story of Jonah doesn't read like this. The fact that all three Abrahamic faiths tell essentially the same story would lead me to conclude that none of the early Jews, Christians, or Muslims had any doubts whatsoever as to the authenticity and historical accuracy of the story. Why would they? What background knowledge would they have had to adequately critique and refute the story? If the original authors, original audience, and modern day fundamentalists take the story of Jonah as a literal telling of a historical event, the logistics involved in making it happen become crucial and open for debate. If the story is false, what other stories are false?

The major problem we encounter reading this in the modern world is that we have to abandon every sense of reason and logic to make this story plausible without invoking the Divine Default. This story could NOT be replicated today. It is utterly impossible without defaulting to supernatural causes. When we finally realize this, the story of Jonah becomes hard to swallow...pun intended.

Chapter 11. The Mystery of Cain's Wife

> "It ain't the parts of the Bible that I can't
> understand that bother me, it is the parts
> that I do understand."—Mark Twain

Those who believe the Bible to be the true word of God often get uneasy when this story comes up, and for good reason. As we recount the story as it is written in the Bible, ask yourself whether it seems plausible or whether the Divine Default becomes the only possible answer. Additionally, I would ask you to please bear in mind the concept I put forth earlier regarding the burden of proof and apply it to this story.

According to Genesis, God created Adam, the first man, from dust and His divine breath.

Our global population is now 1.

Eve, the first woman, is created by God from one of Adam's ribs.

Our global population is now 2.

Adam and Eve have two sons, Cain and Abel.

Our global population is now 4.

Abel was a shepherd and Cain was a farmer. God accepted Abel's sacrifice of "the firstborn of his flock and from their fats," but for whatever reason, God didn't think Cain's offering of the "fruit of the ground" was good enough. This made Cain angry...angry enough that God asked him "Why are you angry?" Genesis never tells us how Cain responded to God, so we can assume he either explained why he felt angry or he simply ignored God in the same way that a pouty child sometimes angrily ignores his/her parent. Regardless of how Cain left things with God, we soon find Cain and his brother Abel in the field. Cain then attacked and killed his brother.

Our global population is now 3.

God asks Cain "Where is your brother Abel?" (Genesis 4:9). Allow me to digress and ask a question that to me seems like common sense. If God is all-knowing, why is it that He has to ask Cain where his brother is? At this point in our history there are only 3 people on our entire planet. If God is all-knowing, surely a global population of 3 isn't too much for an omniscient being to keep track of, is it?

Here's where things get interesting. The conversation between Cain and God comprises Genesis 4:9—4:15, with Cain leaving God's presence and moving to the land of Nod, which was located east of Eden, in 4:16. In the very next sentence, Genesis 4:17, we learn that Cain made love to his wife who became pregnant and gave birth to a son named Enoch.

What? WAIT A MINUTE! How could this be? If the Bible is the word of God and it is an accurate representation of the creation of man, where did this mysterious wife come from? Even an elementary understanding of math tells us that the entire global population was only 3—Adam, Eve, and Cain. So who is this woman and how did she get here? We can look as hard as we like, but the Bible never mentions another race of people or even what her name was.

To be fair, I'll present the most-often cited reason for what clearly appears to be a major oversight on behalf of the author. In order to make this work, Adam and Eve "must have" had other children who moved away from them and for whom the Bible never speaks of. Biblical literalists claim that God's law against brother-sister marriage wasn't yet applicable, and that there would be no genetic deformities or issues with this close inbreeding because Adam and Eve "must have" had "perfect" DNA. The Bible of course makes no such reference, but according to this theory, Cain "must have" married either his sister or his niece. Again, in the interest of being fair, it is worth noting that no credible geneticist alive today would agree with that conclusion, nor do Biblical pseudoscientists like Ken Ham at Answers in Genesis present any critical evidence to support this theory. We are forced to make assumptions that are never mentioned in the Bible just to support an obvious oversight. Without making these wild assumptions, the Bible would clearly be inaccurate, and if the Bible is inaccurate...

Adam's next son, Seth, was born when Adam reached the age of 130 (Genesis 5:3). First, we need to believe that a human being could live to that age during a point in time when not a single person on Earth knew what a germ was or how to prevent/treat illness and disease. God gave man dominion over fish, birds, livestock, and every creeping thing, however God never gave man dominion over germs. It would be millennia before we had an adequate handle on these little guys (and still no dominion). Germs have always had a say in how healthy a human could be, however it is historically apparent that old age was somewhat of a banality back then as Sumerian and Babylonian kings were said to have lived for tens of thousands of years. According to the Bible, Adam lived to be 930 years old. The vast majority of the non-royal humans were lucky to see their twenties or thirties, so the idea that humans could live for hundreds of years requires a rational person to suspend a tremendous amount of disbelief. I digress one last time. The believer's theory suggests that Cain was in Nod for many years while a great deal of inbreeding occurred giving us a global population of more than 3. Therefore there "must have" been plenty of people on the planet for Cain to have chosen a nameless wife.

To my Christian readers, I have to ask whether or not you are you comfortable with this explanation? Mind you that there is nothing in the Bible or any outside reference that explicitly supports a theory like this. If the Bible is the infallible word of God, why do literalists have to make conjectures and assumptions to try and explain away the contradiction? The Bible literally goes from Cain leaving God's presence right to us meeting his wife. Read Genesis for yourself. The math is fairly straightforward on this one.

Most believers will find any way that they can to try and continue to support the original conclusion, even if it means trying to extrapolate information that isn't directly in the Bible. In our example of Cain and his mysterious wife, literalists like Ken Ham conjure up a bloodline that is never mentioned anywhere in the Bible or in any other texts, because the alternative is unthinkable to them. Now if only they could conjure up a name for her...

Chapter 12. Noah's Ark

"I do not think it is necessary to believe that the same God who has given us our senses, reason, and intelligence wished us to abandon their use, giving us by some other means the information that we could gain through them."—Galileo Galilei

Perhaps one of my favorite stories from the Bible is that of Noah and his life-saving Ark. I've always marveled at the speed with which many Christians will readily accept this story as literal and factual. It seems as if a new expedition is undertaken each year to find the long lost Ark. Pseudoscientists like Ken Ham, the president of Answers in Genesis (AiG), make their living off of a population that readily accepts a literal interpretation of the Bible. Ken Ham and his company have published their own account of how the story of Noah's Ark would be possible and present it as historical and scientific proof for the literal interpretation of the story. The Creation Museum in Kentucky which purports to "bring the pages of the Bible to life" is the work of Ham's company. It is here that children and dinosaurs play and roam freely together. If it seems like I am picking on Ken Ham, that's because I am. I liken people like him to snake oil salesmen, but Ham has taken it to a whole new level, bringing in millions of dollars in the process. It is interesting to note that at the time of this writing, Ham and AiG have had to postpone the ground breaking of their newest attraction, Ark Encounter, complete with a life-size replica of Noah's Ark, due to insufficient funds. The group is still $20 million short. Somehow I just can't picture Noah asking God to postpone the flood until he had enough money and resources.

Before we take a look at the plausibility of Noah's story through the lens of Ken Ham and AiG[1], have you ever thought to ask what the moral of this story is supposed to be? God saw how widespread wickedness had become and his *only* solution was to destroy all of mankind? Have you ever wondered how "wicked" our world must have been and compared that to our world today? If the moral of the story is to convey upon us the seriousness with which God takes sin or to teach us obedience, I have to ask why He didn't just strike everyone dead in a flash. It would have been just as impressive, not to mention faster and more efficient, to kill everyone in a flash of light. It certainly would have been more moral to send Jesus down to Earth sooner to save mankind than to drown everyone. Why go through the trouble of a global flood? What did all of the non-Ark riding animals do to warrant a death sentence? Were they as wicked as man? Surely there had to be at least one good, moral person or animal on the planet somewhere. Does God consider a tremendously perverted amount of collateral damage to be acceptable? What moral basis existed for killing everyone? No theologian has ever been able to convince me of the positive moral undertone to mass genocide. If we were to place the atrocities of Adolf Hitler, Joseph Stalin, and Mao Zedong on our Moral Ladder, they would absolutely be found near the Moral Void. With that in mind, where do you think the genocide of an entire planet belongs? The men I just mentioned are responsible for the deaths of tens of millions of people, but none ever came close to the extinction of human beings as a species. If the story of Noah holds even a kernel of truth, it is by far the single closest example that we have to the Moral Void. Literally every other act conducted throughout the course of human history warrants a higher placement on our Moral Ladder. Nothing before or since has ever come close to dethroning the story of Noah as the most despicable act of immorality in the history of our world. If this story belongs at the bottom of our Moral Ladder, the God that our neighbors pray to is the single most immoral being ever conceived. The most ambitious, psychopathic serial killer would blush with embarrassment and envy at the totality of God's killing spree. As we explore the plausibility of the Noah story, please don't forget the immorality of this story. We're going to have a little bit of fun with the plausibility but there's nothing fun about the undertone of genocide.

Let's deconstruct this famously immoral tale by starting with the size of the Ark from the Bible: 300 cubits long x 50 cubits wide x 30 cubits tall. A cubit is essentially the length of a man's arm starting from his elbow and ending at the tip of his fingers. The generally agreed upon dimensions are 450 feet long, 75 feet wide, and 45 feet tall. For comparison purposes, this would put it at more than half the size of the Titanic with a displacement tonnage of roughly 22,000 tons. This was a rather large ship built at a moment in time where something of that size was certainly not the norm. In fact, the next time a ship of that size would be built would be thousands of years later. For the purpose of our discussion, let's go with Ken Ham on this and assume that the people in Noah's time had both the skills and the means

---

1 http://www.answersingenesis.org/get-answers/topic/noahs-ark Retrieved 2/10/2012

to build something of this magnitude that was both seaworthy in the face of a flood of biblical proportions as well as capable of sufficiently holding and maintaining the animals for an extended period of time.

Let's keep in mind that while we don't know for sure whether Noah was an active participant in the physical process of building the ship or merely took on a supervisory role, we know from Genesis 9:28-29 that Noah was extremely old by today's standards.

> "And Noah lived after the flood three hundred and fifty years. And all the days of Noah were nine hundred and fifty years: and he died."

That's right. Noah, in whatever capacity he chose to participate in, was 600 years old during the building of the Ark. In the documented world, nobody has come close to Noah. Madame Jeanne Louise Calment passed away in Arles, France, at the age of 122 years 164 days old, and she is widely regarded as the oldest recorded human that ever lived. In 1900, the human life expectancy in the United States was 47.3 years. Life expectancy rose to 77.7 years by 2006. According to the Human Mortality Database, administered by the University of California, Berkeley and the Max Planck Institute for Demographic Research in Germany, human life expectancy has begun leveling off. By 2055, the average U.S. life expectancy will be 78.49 years.

Given all of our scientific advances in medicine since Noah's time, we are unable to come anywhere close to reaching an age of 950 years. In fact, we would be hard pressed to find a credible medical doctor willing to commit to the possibility of a human being not only reaching that age today but also during any point in verified, recorded human history. Somehow people like Ken Ham readily accept these ages as legitimate and attribute the decline in our life expectancy post-Flood to a less scientific and more vague "environmental change" and "other changes"[1]. While Ham presents absolutely no proof that would hold up to scientific scrutiny to support that claim, let's make another assumption here. Let's assume that the majority of medical doctors the world over are wrong and that the Bible and Ken Ham are correct in that a man could live to be 950 years old.

So now we have a 600-year-old man involved in building a seaworthy wooden ship more than half the size of the Titanic. The next step for Noah and his family is to prepare for the arrival of the animals. There has never been any documented activity throughout history where every type of animal migrated in unison to one location against their natural instincts either before or after this story. Even with his scientific background, Ken Ham is unable to explain how this could have happened, instead choosing to attribute it to a "supernatural event." This, my friends, is a classic example of the Divine Default. He and other creationists have to use the Divine Default to explain this, because without it, the entire story falls apart. What becomes plainly obvious to me is that folks like Ham make regular use of scientific principles (even if he has to stretch them) but when he can't stretch the principles far enough, he invokes the Divine Default. Let's make another assump-

---

1 http://www.answersingenesis.org/articles/nab2/adam-and-noah-live Retrieved 2/10/2012

tion here and say that while *no evidence has ever existed* for the migration of every type of animal to a single spot on Earth at the exact same time, these animals disobeyed their natural instincts and all did just that.

In keeping with the assertions of Ken Ham and the AiG scientists, dinosaurs were also on the Ark. According to the Book of Genesis, all the land-dwelling creatures were made on Day 6. Taking into account the creationist assertion that the Earth is between 6,000 and 9,000 years old, dinosaurs simply had to be on the Ark for the numbers to work out. I'm reminded of the comedian Lewis Black when he said that Bible literalists watch the Flintstones as if it were a documentary. Ham and other creationists attribute the extinction of the dinosaurs post-Flood to a "much more difficult world in which to survive" and that to survive, the "once easily obtained plant nutrition would now have to be supplemented by animal sources"[1]. This would assume that of all the animals on the Ark, dinosaurs were one of the least able to survive and would likely be preyed upon or unable to find food once they got off the Ark (more on this later). Based on the number, sheer size, and varied types of dinosaur fossils that we have today, one has to question Mr. Ham on the merits of that hypothesis. By what evidence is there to suggest that the adaptability and superior place on the food chain in which dinosaurs existed would render them less likely to survive than the common cow or pig?

Please note that paleontologists overwhelmingly disagree with Ken Ham and AiG. Legitimate scientists use techniques like radiometric dating to determine the age of the fossils and rocks. All of those ages are significantly older than the few thousand years that creationists advocate. Creationists try to discredit radiometric dating, without a valid alternative. Scientists use tools like mass spectrometers while creationists use tools like the Bible. Considering this "arsenal of tools," is it any surprise that these two groups arrive at very different conclusions? It's worth noting here that most creationists object to the use of carbon dating as inaccurate beyond a certain amount of half-lives. They always seem to go there without recognizing that other methods of radiometric dating like uranium-lead radiometric dating which has an error margin as low as less than 2 million years in two and a half billion years, with an error margin of 2–5% on Mesozoic rocks[2]. Scientists can use uranium-lead radiometric dating, the popular potassium-argon dating, rubidium-strontium dating, and uranium-thorium dating to arrive at the age of the planet as well as stone tools and fossils.

At this point in the story, a large number of animals are all in the process of migrating toward the Ark. The next question becomes, "How many animals were on the Ark?" The Bible never definitively gives a total number, so we're left to do some educated guessing. Creationists and scientists alike will agree that estimating the number of animal species on our planet

1   http://www.answersingenesis.org/articles/nab/what-happened-to-the-dinosaurs Retrieved 2/10/2012

2   Li, Xian-hua; Xi-rong Liang, Min Sun, Hong Guan and J. G. Malpas (2001). "Precise 206Pb/238U age determination on zircons by laser ablation microprobe-inductively coupled plasma-mass spectrometry using continuous linear ablation." *Chemical Geology* 175 (3-4): 209–219. doi:10.1016/S0009-2541(00)00394-6.

is a challenge. Things like habitat and differences in scientific classifications impact the estimates. Even though there are tens of millions of different species on our planet today, the creationist argument is that not every species needed to be represented on the Ark for it to be visible in our world today. For example, aquatic animals need not be on the Ark, for they would have been capable of surviving a global flood (more on this in a moment). Of the air-breathing, land-dwelling animals, only a male and female of each species had to be on the Ark. To highlight this in layman's terms, this means that a male and female dog had to be on the Ark. Once they got off the Ark, that pair of animals would be the incestuous parents to every kind of subsequent dog that we see today. From the Chihuahua to the Great Dane, it is asserted by creationists that all are direct descendants from that one pair of dogs on the Ark. While creationists will argue at the top of their lungs that evolution is invalid, they will gladly use evolutionary theory to help explain how their 2-dog theory is possible. They will happily use the theory of natural selection to explain why we don't find Chihuahuas in Siberia and St. Bernards in the tropics. For the purposes of our discussion, let's make another assumption that the subsequent inbreeding of these animal pairs would not adversely affect future generations.

While it's important to recognize the hypocrisy with regards to the creationists' use of evolution to explain how a core group of parent animals could repopulate our planet with such amazing diversity, it's even more important to recognize that they envision evolution taking place on an accelerated scale never before seen on Earth. According to creationists, the rediversification of species occurred in the course of a few thousand years as opposed to either tens of thousands (or even millions) of years in the theory supported by modern-day scientists. If all of these animals have evolved over such a short period of time to create literally millions of subspecies, does it not beg the question, "why don't we continue to see that same rate of rapid evolution"? Why did this amazingly rapid rate of evolution proposed by creationists suddenly drop off essentially when modern organized religion began?

Once we factor in the combination of inbreeding and natural selection, we can arrive at a more manageable number of animal species for the Ark. Estimates on this number range from as few as 2,000 animals to more than 100,000. Some creationists like AiG have estimated 16,000 while other places like ChristianAnswers.net suggest a number closer to 50,000 animals. The numbers are subject to interpretation and remain wholly dependent upon how far a creationist can creatively pare down the various species. For land-dwelling animals, 35,000 different species is a number that tends to be repeated and it isn't too far off from most suggestions, so let's use it for the purposes of our discussion.

The 600-year-old Noah and his seven family members had seven 24-hour days to load all of these animals that have amazingly migrated together into the Ark. Let's break out our calculators for a simple math problem. We have 70,000 individual creatures (35,000 species x 2 (1 male and 1 female)) completely loaded over the course of 168 hours (7 days x 24 hours per day). If we have 604,800 seconds in a week and Noah and his family worked every second of every day for that entire week, they would have had to load and stow 1 animal every 8.64 seconds. I'm sure creatures like the snail, spider, and worm took their time so the larger creatures would have had to move faster in order for us to keep that ratio. Can you picture an elephant, hippo, or dinosaur sprinting into the Ark and getting safely stowed in a matter of seconds?

Let's put this in perspective. The San Diego Zoo has over 4,000 animals comprising more than 800 species. They have 2,000 employees[1] (albeit not all of them directly involved with the care and feeding of the animals). If we estimate half of the San Diego Zoo staff to be involved in some fashion with caring for the animals, they would have 1 worker (curators, keepers and vet staff) for every 4 animals. For comparison purposes, 24% of the San Antonio Zoo's staff is involved in the care and feeding of the animals. In Atlanta, it's 42%. Assuming that Noah was not just serving in a supervisory capacity, but rather his 600-year-old body allowed him to actively participate in the care and feeding of the animals for months at a time, this means that 8 people on the Ark took care of 70,000 individual animals each with varied dietary requirements. Noah's ratio is 1 worker for every 8,750 animals—a nontrivial difference. There is no Biblical evidence to support that Noah and his family had any of the modern conveniences of the San Diego Zoo, so imagine the amount of work that Noah and his family had on a daily basis! If this was ever brought to the attention of the San Diego Zoo's Board of Trustees, surely they would have ample evidence for cutting back on their labor costs.

Let's assume that Noah and his family could load and care for all of those animals in the time allotted. Even though the Bible never makes any kind of reference to this, let's further assume that AiG is correct that Noah didn't take fully grown animals[2] on the Ark, as they would have certainly taken up more room and required more food and care. So now we have 35,000 pairs of juvenile animals completely loaded every few seconds over the course of a week.

Genesis 6:21 tells us that God commanded Noah to take food for every animal along with his family. I hope you didn't put your calculator away yet, because we're going to need it. If a pair of elephants consumes 800 pounds of food per day (400 lbs x 2 elephants) and roughly 3/4 of it is converted to waste per day, Noah and his family would have had to acquire approximately 120 TONS of food for JUST our elephants. Try extrapolating the amount of food necessary to care for 35,000 pairs of animals, some as big and diverse as the hippo, giraffe, or the dinosaur. According to Ken Ham and the Biblical scientists at AiG, the dinosaurs most likely "could have eaten dried meat, reconstituted dried meat, or slaughtered animals." While the Bible spells out in great detail the exact dimensions of the ark, it never once spells out the types and sheer quantities of food that would have been required. In fact, the amount of space required to store the food for an entire year is colossal!

1 Better Business Bureau profile. Retrieved 3/16/2012
2 http://www.answersingenesis.org/articles/nab/really-a-flood-and-ark Retrieved 2/11/2012

The space required to store the food would well surpass the space required for the animals. This means that there would be even less room on the Ark to store the animals and makes the plausibility of the whole story even more questionable.

In keeping with the theme of our argument, let's assume that Noah and his family knew all of this and did in fact acquire the necessary staples as commanded by God for every type of animal and in the necessary quantities. Let's further assume that all these hundreds or thousands of tons of food had enough storage space and didn't dry out or spoil in the weeks or months leading up to the big boarding or for the year that they would have been stored onboard.

Ham and AiG also make an assertion that the key to all of this was to have the animals avoid any unnecessary walking. Animals were most likely stored in pens which would prevent the predators from preying on the weaker animals, while it's generally understood that the animals did not spend their time hibernating. If they hibernated, why would God command Noah to bring food? Again, did anyone pause to ask how this would affect the animals? Surely standing still or lying in a pen for so many months would have caused their muscles to atrophy. Ask anyone who has had to wear a cast for a period of time what their limb looks like after the cast is removed. Ask anyone who has been bed-ridden for months what changes their body went through. Did the animals magically not get sick or develop sores from months of lying down or remaining in an inactive state? A fully trained and educated staff with expert knowledge in biology, zoology, botany, and ecology would have a tough time caring for these animals in this type of environment for that length of time, but we don't read about any difficulties experienced by Noah and his family. Again, let's make a few more assumptions and say that the Ark and Noah's family could easily handle the ventilation, waste, food, and medical needs of all of these animals for an extended period of time and that every animal would emerge from the Ark in a healthy condition free of atrophy, sickness, and sores. They would have to be healthy during the time afloat or else face possible death while onboard the Ark, eliminating them from the future food chain.

After a grueling week, Noah and his family have the Ark fully loaded and ready to go. Genesis 7:12 tells us that the rain that God promised began to fall for forty days and forty nights. So much rain fell that it covered *"all the high hills under the whole heaven. The waters prevailed fifteen cubits upward, and the mountains were covered"* (Genesis 7:19-20). This would have been quite a sight for every single person in the world because Genesis 2:4-6 tells us that God had never sent rain before the flood. According to Scripture, Noah wouldn't have even seen rain before the flood. Perhaps God irrigated the Earth from the ground up. Geologists from around the world generally agree that there is little to no evidence that the Earth's atmosphere held all of the flood's water in the air (in the form of mist) or that a global flood even occurred during the time period that Noah's flood was supposed to have happened. There is ample evidence to support localized flooding, but if we are to believe modern day geologists, the Biblical account has to be rejected. I hate to point this out, but creationists discount radiometric dating for determining the age of our planet, but they readily accept it when dating rocks from a flood or documents supporting the Bible. Oh, the hypocrisy...

The conditions described in Genesis for the flood are extreme and like nothing seen before or since, so let's try and put some context around this. In order to cover just Mount Ararat, where Noah's Ark finally came to a rest, the amount of water required to accomplish that would be in excess of 400 feet each day for 40 consecutive days. That's enough water to rise up 3 stories every hour! 400 feet of water every day is something that has never been replicated in nature and there isn't enough water in our atmosphere to even come close to it today. There is no scientific basis of explanation to support the actual 40 days of rain and the resulting water levels, so once again we have to go to the Divine Default as our explanation. If it really happened, our "loving" God is the only thing capable of producing such a destructive event, right? Let's further assume that the overwhelming majority of modern day geologists are completely wrong and that enough credible evidence really does exist to support a global flood that covered all of the mountaintops. We've had to make quite a few assumptions and take a number of liberties to get to this point, so why stop now?

If you'll recall, only the land-dwelling animals needed refuge aboard the Ark. Aquatic animals didn't need to be accommodated. While a handy piece of information, the Bible never says what kind of water filled the Earth. If the rain were fresh water as it is today, the salinity of the oceans would change drastically in a very rapid manner. This would destabilize the environment and kill off billions of saltwater fish and creatures, but it would allow Noah to give fresh water to our 35,000 pairs of animals currently floating on the Ark. With fresh water raining down, it's reasonable to assume that God would have required Noah to make accommodations for those aquatic animals living in salt water, or else they would have perished and we wouldn't have them in our oceans today. Of course, if the rain was salt water (a scientifically implausible scenario), the freshwater fish and creatures would have died. A third scenario is that the change in salinity didn't impact any of those fish and creatures, but of course, this is only possible if you subscribe to the Divine Default for a temporary suspension of the laws of chemistry. For the purposes of our discussion, let's ignore the fact that a drastic and dangerous change in salinity would kill off billions of unfortunate aquatic creatures and instead assume that the creatures of Noah's era were supernaturally able to rapidly adapt. If men could live for 900 years, surely the animals had to be heartier as well!

At this point, torrential non-stop rains are literally filling up the entire Earth covering all of the land up to and beyond the tallest mountaintops drowning all the non-Ark people and animals. Obviously, if this is happening, everyone is being impacted including those people located as close as 800 miles southeast in Egypt as well as those living 3,700 miles to the east in China. If we look at the Great Pyramid of Giza in Egypt, we should expect to find evidence of this global killer. The Great Pyramid was completed approximately 200 years after the flood. If the Bible is to be believed, people repopulated extremely quickly in Egypt and in great numbers. This would have had to occur all over Asia, Africa, and the rest of the world as well. I'm happy to continue conceding items to Ken Ham and AiG, however the numbers simply do not add up when trying to calculate population amounts and diversity in that kind of time frame.

Why is it that there is no archeological evidence whatsoever for a global flood completely covering Egypt at this point in time? Why doesn't this area show any sort of evidence of the waters that supposedly killed everyone including every Egyptian? Considering conventional Egyptian chronology, why don't the texts from this point in Egyptian history make any reference to this massive, global-killing flood? Frankly, how could there even be any texts created in Egypt from this time period if everyone died (along with their language)? We can look as hard as we like, but we will not find any credible evidence of a global flood during that time in this part of the world, nor will we find any credible evidence that this massive global killer even registered among the people of Egypt. Apparently they didn't find the flood terribly inconvenient. Nobody in Asia, with a more literate populace, was inconvenienced by this global killer, either. In addition to the Chinese and the Egyptians, there were other well-established civilizations during Noah's Flood. Evidence supporting the worldwide extinction of the human race by a global flood cannot be found among the Sumerians of Mesopotamia, the Minoan, or the Indus Valley even though the Bible tells us that these people should have been drowning. No evidence exists for the elimination of either culture or infrastructure in Mesopotamia. The same applies to the prosperous Chinese period during the early Yao Dynasty. It would appear that the global killer known as Noah's Flood barely got their feet wet.

There are some language and cultural issues that we're going to have to deal with as well. If everyone in the world died and the global population was then rapidly replenished starting with Noah and his family, why do we have such a multitude of languages? If all of humanity were suddenly repopulated quickly from this single spot, it would stand to reason that we wouldn't have seen such a varied number of languages. Surely the language of Noah would have been passed down to each subsequent generation and yet there is no evidence to support the theory that anyone in China, Australia, or the Americas spoke Hebrew...ever. We can be reasonably certain that Noah would have passed down such concepts as the Ten Commandments and the prohibition of working on the Sabbath, yet many of the Old Testament concepts didn't make their way to the rest of the world which, if the story is accurate, would have been entirely populated by Noah's descendants in an astonishingly rapid manner.

Let's make another assumption, to keep the story moving. Let's assume that evidence of this global killer wiped out all of the people of Egypt, Asia, and the rest of the planet. Let's further assume that Noah's family was able to repopulate an entire planet with a multitude of languages and that historians are completely wrong about Egyptian and Asian texts/technology created during both the time of Noah as well as immediately after. Let's assume that evidence for all of the global language and cultural issues simply hasn't been discovered yet.

"*And the waters receded continually from the earth. At the end of the hundred and fifty days the waters decreased*" (Genesis 8:3).

So now the waters have receded and comprise the oceans we see today. While scientists make claims that such processes as plate tectonics are responsible for the formation of our continents, creationists chalk that up to the receding flood waters. Let's assume that the scientists are wrong and that the flood's receding waters filled our oceans and lakes (perhaps the Ice Age was a hoax as well). The Ark has finally come to a rest "*on the seventeenth day of the seventh month...on the mountains of Ararat*" (Genesis 8:4). Many believe that the mountain referred to in Genesis is the same Mount Ararat in eastern Turkey. The Qur'an, Islam's holy book, places the Ark on Al-Judi. Regardless of where the Ark apparently finally came to rest, we're left with a few sticky issues that we have to deal with.

At the ripe old age of 601, Noah removed the covering from the Ark and "*by the twenty-seventh day of the second month the earth was completely dry*" (Genesis 8:14). Ken Ham and other creationists never seem to follow the story of Noah through to its logical conclusion. If the Ark came to rest on the mountains of Ararat, how did the animals safely get down the mountain, which is a difficult task for even experienced climbers? Let's assume that all the animals (including the dinosaurs) made it safely down the mountain. What kind of environment would they find themselves in once they reached the bottom?

The plants that would have been prevalent before the flood would not have survived the flood. Plants adapted to water-logged conditions will survive, however there's no reason to believe that plants and other vegetation would have found themselves as equally adapted to that environment back then any more than they would today. Basic biology tells us that roots need oxygen to carry out aerobic respiration to produce ATP for root functions. Water does not hold as much oxygen as air and when the soil becomes saturated it also becomes anaerobic leaving the roots of non-aquatic plants to die. With water levels reaching the types of proportions mentioned in the Bible, how much sunlight could possibly pierce these depths? Remember earlier when we discussed the change in salinity that would most certainly impact aquatic life? Plants would be just as affected. Seeds would have also been exposed and soaked in salt water for many months. The post-flood world would be a very harsh environment for plants to try and not only survive but thrive in a very short amount of time.

OK—I think we've given creationists like Ken Ham enough liberties with their theories to support the story of Noah. If you're keeping tally, we likely passed the "ridiculous" level several assumptions ago.

The animals that have made the difficult descent down from Mount Ararat have now found themselves in a silty, barren wasteland completely devoid of a food chain. With a maximum of seven of any species (another

Biblical contradiction), and most often only two members left alive, entire species (and the millions of future sub-species) would have been wiped out very quickly if even one of them were killed by a predator or died from lack of vegetation to feed on. All of these animals would be in a small, concentrated place fighting for extremely limited resources. Common sense should tell us that animals that don't eat can't live long enough to repopulate our world.

If the Bible is to be believed, all of these animals dispersed from this one central location to spots around the globe. Why is it that marsupials can only be found in abundance in Australia and the abundance of the fossils of their ancestors are only found on that continent? Additionally, how did these marsupials get to Australia in the first place? If you recall, the creationist argument for our continents is that the receding flood waters, not plate tectonics, created them. Did the kangaroos and koalas swim alongside the Tasmanian devils across the ocean, and if so, for what purpose? Why leave dry land? There are literally hundreds of these types of examples and they all become increasingly difficult to explain when limited pairs of animals are all placed and dispersed from one geographic spot.

There's little use for a creationist to argue most of the scenarios in this chapter as I have conceded most of their assertions to an annoyingly ridiculous degree. I would however challenge any creationist to explain how an entire food chain not only survived but thrived, expanded, and dispersed across the globe in rapid order in that post-flood world. The problem is that, just like the initial migration of every animal species to the Ark, they can't unless they invoke the Divine Default.

CHAPTER 13. PUTTING FAITH TO THE TEST

> "The fact that a believer is happier than a skeptic is
> no more to the point than the fact that a drunken man
> is happier than a sober one."—George Bernard Shaw

There is perhaps no greater test of faith than when it comes to health. Health concerns can very often have life-threatening consequences. It's within this realm that I'd like to put faith and the power of prayer to the test. Imagine for a moment that a loved one is deathly sick or injured. If you had one choice, would you take him/her to the doctor, or would you instead opt for prayer? It's a simple question with real consequences. The answer should give us some indication on just how much faith we really have. Most people, even most religious people, would choose the doctor over prayer every time and this answer should tell us something.

When faced with a life and death situation, a rational person will choose something tangible because of the significantly greater likelihood of success. In the case of religious people, their actions speak much louder than their words. A religious person may say (and perhaps believe) that God can heal the sick, but that faith is only worthy of words. The actions of a religious person in our scenario are completely different. If they truly believed that God can have a physical impact in our world, then why would they make Him the backup plan? Why would their actions conflict with their stated beliefs?

This scenario takes away all ontological positions and arguments. It forces us to examine God in a "rubber hits the road" type of fashion. Arguing over the validity of Noah's Ark, Muhammad's revelations, or Krishna's contributions to our life on Earth becomes absolutely irrelevant. A rational person recognizes this and this is why we'll find a rational person rushing to see a doctor instead of a priest. The most devout religious believers may probably cry "foul" with the question of choice being asked in the first place, but why? Is this not a legitimate question? If we apply the Omni Paradox to the situation, we could come to the conclusion that if He wanted to save someone, He could. God is all-powerful, all-knowing, and all-loving, correct? If someone legitimately believed that God could save a life, the doctor then becomes unnecessary on the simple premise that no doctor could ever be more powerful than God. If God has time to listen and answer prayers, surely He has time to save a life. The "religion vs. medicine" argument is the ideal topic precisely because of the seriousness of the outcome.

In 2009, Dale and Leilani Neumann of Weston, WI, were found guilty of homicide in the March 2008 death of their daughter Madeline. Madeline, also known as Kara, had a treatable form of diabetes. The Neumanns relied on prayer for treatment. As their daughter became so weak that she couldn't eat, drink, walk, or even speak, people surrounded her and prayed as she lay on the family's floor. Only when she stopped breathing did anyone bother to call emergency personnel. While the courts questioned their decision, nobody could question their faith in Jesus Christ. After the trial, Dale said, "We live by faith. We are completely content with what the Lord has allowed to come down, but he is not done yet." So here we have a deeply religious couple who believed in Jesus and prayed in his name (*"If you believe, you will receive whatever you ask for in prayer,"* Matthew 21:22) for the health of their daughter. The Neumanns put their faith in Jesus to the test. The outcome was tragic and completely avoidable. Jesus did not come. Their prayers were not answered. Their child could have been saved by qualified medical personnel. As I have stated multiple times in this book, religion is dangerous and has the power to warp minds. The Neumanns are perfect examples of this.

Carl and Raylene Worthington of Oregon chose God instead of a doctor for their sick 15-month-old daughter, Ava. Church members gathered at the Worthington's home to pray for Ava. They gave her a dab of wine with water, anointed her with oil, fasted, and prayed. They believed in the "power of prayer," and as the Neumanns did, they put faith above medicine with the same tragic and avoidable outcome. This example, and every example like it, completely contradicts the Bible. James 5:14–15 says that a prayer offered in faith will make the sick person well and the Lord will raise them up. The Lord did not raise this child up and make her well. God did nothing.

Prayer alone is incapable of saving someone requiring serious medical attention. We can't pray away cancer. We can't pray away a heart attack. We can't pray away diabetes. When someone's life is on the line, their survival instinct will take over and God, correctly, becomes an impotent afterthought. What should this tell us about the true power of God and the true power of prayer to produce tangible results?

The most scientifically rigorous study ever conducted into the power of prayer was done by the John Templeton Foundation, which funds and conducts research relating to the questions of human purpose and ultimate reality. They generally do this by providing grants for high-level scientific research projects. Before you subconsciously (or consciously) place the atheist moniker on the Templeton Foundation because of their focus on science, realize that this is not the case as demonstrated by some of their critics. Richard Dawkins, perhaps the most well-known atheist in the world, criticizes the Templeton Foundation in his book *The God Delusion* by saying that the Templeton Prize is "a very large sum of money given...usually to a scientist who is prepared to say something nice about religion." Peter Woit, a mathematical physicist at Columbia University, has stated, "they unambiguously are devoted to trying to bring science and religion together, and that's my main problem with them." Neil DeGrasse Tyson once said, "Templeton seeks out widely published religion-friendly scientists to receive an annual award whose cash value exceeds that of the Nobel Prize." Paul Davies, a Templeton Foundation Board of Trustees member, refuted these perceptions, saying, "The benefactor, Sir John Templeton, bemoans the way that religious leaders often claim to have all the answers. Imagine, he says, consulting a doctor about an ailment, only to find him reaching for a volume of Hippocrates. Yet priests rely on ancient scriptures to deliver spiritual guidance...In none of these projects is anything like a preferred religious position encouraged or an obligation imposed to support any religious group."

When the voices of the critics are considered alongside the results of the study, I believe that the results become even more interesting and illuminating.

The goal of the study was to determine the effects of prayer on the recovery of people who underwent heart surgery. This $2.4 million study was led by Harvard professor Herbert Benson over the course of nearly a decade and included 1,802 patients from six different hospitals undergoing coronary artery bypass surgery. The patients were randomly placed into three groups. As a control, Groups 1 and 2 were told that they may or may not receive prayers for their quick recovery. Group 1 received prayers and Group 2 did not. Group 3 was told that they were going to receive prayers, and in fact, they did. Three Christian churches were used for the prayers. As a scientific control, the congregations were given only the patients' first names and last initials. Each member of the church could pray in their own way, but each had to include the following phrase in their prayers: 'for a successful surgery with a quick, healthy recovery and no complications.' The goal was to evaluate the effects that intercessory prayer would have on the patients.

- Group 1, which received prayers but were not certain about receiving them, saw complications occur in 52% of the patients.

- Group 2, which did not receive prayers but were also not certain about receiving them, saw complications occur in 51% of the patients.

- Group 3, which received prayers and knew that other Christians were praying for them, saw complications occur in 59% of the patients.

The results were pretty clear. Not only did prayer not help those patients, it actually made things worse. Patients who were prayed for saw more complications than those who had no prayer. The reason most often cited by critics is that of "performance anxiety." If Jesus is not just a spiritual

God, but rather one that has the ability to directly intervene in our lives, what conclusion can we draw from the most scientifically rigorous study ever conducted?

If someone uses prayer and it makes them feel good or it gives them the motivation to keep a positive attitude, then there can be a beneficial element to it but that doesn't mean that a divine entity was involved. The same effect can be reached regardless of the specific god being prayed to. There is value in the comfort that one feels when asking for help from a divine power, particularly when help seems so far out of reach. Positive thinking is no substitute for qualified medical care though. Likewise prayer is no substitute for qualified medical care either. Prayer alone is medically and tangibly ineffective.

I encourage every religious person to put faith to the test by keeping track of their prayers and the associated results. I would suggest assigning a difficulty level next to each prayer request where 1 is a simple prayer request and 10 is an impossible request without divine intervention. If a prayer is for someone who happens to be sick or hurt but is being medically attended to, that's a 1 or 2 due to the fact that qualified medical personnel and the person's own body figure heavily in the outcome. If a prayer is for someone who has lost a limb to have God give that person his/her limb back without medical attention, that's a 10. Adjust the situation accordingly and examine the results. How many high number prayer requests did God "answer"? How many prayers went unanswered? The point behind this exercise is to call attention to all of the unanswered prayers. This becomes much easier the moment we bring some accountability to it. It also allows us to see the impact of cognitive dissonance. If God doesn't answer, it's because His ways are mysterious or He has something better in mind. As George Carlin once said, "Fine, but if it's God's will, and He's going to do what He wants to anyway, why...bother praying in the first place? Seems like a big waste of time to me! Couldn't you just skip the praying part and go right to His Will?"

The simple fact of the matter is that God doesn't answer prayers that are impossible. He never has and He never will. Jesus lies to his disciples in Mark 11:24. It does not matter what someone prays for, how hard they pray, how many people pray for the same thing, how righteous the believer is, or how honorable the prayer is. Prayer might make someone feel better, as a coping mechanism, but it doesn't provide tangible, meaningful results. Prayer is nothing more than mental self-gratification. If someone prays for something impossible like the re-growing of a lost limb, those prayers will always go unanswered. In fact, there is no single recorded case where an amputee's prayer has ever been answered. The key here is probability. An "answered" prayer will always have the potential to occur within the normal laws of probability. For example, cancer has been known to go into remission on its own, therefore we shouldn't automatically assign God as the reason when someone's cancer goes into remission. It's estimated that cancer will go into remission on its own in approximately 1 out of every 100,000 cases[1]. It's es-

1 Hobohm U (October 2001). *"Fever and cancer in perspective."* Cancer Immunol. Immunother. 50 (8): 391–6. PMID 11726133

timated that 22% of all breast cancer cases will experience spontaneous regression, so it would be intellectually dishonest to rush to insert God as the reason when we find ourselves on the receiving end of a positive result like this. Someone from another faith or even an atheist could achieve the same result. Coincidences are rarely meaningful but our ability to notice and associate meaning to them is a phenomenon that fascinates both believers and skeptics. The "power of prayer" can be more accurately described as the "power of coincidence".

Answered prayers are a big part of validating religion. Many prayers in-volve asking for a miracle, so it's worth asking what exactly is a miracle? The Scottish philosopher David Hume sums it up nicely by saying that a miracle is not just the suspension of the laws of nature, but it's a suspension of the laws of nature in favor of the person asking for the miracle. This pres-ents an egotistical challenge however. As Hume proposes, either the laws of the universe have just been suspended for someone's personal benefit or the person reporting such a miracle is either simply mistaken or unaware of the event's natural probability. It seems to me that there is something quite arrogant about claiming a miracle. If I were to make a miraculous claim, I would essentially be saying that my miracle was so important that it was worthy of suspending the laws of the universe to produce. With the sheer number of miracles being claimed on a daily basis around the world, the laws of the universe would appear to be far looser than one might imagine—mere guidelines in fact. Fortunately there is no empirical evidence of any sort to support this outcome and therefore there is no empirical evidence to support belief in miracles.

When He's not killing them in a global flood, it is often said that God has a soft spot for children. I have difficulty reconciling God's love of children to the child mortality rate in our world. In 2010, 7.6 million children under the age of 5 died[1]. Two thirds of those deaths were preventable. In the time it will take you to read this paragraph, 10 children under the age of 5 will have died of a preventable death. Most of the parents of these children will pray to God and their prayers will not be answered. What if their prayers are unanswered because they're praying to the wrong God? What if their geography prevented them from being "saved" by Jesus because they never heard the story in the first place? Those children get rewarded with hell on earth as well as hell in the afterlife. I question the morality in believing this.

When it matters most, rational people will, either consciously or sub-consciously, dismiss prayer as an ineffectual solution. Whether they want to admit it or not, they know that God is impotent to affect real change. That is the real takeaway. God doesn't regrow limbs, no matter how many people might pray for it. He never has. He never will, and actions always speak louder than words.

1 UNICEF press release Sept. 2011

Chapter 14. Our Christian Nation

"Everyone is entitled to their own opinions, but
not their own facts."—Daniel Patrick Moynihan

It is a rather common perception that the United States of America is a "Christian Nation." Whether people are Baptist, Catholic, Lutheran, or Anglican, they often believe that their denomination had a major, fundamental influence on our Founding Fathers and the establishment of the United States. Whether they were Christians or deists, the truth is that many of our founding fathers held some sort of religious belief. A deist is someone who holds the belief that reason and observation of the natural world can lead to the determination of a creator[1]. The creator built the universe but does not generally intervene in human affairs. A deist does not believe in the need for organized religion. Deism became prominent during the 17th and 18th centuries among those who were raised as Christians but who couldn't logically believe in miracles, the innate "truth" of the Bible, and the concept of the Holy Trinity. Deists from that time period believed in a God but did not put their faith in the infallible word of the Bible. The people who tend to use the term "Christian Nation" do so under the belief that Christianity is not just the most popular religion but that the country itself was founded *by* and *for* Christians. Here's where I take issue.

Instead of rhetoric, I'd like to look at real actions. There's merit in the cliché that actions speak louder than words. I'd also like to debunk some of the common myths that many Christian revisionists try to spread. Before we dial back our clocks and take a look at the initial history of our country, let's deal with some of the common misconceptions that the religiously-motivated often pontificate today to support their notion of a Christian Nation.

---

1 http://en.wikipedia.org/wiki/Deism Retrieved 12/6/2011

During the many discussions I've had with Christians, they always offer up such things as our currency as proof that we're a Christian Nation. "In God We Trust" is on our coins and dollar bills. It's true. It's absolutely true. Look at the back of a twenty dollar bill and you will see those words. I can't argue that. What I can and will argue, and what these people never seem to recognize, is that those words weren't always there. Those words began appearing on coins in 1864 and on paper dollars in 1957. For those who like to credit our Founding Fathers for establishing this Christian Nation, that's an awful long time after their deaths to support such "evidence".

I don't expect those words to be on there forever, however they will remain there for the time being. The United States Court of Appeals for the Ninth Circuit issued a ruling that said:

> "It is quite obvious that the national motto and the slogan on coinage and currency 'In God We Trust' has nothing whatsoever to do with the establishment of religion. Its use is of patriotic or ceremonial character and bears no true resemblance to a governmental sponsorship of a religious exercise."

While Christian revisionists often assume that the words "In God We Trust" have always existed on our currency, they're incorrect. Even though the courts have said that it does not indicate that the government sponsors this for anything more than "patriotic or ceremonial character," our Founding Fathers did not intend to have this on our currency. If they did, they would have put it on there in the first place. All the evidence is to the contrary.

Another misconception offered up by Christian Revisionists deals with the Pledge of Allegiance. Perhaps you've seen the email forwards or heard someone make reference to it as part of their Christian Nation support. When Francis Bellamy wrote the Pledge in 1892, it read,

> "I pledge allegiance to my flag and the republic for which it stands: one nation indivisible with liberty and justice for all."

It went through four changes since Bellamy originally wrote it. In 1954, 62 years later and 23 years after his death, Congress added the words "under God" to the Pledge as a way to differentiate the United States from the concept of communist state atheism[1]. Just like our currency, the reference to God was not originally intended to be there. If Bellamy wanted a religious reference included in the Pledge, he could have put it there. All the evidence is to the contrary.

For many people who lay claim to the title of Christian Nation, they often forget about the world that our Founding Fathers lived in. They had fled England where the power of the government was derived from God, not the people. That is a pretty inconvenient fact for many Christian revisionists, but it's important to keep that in mind as a backdrop when discussing this topic. If we consider the actions of our Founding Fathers within the context of the world that they lived in, it becomes easier to understand why they did (or didn't) do certain things.

---

1   Merriman, Scott A. (2007). *Religion and the Law in America: An Encyclopedia of Personal Belief*. ABC-CLIO. p. 111. ISBN 9781851098637.

One would assume that if we were a Christian Nation, the Constitution should provide ample evidence to support such an assumption. The Constitution is perhaps the single most important document in our country's history. It is the underlying foundation for the rules that we as a society live by. Let's test this assumption. Do me a favor and put this book down for a few minutes. I'd like you to go to a computer and go online to the Internet. Do a search for "full text US Constitution." Google provided me with more than 59 million results, but we only need one. Take your pick and look for the words "God," "Jesus," "Christianity," "Divine," "Creator," or "Bible" within our Constitution. Take your time. I'll be here when you return.

Back already? Good. How many instances did you find of those words in our Constitution? None? Really? Perhaps you should read it again, because surely if we are a Christian Nation, our Founding Fathers should have included at least some of those words. How can we be a Christian Nation without any mention of Christ?

Article 6, section 3 says that "no religious test shall ever be required as a qualification to any office or public trust under the United States." This means that religion cannot be used as a condition for public office, which provides equal opportunity for those with faith and those without. We have even seen early state constitutions like those in Delaware (1776), South Carolina (1778), and Georgia (1777) where religious belief was a defined requirement for public office and many explicitly required the person to be a Protestant. Each of these would be repealed. If our founders wanted a Christian Nation, wouldn't it be in our best interest to make sure that our public leaders were Christians? Why would the U.S. Constitution and state constitutions explicitly ban Christian (or any religious) beliefs as a potential requirement? This seems detrimental to the belief that we were intended to be a Christian nation.

You'll also notice religion mentioned in the First Amendment where it clearly prohibits the government from adopting any religion as its own, nor can it promote one over the other. It cannot dictate what religion its citizens must adhere to. Citizens were able to choose for themselves. The First Amendment prevents us from elevating Christianity over any other religion. The Founding Fathers could have very easily made us an official Christian Nation if they wanted to. All the evidence is to the contrary.

Let's look at the Declaration of Independence. While it isn't a governing document like the Constitution, it is still a historical document of incredible importance. The Declaration of Independence was used to make a moral case as to why the colonies were severing their ties to England. The Declaration makes reference to "Nature's God" and the "Creator," but before you jump to any conclusions, consider the time period that our Founding Fathers were in and the term "deist" that I defined earlier. "Nature's God" and "Creator" were synonymous with deism and not specifically Christianity. What would prevent any other faith from claiming that "Nature's God" and "Creator" weren't references to their God? The Founding Fathers never once mention "Jesus Christ" or "Christ our Savior." It seems to me that if one wants to make a case for a "Christian Nation," one should find exclusive reference to Christ, or at least one reference to Christ at a minimum. All evidence to the contrary.

Thomas Jefferson, the principal author of the Declaration of Independence, was a deist and any attempt to portray him as anything but is both wrong and insulting to the man's honor. Jefferson did not believe in any of the miracles of Jesus Christ, nor did he believe that Jesus was the son of God. He thought very highly of the moral teachings of Jesus, which is why he took a razor, cut and pasted selected verses from the Bible, and created his own book called the *The Life and Morals of Jesus of Nazareth*. Today we commonly refer to it as *The Jefferson Bible* and you can go online and purchase a copy of it yourself. You will not find any references to angels, prophecies, miracles, the Holy Trinity, or Jesus' divinity. In a letter to John Adams in 1813, he referred to these things as "nonsense." The book ends with Jesus dead in a tomb sealed with a great stone. No resurrection. Imagine the will, effort, and time it took for a man to painstakingly remove all of the "nonsense" from the New Testament. For a man who didn't believe in Jesus' divinity, why would anyone think that he was referring to Jesus Christ when he wrote the words "Nature's God" in the Declaration of Independence? If Jefferson wanted to reference Jesus in the Declaration, he could have written "Christ," "Jesus Christ," or "Christ our Lord" instead of the more generic, deistic God. All the evidence is to the contrary.

So if the Constitution and the Declaration of Independence never make any type of reference to us being a Christian Nation, surely there must be some other evidence to support such a conclusion, right? The Treaty of Tripoli, negotiated during the presidency of George Washington and signed by President John Adams was very explicit about America and religion.

> As the Government of the United States of America is not, in any sense, founded on the Christian religion,—as it has in itself no character of enmity against the laws, religion, or tranquility, of Mussulmen,—and as the said States never entered into any war or act of hostility against any Mahometan nation, it is declared by the parties that no pretext arising from religious opinions shall ever produce an interruption of the harmony existing between the two countries.

There's nothing to try and interpret here. It is very clear that we are NOT a nation founded on the Christian religion. The official treaty was read aloud on the Senate floor. Copies were given to every Senator. When the vote was taken to ratify the treaty, it was unanimous. Let me highlight that last part. When given the opportunity to vote on the treaty, not a single Senator voted "no." It was ratified unanimously. Our early government could have removed the reference to our lack of Christian foundation if they wanted to. If we were truly a Christian Nation, they would have said so. All the evidence is to the contrary.

It is not my intention to persuade anyone that religion, and Christianity in particular, hasn't played a role in our country and its development. I gladly offer that it has and it continues to do so to this day. President Harry Truman once wrote "This is a Christian Nation" in a letter to Pope Pius XII. Woodrow Wilson has made similar comments. We can find Supreme Court opinions that make reference to Christian values. Many of our Founding Fathers were Christians, but I have to ask, if they didn't see fit to officially make us a Christian Nation, why are we trying to rewrite history against their intentions? If they wanted us to be a Christian Nation, they could have easily done so. All the evidence is to the contrary.

Let's review where we're at. The Constitution makes no reference to Christianity or religion in general, except in exclusionary terms. The Declaration of Independence, written by one of the most influential people in the founding of our country who did not believe in Jesus' divinity, makes no reference to Christianity, but instead to a more generic "Nature's God." One of our earliest official treaties explicitly states that we are *not in any way* a Christian Nation. We do not find "Jesus," "Jesus Christ," or "Christ" in any of those works, which makes it awfully difficult to put the "Christian" label on any of them. None of these items are debatable. Christians can research and verify every example I've provided for themselves and I would encourage them to do so. So what else is there?

Christians not satisfied with the above information often resort to "Christian values." They will often argue that our founders, while not explicitly endorsing Christianity, used Christian morals as the underpinnings of our country. Harry Truman once said "The fundamental basis of this nation's laws was given to Moses on the Mount. The fundamental basis of our Bill of Rights comes from the teachings we get from Exodus and Saint Matthew, from Isaiah and Saint Paul."

I take no joy in disparaging a great American like Harry Truman, but our country would be a hotbed of intolerance and hatred if indeed he was even remotely correct. If someone wants to claim, as Truman did, that our laws were based upon Christian values, what values exactly are we talking about? President Truman made reference to Moses and the Book of Exodus. These references come from the Old Testament. The God of the Old Testament is very different from the God of the New Testament. The Old Testament God is capricious, petty, mean, jealous, and vengeful. He watches with indifference as people are murdered, enslaved, and raped. He himself is responsible for the murder of many! Jesus in the New Testament is quite the opposite. He's for the most part very loving, caring, and peaceful. If President Truman is to be believed, our Christian values would be associated with slavery, murder, and rape. If we overlook his Old Testament references and choose to base our definition of "Christian values" on the teachings of Jesus Christ instead, I think we would find more universally-accepted "values."

Using the New Testament as our basis for Christian values, we can use the following traits[1] to help us identify the principles of Christianity and their relation to the notion of a Christian Nation.

---

1 http://en.wikipedia.org/wiki/Christian_values (*The Holy Bible, King James Version*, Meridian, 1974.) Retrieved 1/8/2012

— Love of God —
"You shall love the Lord your God with all of your heart,
and with all your soul, and with all your mind"

— Fidelity in Marriage —
"Whom God has joined together let no man put asunder"

— Renunciation of Worldly Goods —
"Gather not your riches up upon this earth,
for there your heart will be also"

— Renunciation of Violence —
"If a man strikes you on one cheek, turn the other cheek"

— Forgiveness of Sins —
"Forgive us our trespasses, as we forgive those who trespass against us"

— Unconditional Love —
"Love your enemies and pray for those who persecute you"

I'm confident that if I presented the list above to any Christian, they would universally agree that these are all qualities that describe "Christian values." I could even add broader qualities like love, family, charity, honor, and kindness. All of these seem logical in relation to Jesus' teachings.

But in order to make the claim that these are Christian values used as the basis for a Christian Nation, these qualities need to be unique to Christianity, otherwise why bother with the "Christian" label? In that respect, we'd better not find any of these qualities in any non-Christian society or else they can't be claimed exclusively by Christianity.

Unfortunately, the values represented here are present in human societies throughout the course of history. Not a single one of them is unique to Christianity.

- "Love of God" is not unique to Christianity. Every religion with a deity lays claim to this one.

- "Fidelity in Marriage" is not unique to Christianity. Roman law was very strict on adultery. Adultery is a major violation of the Islamic marital contract and considered a sin condemned by God himself. Both Buddhism and Jainism clearly forbid it.

- "Renunciation of Worldly Goods" is not unique to Christianity and seems to contradict the capitalist society that the United States has become, doesn't it? How many Christian Americans, or more specifically Founding Fathers, can we name who have given up all of their worldly possessions? The concept doesn't belong solely to Christianity. The Qur'an says *"Such are the possessions of this world's life; but in nearness to Allah is the best of the goals"* (Surah Aali-

'Imran: 14). The Prophet Muhammad once said, "What have I to do with worldly things? My connection with the world is like that of a traveler resting for a while underneath the shade of a tree and then moving on." Renunciation of worldly goods is the true mark of Hinduism and is the most direct way to find moksha (liberation).

- "Renunciation of Violence" is not unique to Christianity. One cannot read the news and give serious consideration to that value, particularly when it's used to support the founding of a nation that currently spends almost half of the world's military expenditures. The United States currently spends more on its military than the next closest 15 countries *combined*. Renunciation of violence can be found in Jainism and Hinduism as well. In Jainism, Acaranga Sutra 4.25–26 tells us "One should not injure, subjugate, enslave, torture, or kill any animal, living being, organism, or sentient being. This doctrine of nonviolence is immaculate, immutable, and eternal. Just as suffering is painful to you, in the same way it is painful, disquieting, and terrifying to all animals, living beings, organisms, and sentient beings." Imagine if Christianity actually operated like this!

- "Forgiveness of Sins" isn't unique to Christianity either. Hindus and Buddhists regularly preach this concept. Examples of the Prophet Muhammad's forgiveness can be found in the Hadith.

- "Unconditional Love" is not unique to Christianity, nor was it a tactic used by our Founding Fathers. In Islam, unconditional love forms the basis for all morality. Unconditional love can also be found in Sikhism, Confucianism, Jainism, Taoism, and Buddhism.

- Finally, if using the generic concepts of love, family, charity, honor, and kindness, which of these are strictly Christian?

I would propose that none of the universally-accepted qualities that we associate with Christian values are uniquely Christian. In fact, the only thing that is unique to Christianity is the story vicarious redemption, but this is in direct conflict with both the founding of and the current existence of the United States. If I commit a crime as a US citizen today, my children and their future children bear no responsibility for my crime. The responsibility is mine. In Christianity, Jesus plays the role of scapegoat taking away the sins of his followers. In the United States, we are all held accountable for our actions. If I commit a crime today, someone else isn't responsible for paying my debt. There are no scapegoats. The responsibility is mine. Ultimately, there is no accountability in Christianity so I fail to see how the only real quality that is absolutely unique to Christianity has anything at all to do with a "Christian" nation.

The evidence would suggest that our Founding Fathers were clearly against the notion of a "Christian Nation," instead intending for our government to maintain a neutral position in this matter. The simple, non-debatable fact is that the United States is a democracy and not a theocracy. We are a secular country by choice with absolutely no room for divine authority. The people are the authority—not God. If someone truly wanted to live under a government that is based upon religious text, they always have the option to move to Iran or Saudi Arabia. Those countries truly do operate upon religious texts. One need only look at the case of Raif Badawi, the editor of a Saudi Arabian website critical of the role that religion plays in that country, who was cited in 2012 for blasphemy and apostasy, which carries an automatic death sentence if convicted to realize the dangers of infusing government with religion. Imagine if a United States citizen could be put to death for the simple "crime" of changing religions. That is clearly not something that our Founding Fathers ever wished for us.

If our Founding Fathers did not call us a Christian Nation, and if the principles that we'd like to believe we were founded upon are not uniquely Christian, by what basis can anyone logically conclude that we are a Christian Nation? What other criteria exists that would overwhelmingly refute the U.S. Constitution, Declaration of Independence, and the Treaty of Tripoli? Once all of the rhetoric subsides and someone has given ample consideration to all of the facts, it becomes pretty clear that the United States was not based upon the values of any one specific religion. Our country is often referred to as a "melting pot." Our Founding Fathers were brilliant and made sure that there would be room for every religion, or even no religion at all. The basic concept for our country's founding had nothing to do with submitting oneself to God. The basic concept for our country's founding is that our citizens were capable of governing themselves. Throughout history, and with special focus on the Catholic Church, this type of openness and freedom of religion would have often been met with prejudicial intolerance.

It seems to me that we can't have Christianity without Jesus Christ, and considering the lack of references to Jesus Christ in our official foundation, it's hard to tie the two of them together without making an absurd number of assumptions and conjectures. There is simply no logical argument that can withstand the scrutiny in justifying the United States of America as a purely Christian Nation. The sad fact of the matter is that many Christians would have us believe that elevating Christianity is what our Founding Fathers wanted, and those who don't know the difference buy into it. If our Founding Fathers wanted us to be a Christian Nation, they could have created our country that way. All evidence to the contrary.

CHAPTER 15. THE SAUDI ARABIA EXAMPLE

> "So far as I can remember, there is not one word in
> the Gospels in praise of intelligence."—Bertrand Russell

Billions of people around the world remain steadfast in their conviction for the truth of their chosen faith while remaining essentially ignorant about virtually every other faith. They have no foundational basis for this position other than their respective holy book(s). This conviction is both disingenuous and intellectually dishonest. Most Christians have never read a page of the Qur'an and yet find no difficulty dismissing its claims. Most Muslims have never read a page from the Book of Mormon and yet find no difficulty dismissing its claims. Additionally, these billions of people will never give conscientious thought as to the arbitrary factors leading up to their chosen belief.

Here's a little elementary algebra experiment designed with religious believers in mind. For argument's sake, let's say that you (Y) were born and raised in the United States (U). You are Christian (C) and believe with 100% certainty that Jesus, well, the Holy Trinity, is the "one and only" true god. Our equation might look something like:

$$Y + U = 100C$$
You + United States = 100% certainty in Christianity

What would happen if we changed the variable U and replaced the United States with Saudi Arabia? Would your belief change if you were born and raised somewhere else?

$$Y + S = ???$$
You + Saudi Arabia = ?

Saudi Arabia is an Islamist state that is officially listed as 100% Muslim (M)[1], so with relative certainty we
can conclude that our equation would look like:

$$Y + S = 100M$$

You + Saudi Arabia = 100% certainty in Islam

Keep in mind that you are still you and you still believe with 100% certainty that your god is the one and only true god. The difference lies with the
god that you are absolutely certain of. If you were born and raised in Saudi
Arabia, you would most likely not worship Jesus, but Allah and his prophet
Muhammad instead. A Christian who was born and raised in Saudi Arabia
instead of the U.S. would be a Muslim.

What is common to all religious beliefs, regardless of the geographic location from which they spring forth, is the assertion that divine revelation
has occurred between god(s) and humans. Visions and miracles are in abundant supply irrespective of the god being prayed to. Childhood indoctrination is a major component to the continuation of religious beliefs and that
tactic remains the same whether someone is raised in Saudi Arabia, Israel,
or the United States. Often the only piece that changes is the specific revelation delivered to man. Depending on where someone is born and raised,
their belief in both the creation of man as well as the eventual capitulation of
man will be molded by sociological influences. While this influence doesn't
immediately warrant dismissal of the religious belief, the point behind this
exercise is to highlight the strength, irrationality, and arbitrary nature of the
conviction. A Hindu's conviction on religious truth can be equal to that of a
Jew, Sikh, Muslim, Jain, or Christian, but conviction alone isn't sufficient to
make a religious belief true. The revelations man claims to have had are often
contradictory which leads us to the conclusion that a person's religious conviction is more heavily influenced by the factors we've listed than by truth
itself.

If we don't allow our brains to take a mental shortcut here, we'll see that
something as trivial as our geographic location can completely alter our religious choice without affecting the degree to which we believe it. The mere
fact that geographical and cultural factors can be such a strong influence
strains the credibility of the passion with which a believer professes in their
faith. If we were born in India, we would likely be Hindu. If we were born
in ancient Greece, we would likely believe in Zeus. If we were born in West
Africa, we might believe in the earth goddess Ala. It is nothing more than
a roll of the dice that we are born into whatever culture we find ourselves,
and for the vast majority of our neighbors, it's that same roll of the dice that
determines their religion.

---

1 United States Department of State

CHAPTER 16. CHRISTIAN HYPOCRISY

> "I contend we are both atheists, I just believe in
> one fewer god than you do. When you understand why
> you dismiss all the other possible gods, you will un-
> derstand why I dismiss yours."—Stephen F Roberts

When discussing religion, I've always found it interesting and ironic that most believers tend to know the least about their chosen religion. The Pew Research Center conducted a study entitled the "U.S. Religious Knowledge Survey" in September of 2010. The goal was to determine how much Americans from each belief system knew about not only their chosen religion, but others as well. Atheists and agnostics scored the highest of all of those interviewed. Jews and Mormons followed closely behind with Christian denominations collectively scoring the worst.

The study demonstrated that most Americans are uninformed about the world's major religions. Sadly, American Christians knew far less about their own religion than those who don't practice it. This should speak volumes. Atheists and agnostics, the most religiously-knowledgeable group, dismiss organized religion while those who are less religiously-knowledgeable swear to the authenticity of things they aren't even aware of. With that in mind, it becomes easier to understand why Christians willfully ignore the parts of the Bible that might not fit with their preferred interpretation. They most likely don't even know that those parts exist.

Here are some of my favorite examples of Christian hypocrisy.

~ The Positive God ~

God is good, just, and kind. These are characteristics that virtually every person of faith will agree with; however there is ample evidence every minute of every day where God is not good, just, or kind. Often these acts are easily dismissed with the statement "God is mysterious."

I've heard people say that God has three answers to every prayer: Yes, not yet, and I have something better in mind. This should sound somewhat familiar to most Christians. If one asks for something from God and gets it, then He must have answered the prayer with "yes." If one doesn't get it right away, but it happens at a later date, then He must have answered it with "not yet." If one didn't get it at all, then He must have a better plan in place. That might sound nice and it likely gives a religious person comfort in their ability to reconcile the lack of a direct response from God; however, as I do frequently in this book, I'm going to compare this to a real world example. If we look at the situation in the countries across East Africa, we see children so malnourished that they are the very definition of "skin and bones." As they and their parents cry out to God in desperate prayer for help, what is God's response? He surely hasn't said "yes." All evidence to the contrary. He hasn't said "not yet" because children have been dying like this for years. So, we're left with "I have something better in mind." What "something better" could He possibly have in mind? Is God telling us that he'd rather let these children starve to death so that they can spend eternity with Him in heaven? If someone can have faith in a loving god in the face of this kind of abject suffering, that kind of faith is both callous and obscene. When a religious person says that God will never give us more than we can handle, a statement like that shows a level of ignorance that is simply astounding. Are we to believe that a child dying of starvation can handle it? Can its parents? To see children dying like this from absolutely preventable causes should be enough to demonstrate the heartless and cruel nature of the all-too prevalent belief that God would never give us more than we can handle.

God loves us unconditionally...as long as we believe in Him, worship Him, and aren't born into third world poverty.

-- The Bible --

If one is interested in finding examples of Christian hypocrisy, one does not need to look any further than the Bible itself. Biblical scholars overwhelmingly agree that the canonized Gospels are copies of copies of stories told by fallible people over the course of decades or even centuries. Original manuscripts do not exist. The hypocrisy here is in holding up a book and claiming it to be infallible while at the same time knowing the entire thing was written by fallible people who heard the stories from other fallible people. Not a single word was ever written by God Himself. No supreme being ever put pen to paper. There isn't a single sheet of papyrus with writings from Jesus himself. No matter how someone tries to support the infallibility of the Gospels, the fact cannot be dismissed that they were written decades later by imperfect men who were already biased to believing in Jesus and his "miracles".

I'd like to put the infallibility of the Bible to the test. If the Bible is both infallible and inerrant, then logically it must be perfect. If it is perfect, then by definition it cannot be improved upon. Is that true? What areas of the

Bible couldn't be improved either historically, ethically, or scientifically by virtually any modern-day person? You will find examples throughout this book highlighting examples of Biblical deficiencies under each one of those topics. It is a rather easy exercise to find such examples because there isn't a single line in the Bible that doesn't appear to have been written by a 1st or 2nd-century person. Take a moment and just think about how good a book would really be if authored by a perfect omniscient being who knows everything there is to possibly know. This book is supposed to be the perfect word of God with instructions for mankind. Oddly enough, we can find guidance on what to do in the unlikely event that two men are fighting and the wife of one of them comes to her husband's rescue. If she reaches out and seizes him by his private parts, we are supposed to cut off her hand and show her no pity (Deuteronomy 25:11-12). A situation like that warrants mention in a perfectly-authored book but not a single word is ever uttered about DNA, germs, electricity, atoms, or anything else that might actually be useful centuries later. If the Bible is the word of God, He never thought it worthy to devote even a single sentence to cancer or how to overcome it knowing that millions of His pious children will suffer and die from it. This shouldn't surprise us if the Bible was authored by 1st-century people. If it's divinely inspired, it should give us cause for great concern. Would we have nuclear bombs if Jesus told his disciples that the power of the atom could only be used for peaceful purposes? What would have changed if an Old Testament figure like Abraham commanded man to never use flying machines to inflict terrorism? Show me a man who truly believes the Bible to be the word of God and I'll show you a man who hasn't read the Bible critically.

-- The Poor --

How many of today's Christians would willingly follow Jesus if he told them to sell off everything they own and give the proceeds to the poor? Imagine where Christians would find themselves if indeed he ever uttered such words and if indeed any Christians were to follow that command. The truth is that today's Christians willfully ignore Jesus. Mark 10:21 clearly tells us, *"Jesus looked at him and loved him. 'One thing you lack,' he said. 'Go, sell everything you have and give to the poor, and you will have treasure in heaven. Then come, follow me.'"*

Rare is the Christian who has done this in the manner that Jesus suggests. The hypocrisy lies with Christians elevating the teachings of Jesus as the standard by which we should live and then summarily dismissing those teachings that they either don't agree with or simply don't want to live up to. Jesus not only said *"Take therefore no thought for the morrow,"* he apparently lived that mantra. Christians completely ignore Jesus' command in favor of building personal wealth. This hypocrisy is evident any time we see a Christian driving around in a Cadillac or BMW instead of buying a used Ford or Chevrolet and giving the difference to the poor. This hypocrisy is evident any time we see Christians dumping money into a 401K or other investment instead of giving to the poor and following Jesus. Jesus did not have a savings account, and the Biblical account of his life leads us to believe that he was both frugal and dependent on others. If Jesus were alive today, can you imagine seeing him drive through town in a Lexus?

Lest you think that the hypocrisy extends only to the average Christian, let's look at the Vatican. In 2010 the Vatican reported revenues of 245.2 million euros ($356 million) and profit of 9.8 million euros ($14.2 million). In all sincerity, these financial numbers are nothing in comparison to many of today's global businesses, which was the outcome that Pope John Paul II hoped for when he ordered the Vatican to begin publishing its annual financial reports in 1981. Don't give in to your mind's mental shortcuts though, and assume that this is what the Vatican is worth. When we shine a light on the Vatican's books, we'll find that they list all of their artwork and ornate buildings with a value of just 1 euro each. As funny as this might sound, it is tragically true. The Sistine Chapel, while officially valued at 1 euro, could be worth as much as $500 billion. Estimating the worth of the many pieces of artwork is not an exact science. Many of the items owned by the Vatican are considered "priceless" and non-commercial, which is why they get the 1 euro label. Regardless of the official reason, there is inherent hypocrisy in valuing such assets so ridiculously low when the real value is so ridiculously high.

If we're being intellectually honest, it doesn't take long to reach trillions of dollars when adding up the potential value of the Vatican's assets. Even conservative estimates will put the value in the billions of dollars, and yet the Vatican ignores Mark 10:21 in the same way that the average Christian does. There are poor people all over the world who would benefit considerably from the sale of even a handful of Church assets, but we won't see that happen. So I ask, why the hypocrisy? Is a life not worth more than a painting? I am not alone in asking this question. Pope John Paul I asked himself the same question in 1978 and remarked:

> "... this morning, I flushed my toilet with a solid gold lever edged with diamonds and at this very moment, bishops and cardinals are using a bathroom on the second floor of the papal palace which trappings, I am told, would draw more than fifty million dollars at auction ... Believe me, one day, we who live in opulence, while so many are dying because they have nothing, will have to answer to Jesus as to why we have not carried out His instruction, 'Love thy neighbor as thyself.' We, the clergy of the Church together with our congregations, who substitute gold and pomp and ceremony in place of Christ's instruction, who judge our masquerade of singing His praises to be more precious than human life, will have the most to explain."

Pope John Paul I was a man who, more often than not, appears to have actually lived what he preached. He was perhaps one of the most fiscally conscious and responsible popes—even though his papacy only lasted 33 days. Pope John Paul I embodied Luke 3:11, which says "Anyone who has two shirts should share with the one who has none, and anyone who has food should do the same." There are more than a billion Christian hypocrites walking the world today either willfully ignoring or barely scratching the surface of one of Jesus' most basic teachings.

-- How Strong Is Your Faith? --

Genesis 22 is the type of story that every Christian parent should read and ponder. This is the story of Abraham and his son Isaac. The abridged version goes something like this: God told Abraham (a character whose historicity still remains a question) to take his son Isaac to a mountain to sacrifice him. Abraham, Isaac, and two servants loaded the donkey with enough wood for the sacrifice. Once they got to the point where Abraham could see the spot that God had told him to go, he told the servants to stay back while he and his son went ahead to worship. Isaac started to get a little nervous and asked his father where the lamb was for the burnt offering, upon which his father lied to him and said that God would provide it. When they arrived at the sacrificial spot, Abraham tied his son up and put him on top of the "altar." As Abraham grabbed his knife and prepared to slit his son's throat, an angel apparently cried out from the heavens instructing Abraham not to go any further. God was now satisfied with Abraham's commitment.

We are told that we should put God first and our love for God should transcend that of even our own family. How many Judeo–Christian parents could sacrifice their child as Abraham was prepared to do? How strong is their faith? How many could physically put a knife to their child's throat with the intent of slicing it open? A Christian hypocrite is one who pretends to believe in God as long as it doesn't require them to do anything this serious. But is a reasonable person supposed to admire Abraham and his level of faith?

People like Deanna Laney and Andrea Yates have heard the voice of God. Deanna stoned two of her sons to death while critically injuring the third. Andrea drowned her children in the bathtub. Both women were eventually found to be not guilty...by reason of insanity. That means that a jury of their peers found them to be insane. Christian parents: if you ever hear the voice of God telling you to do something, it is my everlasting hope that you immediately seek help from competent medical personnel.

I'd be willing to wager that few if any parents have the type of strength in their faith to allow such a conviction to take hold. Few parents love God so much that they would do as Abraham was told to do; and yet the monotheistic religions tell us to hold this man in high esteem. There is hypocrisy in being told to revere an obvious lunatic but knowing that we couldn't ever bring ourselves to submit to an act of such insanity. If we can't imagine this scenario being virtuous if conducted in modern day, how does the subtraction of thousands of years make it any better? What kind of trauma do you think this put Isaac (and Abraham) through? What kind of trauma do you think a modern child would go through? As Richard Dawkins once quipped, this was the first recorded use of the Nuremberg defense: I was only doing what I was ordered to do. Sadly, that's the only thing funny about it.

~~ Selective Morality ~~

While I covered morality in greater detail in a previous chapter, it's worth mentioning some of the common acts of hypocrisy that we see among Christians every day as it relates to morality. I find that Christians rarely practice what they preach instead picking and choosing the parts of the Bible that they like and disregarding the parts that they don't. For example, tithing has always been important to the church. It's so important that Ananias and his wife Sapphira were killed because they lied about the amount that they tithed. How many Christians honestly give 10% to their church? Leviticus 27:30 tells us to tithe 10%, and yet I know many Christians who do not give this amount, with a varying sense of guilt. This rule is just not that important to them in the same way that desecration of their bodies is not important. Christians with tattoos regularly ignore Leviticus 19:28.

The evangelical pastor Ted Haggard preached about the immorality of homosexuality but engaged in it himself for years. Bishop Gene Robinson, Bishop Otis Charles, Cardinal Hans Hermann Groër, Cardinal Keith O'Brien, Archbishop Rembert Weakland, Bishop Juan Carlos Maccarone, and Bishop Thomas Gumbleton are just some of the thousands of hypocrites dressed up in official religious garb.

Killing is bad, but in über-religious places like Texas, executions are encouraged. Murder violates the Ten Commandments, but many Bible-thumping Texans are proud of their state's attitude towards it.

Cannibalism is immoral but Christians will eat the body of Christ on Sunday.

Christians should not divorce nor should they marry someone who is divorced, unless, of course, one side has committed adultery. If we look at the numbers, 75–80% of Americans are Christians and we have a divorce rate that consistently hovers around 50%. Considering the fact that the majority of divorces are due to "irreconcilable differences," how can they preach about the sanctity of marriage? Technically speaking, this amounts to millions of Christian hypocrites.

In virtually every organized religion, sex outside of marriage is a sin, yet how many people of faith are virgins on their wedding night? Christians hold up the Bible as the will of God, so why don't they stone the bride to death for not being a virgin as Deuteronomy 22:13-21 tells us we must?

In virtually every organized religion, corruption would be immoral, yet we have corruption in every corner of a world where the majority of the people are religious.

Most people would be opposed to torture if you asked them, yet they are OK with people of other faiths being tortured for eternity for being guilty of the simple crime of disbelief. Christians might be opposed to torture, but they have no problem with me burning in a lake of fire forever.

Jesus spoke very clearly and outspokenly against wealth, however, many Christians are more devoted to money than to God. Next time you drive by a church parking lot during weekly service, take a look at the brands of vehicles that belong to the faithful. The hypocrisy is even more apparent if you happen to be driving through a wealthy neighborhood.

Jesus encouraged his followers to forgive those who have wronged them. Do you know any Christians who hold grudges? Yes, so do I.

Jesus preached that we should take care of the poor, yet Republicans, the political party most closely associated with Christianity, are the first to cut funding for social programs. There are more than 300 verses in the Bible that deal directly with the poor and social injustice, and yet we as a "Christian" society don't seem as concerned about them as Jesus does. During the course of writing this book, we've experienced a recession, people have lost their homes, and more people are living below the poverty line than at any time in the past 50 years, and yet we're cutting programs and turning people away at homeless shelters. The religious right will lobby relentlessly for tax credits for wealthy people and at the same time vote to cut funding for those who are poor. The stench of hypocrisy is overwhelming. What would Jesus say?

As Tolstoy once said, "Everybody thinks of changing humanity, but nobody thinks of changing himself." To those who lift their holy book in the air and preach about the actions of others, you may find your time being better spent by looking in the mirror and starting with that person first.

CHAPTER 17. THE BIBLICAL LOTTERY

"I don't believe in heaven and hell. I don't know
if I believe in God. All I know is that as an individual, I won't allow this life—the only thing I know
to exist—to be wasted."—George Clooney

On more than one occasion, I have been asked, "what if you're wrong?"
What if my beliefs are wrong and my Christian counterparts are correct? It's
a good question and deceptively simple. After all, belief is all that is required.
What obstinacy prevents me from just saying "yes" to salvation? If Christians are correct, they get eternal bliss in heaven and I burn in hell. If Christians are wrong, they've lost nothing. Under this premise, believing in Jesus,
for example, would be a win–win situation because the believer stands to
lose nothing. If there was such a thing as an "I told you so" moment in the
afterlife, only the believer would be in a position to use it. Believers would
apparently reap the additional benefit of being comforted in the face of death
by the prospect of eternal life, whereas a non-believer like me wouldn't be
eligible for that kind of comfort.

I refer to this line of questioning as the Biblical Lottery—you can't win
if you don't play. It has a better, more well-known name however: Pascal's
Wager. The 17th-century French mathematician, physicist, and philosopher
Blaise Pascal asked this very question in defense of the Christian religion.
Before his death, Pascal had been working on a book in which he laid out a
set of criteria supporting his religious wager. These criteria were published
posthumously in *Pensées*, which literally translates to "thoughts." Here is the
logic that Pascal laid out in *Pensées*:

1. Either there is a God or there isn't.

2. A game is being played and either heads or tails will turn up.

3. Neither logic nor reason can defend either of the options.

4. You must wager on one or the other.

5. Weigh the potential gain and loss in the event that God is real. If you win, you win everything. If you lose, you lose nothing.

6. Wager, then, that God is real.

According to Pascal, the odds are 50–50, so why not simply play the odds and believe in God? A modern-day example could lie in the scenario of having the odds of winning of the next Powerball lottery at 50–50. If that were the case, wouldn't it make sense to go ahead and buy that lottery ticket?

There is a moral dilemma here that I don't want to overlook—fear of being wrong shouldn't be the reason why we believe in God. That being said, the bigger problem with Pascal's Wager is the faulty premise of an either/or situation. Pascal has only given us two choices: believe in God or don't believe in God. As a Christian, he hasn't given us a choice of any other god beyond the Christian god. If you recall from the introductory chapter of this book, I claimed that it was one thing to believe in the potential for a divine creator, but it was something entirely different to make the definitive claim that we know which one is correct. Keep in mind that it is the Judeo-Christian god who reveals Himself to us and tells us that He is a jealous god and that we may have no other gods before Him. If I believed in the Hindu god Shiva, that belief alone would have satisfied Pascal's Wager in a generic-deity manner, but the end result would not be blissful simply because the god I professed my belief in would be the "wrong" one. There is an unequivocal issue between deism and theism at this point. Once we factor in all of the gods that mankind currently professes belief in along with gods that have long since come and gone, our 50–50 odds have been eviscerated. If our religious options were actually limited to one god, Pascal's Wager might hold some logical weight, but that is not the world that we find ourselves in. Our odds of winning the wager are now much more akin to a Biblical Lottery.

Pascal said, "If there is a God, He is infinitely incomprehensible, since, having, neither parts nor limits, He has no affinity to us. We are then incapable of knowing either what He is or if He is..." As stated earlier, the choice of believing is not optional. We must make a wager. If Pascal was correct, this poses another dilemma. If God is infinitely incomprehensible, there stands to reason that none of our religions are correct and God is ultimately unknowable. An "infinitely incomprehensible" god presents us with an infinite number of potential religious doctrines, each with an equal chance of being correct. Under this scenario, it becomes quite probable that mankind has not yet found the true God. Perhaps the true God rewards those based upon the totality of their lives instead of irrational belief. If, as my Christian friends might say, God has given us the ability to use reason and logic, why would it be virtuous to completely abandon those capabilities in favor of blind faith?

If Pascal's Wager weren't fundamentally flawed, the skeptic would now be confronted with the very real issue of inauthentic belief. Even if I answered the short-sighted question "What if you're wrong" by professing my belief in Jesus Christ, if I can't do it honestly, then why bother with the facade? It wouldn't be genuine faith. I would be faced with the incredible challenge of trying to convince myself to ignore everything that I've ever learned that could potentially conflict with the specific tenets and assertions of my faith. Even if I could deny every rational conflict, wanting something to be true isn't a sufficient basis for actually making it true. As Voltaire said "the interest I have to believe a thing is no proof that such a thing exists."

To those who wish to play the Biblical Lottery, I wish them the best of luck. Their odds of "winning" are roughly equal to mine. The next time I am asked the deceptively simple question "What if you're wrong?" the most appropriate response will simply be "What if *you're* wrong?" As Jay Leno once quipped "How come you never see a headline like 'Psychic Wins Lottery'?" Sometimes a deceptively simple question requires a deceptively simple answer.

CHAPTER 18. EVOLUTION VERSUS CREATIONISM

> "Extraordinary claims require extraor-
> dinary evidence."—Carl Sagan

Where did we come from and how did we get here? They seem like such simple questions. The social controversy that exists in our country pits the scientific answer of evolution as accepted in modern paleontology and evolutionary biology against the religious assertion of *creatio ex nihilo* which is Latin for "creation out of nothing." The scientific position holds that we are the evolutionary product of abiogenesis while the religious position holds that a divine being literally created everything we see from nothing generally by speaking, breathing, or simply willing everything into existence. To a Christian, men were created from dirt and a breath from God. Women were created from the rib of the first man. To Muslims, men were created from a clot of blood (Sura 96:1-2), water (Sura 25:54), clay (Sura 15:26), dust (Sura 30:20), or simply out of nothing (Sura 3:47). There are many stories of creation, which are often classified as myths. Divine word, Earth divers, and cosmic eggs are all examples. The truth is that we don't really know for sure how life began on Earth. We have not been able to create life in our labs and the religious accounts vary dramatically. The topic of creation is something that science hasn't been able to answer definitively and religion arrogantly believes it has.

While we may not be able to answer definitively how life began, we can explain a great deal about how life evolved to what we see today. The debate between evolution and creationism is a scientific one, and as such, the evidence put forth from both should be subject to intense scrutiny. The vast majority of our scientists have concluded that the evidence for evolution is overwhelming while creation myths lack the supporting evidence for their claims. This is applicable to all religions. The difficult side to the religious argument comes from determining which religion's evidence is conclusive. For virtually every religion, the evidence usually consists of a holy book and unsupported inferences. In certain Hindu traditions, we are given Manu (who, it should be noted, saved mankind from a great flood much the same as Noah in the Bible). The Abrahamic faiths give us Adam and Eve. Not a single religion provides the type and sheer amount of evidence that science does. Science is the only unbiased source we have which is precisely why the scientific account of evolution is taught in our school classrooms. It seems fairly straightforward to me—any science curriculum that rejects the scientific process doesn't deserve to be taught in a science class. When religious people push science aside for religious theories by advocating for the teaching of creationism in our classrooms, those acts require a response. Evolution, and the evidence supporting it, cannot be dismissed by a few sentences in an ancient text translated into English from fragments of manuscripts written in dead languages.

Religious doctrine has not put forth sufficient evidence to discard scientific consensus on this topic and the tremendous efforts undertaken over a great many years to reach it. If you remember nothing else about this topic, please remember this. We as a society may argue about evolution, but scientists aren't having the same debate. Unlike such items as string theory which genuinely have scientists divided, the overwhelming majority of our global scientific community supports evolution. Evolution has been debated, dissected, and extrapolated over the course of many, many years by hundreds of thousands of scientists. The biggest differences between those who support evolution versus those who support creationism can be found in the methods used, consensus achieved, and transparency of peer review. The scientific process works and it works reliably well because it has a significant focus on transparency. Before a consensus is reached, vigorous debate occurs. Based upon challenges from other scientists, hypotheses are modified and refined to take into account a wide array of viewpoints and other data sources. A scientific hypothesis is open to debate, criticism, and, in some cases, even ridicule. The end result of this process is a consensus that is fact driven, reasoned, and logical. The mere fact that there is consensus is not enough by itself to warrant belief however. If consensus were the only criteria for believing something to be true, a billion Muslims, Christians, and Hindus could all lay claim to the truth. The reason why the scientific consensus is worthy of mentioning is because it is a scientific consensus reached using the scientific method. Unlike religion, science is not biased to any metaphysical claims. For example, scientists who practice Islam have the same understanding of gravity that scientists practicing Christianity have. An astrophysicist who believes in Shiva can agree on the development of stars with another astrophysicist who believes in Xenu. Scientific facts are factual regardless of and in spite of any metaphysical beliefs. Evolution has already undergone such discussions and debates using the same scientific methods by which we determine other facts about our world.

In 1922, Woodrow Wilson, in a letter to Winterton C. Curtis, said, "Of course, like every other man of intelligence and education, I do believe in organic evolution. It surprises me that at this late date such questions should be raised." Nearly a century later, we're still talking about this topic; however, evolution is not being debated among scientists. So what is the real reason why evolution continues to be such a hotly-debated topic among non-scientists? After all, nothing about our daily lives is dependent upon our acceptance or dismissal of our ancestral link to chimps and apes. We are still going to go to work. We will continue to have bills that have to be paid. Acceptance of evolutionary theory will not change any of these things. The problem for religious people lies within the consequences of acceptance. For example, once a Christian accepts evolution as true, it renders the Genesis account of creation false and thus casts doubt on the rest of the Bible. As the pseudoscientist Ken Ham accurately states:

> Now, if the book of Genesis is an allegory, then sin is an allegory, the Fall is an allegory and the need for a Savior is an allegory—but if we are all descendants of an allegory, where does that leave us? It destroys the foundation of all Christian doctrine—it destroys the foundation of the gospel.

Ham hits it right on the head. This is precisely why so many, either consciously or subconsciously, refuse to acknowledge that the Book of Genesis simply can't be true. If God didn't create the universe and everything in it over the course of six days exactly as the Book of Genesis states, then we would be forced to not only question the Bible but everything that the Bible purports to explain. If evolution is true and God didn't create man exactly as we are today, then the story of Adam and Eve could be false. If the story of Adam and Eve did not actually happen, why should we believe in Original Sin? If Original Sin isn't real, then why should we believe in Jesus and his ability to take away our sins? We can follow this line of questioning all the way down the line. To reject the Book of Genesis and instead believe in evolution dilutes the very core of the Christian faith. For believers in the Abrahamic faiths, there is a very real danger in accepting evolution.

The acceptance of evolution is being granted due to the abundance of scientific evidence supporting such a conclusion and not from a primitive, unscientific account asserted thousands of years ago. Science completely contradicts the Bible on this topic. If someone is unwilling to even consider that the story of Genesis is not a historically accurate representation of the creation of man and universe, then no amount of evidence could possibly convince them otherwise. As Thomas Paine once said, "Attempting to debate with a person who has abandoned reason is like giving medicine to the dead." This is why the debate rages on.

Francis Collins, an evangelical Christian with impeccable scientific and medical credentials, finds himself walking a fine line between scientific consensus and his faith. As the man who helped decode the human genome, he takes a more nuanced approach to faith. For example, he is not a "young earth creationist" nor does he advocate for "intelligent design," but he does interpret the Bible in a convenient manner crediting God for creating the universe 13.7 billion years ago and implementing evolution as the mechanism by which life diversified. He charges creationists with an over literal misreading of Scripture. "I don't think God intended Genesis to teach science," he says, arguing that "the evidence in favor of evolution is utterly compelling."[1] Collins has on multiple occasions stated that even if there were no transitional fossils, DNA evidence would be enough to prove evolution. He has perhaps as much knowledge regarding DNA as any other man on the planet so his words on this topic should carry significant weight. If only he applied the same standards to his faith. In his book *The Language of God*, he follows in the footsteps of Immanuel Kant in trying to reconcile the spiritual and material worlds however he approaches each very differently. His approach to sequencing the human genome was very methodical and rational while his approach to faith was based on emotion. As he "rounded a corner and saw a beautiful and unexpected frozen waterfall, hundreds of feet high, (He) knew the search was over. The next morning, (He) knelt in the dewy grass as the sun rose and surrendered to Jesus Christ."[2] He would later claim that the frozen waterfall was in fact three streams which convinced him of the Holy Trinity. That a man could be so scientifically elegant in his analysis of DNA and evolution while abandoning that elegance in favor of determining religious conclusions based upon emotion demonstrates the double standards by which religion operates. Imagine if Collins or any member of his team had used emotion or inferences to map the human genome in the same manner that three frozen streams of water can be used to infer the Holy Trinity.

Whether we're talking about DNA, evolution, intelligent design, or creationism, it should become plainly obvious that religion, as I've stated, continues to operate by a double standard. It is not only common for our general society to be emphatically critical regarding any scientific claim, it is an expectation, yet we are implored to respect religious belief even when the evidence for such belief is either flimsy or completely vacuous. It seems a rather obvious question, but what is respectable about that? Transparency is one of the biggest reasons why the scientific method has produced so much progress. Creationists on the other hand do not subject themselves to even a fraction of the transparency that science depends upon. Creationism is conceptually based upon faith which renders it unfalsifiable, meaning that it isn't testable by empirical experiments. We cannot scientifically test and verify creationism which is why it remains a matter of faith. Whether we read the opinions from Answers in Genesis, Christian Answers, The Institute for Creation Research, or Creation Ministries International, we are not reading peer-reviewed scientific opinions. Each of these organizations presents itself as science-based, but there's just one problem: scientists overwhelmingly disagree. I've touched on pseudoscience in multiple areas of this book, but it bears repeating. When folks like Ken Ham, Kirk Cameron, and

---

1 Time Magazine: Reconciling God and Science, 2006
2 Francis S. Collis, *The Language of God: A Scientist Presents Evidence for Belief* (Free Press, 2006), 225

Lee Strobel peddle their false science, there are legitimately harmful implica-tions. According to the Stanford Encyclopedia of Philosophy[1]:

> From a practical point of view, the distinction is important for decision guidance in both private and public life. Since science is our most reliable source of knowledge in a wide variety of areas, we need to distinguish sci-entific knowledge from its look-alikes. Due to the high status of science in present-day society, attempts to exaggerate the scientific status of various claims, teachings, and products are common enough to make the demarca-tion issue pressing in many areas.

If you ever find yourself unfortunate enough to be reading an article by Ken Ham at Answers in Genesis, and he's providing a "scientific account" for the creation of the universe, the plausibility of Noah's Ark, or the geological age of our planet, please keep in mind that the "science" that he is present-ing to you as fact has never been offered up to scientists at large for the same type of scrutiny and objective analysis as is common in the actual scientific community. He bears no burden of proof and is only offering it up to a biased audience already predisposed to his outcome. The reason he and others like him will never open their scientific theories up for official scientific peer-review is because 1) they already know the scientific consensus reached on these subjects, and 2) they are not able to scientifically support their "scien-tific" claims. It's one thing to present pseudoscience to the religious faithful who don't have an adequate level of scientific knowledge to fully understand what's being presented to them. It's something entirely different to present the same pseudoscience to a group of people who possess the scientific back-ground to not only question the assertions and methods, but systematically negate each of them. When a pseudoscientist attempts to make a scientific claim where only a faith-based claim is appropriate, they are truly the ones guilty of blasphemy.

When 38 Nobel laureates issue a statement saying "Intelligent design is fundamentally unscientific; it cannot be tested as scientific theory because its central conclusion is based on belief in the intervention of a supernatural agent," it becomes difficult to take pseudoscientific "evidence" seriously. I assure you that if Ken Ham, Kirk Cameron, Lee Strobel, William Lane Craig, or any other Christian apologetic had sufficient, overwhelming evidence to support their claims, they would be embraced by the scientific community because their work would fundamentally alter the way in which we view our world and our place within it. Think about that for a moment. If these men had enough evidence to even create "reasonable doubt" in evolution and elevate creationism, wouldn't it be logical to conclude that there would be a greater divide among the elite scientific community? Why, 93% of the mem-bers of the National Academy of Sciences and 97% of the UK's Royal Society are either atheist or agnostic and overwhelmingly disagree with people like Ken Ham and Lee Strobel on their creationist views. If sufficient evidence existed to support the creationist view, imagine the cheering section they

---

1 http://plato.stanford.edu/entries/pseudo-science/ Retrieved 3/15/2012

could obtain from the scientific community! There's a reason why creationists are laughed at. If evolution could be proven false, pseudoscientists and creationists should take the time to write it down, get it peer reviewed, and prepare to collect their Nobel Prize. We could then stop using the word "faith" and instead refer to it as the science of Christianity.

Apologetics like Ken Ham and Lee Strobel don't even need to have physical proof to gain scientific support. For example, we don't know with absolute certainty what happens beyond the event horizon inside a black hole, but we have enough observed evidence to support the conclusion that black holes exist and that they are very powerful. Ham, Strobel, and other creationists don't even have what I would call "black hole support." They have offered up next to nothing of any substance that hasn't already been refuted elsewhere. Scientists from around the world would readily endorse them if their theories and conjectures had any hint of real science to them. That, of course, is not the case and that's why the scientific community shuns them.

We don't have to be particularly scientific to appreciate and embrace evolution. We can find support, even if it's tacit support, from religious leaders. When Pope John Paul II gave a speech to the Pontifical Academy of Sciences on October 23, 1996, he very clearly stated "Today, almost half a century after publication of the encyclical, new knowledge has led to the recognition of the theory of evolution as more than a hypothesis." In July 2004, then Cardinal Ratzinger, who would later become Pope Benedict XVI, was serving as the President of the International Theological Commission. The Commission said, "Converging evidence from many studies in the physical and biological sciences furnishes mounting support for some theory of evolution to account for the development and diversification of life on earth, while controversy continues over the pace and mechanisms of evolution." While neither Pope John Paul II nor Pope Benedict XVI has obviously budged on their belief in the divine for the initial creation of life, both have concluded that the evolutionary process of natural selection is responsible for the diversity of life that we see around us. The caveat is that this process is believed to be guided by the hand of God. It's laughable that many creationists have now modified their views in light of this progress by announcing that evolution by natural selection was actually part of God's plan all along. What a convenient discovery! What remains inconvenient however is when someone embraces the literal story of Genesis. When people do this, they are essentially saying to theoretical physicists like Stephen Hawking that their knowledge of cosmology is far greater than his. This is of course an absurd proposition. Not a single person throughout the course of human history has ever been able to adequately make the connection and dependency between physics and God. In fact, nobody has even tried.

As I will do several times in this book, I'd like to present you with a statement or condition. Once we agree on the validity of the statement or condition, we'll apply it to a scenario and see how well it holds up. I'd like to present the following statement from Richard Dawkins:

> The power of a scientific theory may be measured as a ratio: the number of facts that it explains divided by the number of assumptions it needs to postulate in order to do the explaining. A theory that assumes most of what it is trying to explain is a bad theory.

The concept is simple and straightforward. If we say something is true, but it takes a lot of assuming to get to that conclusion, it probably isn't a very good conclusion. If we say something is true, and we don't have to make a lot of assumptions to get to that conclusion, it is most likely a much better and more plausible conclusion. If we apply this concept to evolution and creationism. Darwin's theory explains a tremendous amount (the current and past state of every living thing we see) through one simple, yet powerful idea: natural selection. A species gradually evolves over a long period of time with adaptations that help ensure its future survival. Using the agreed-upon concept of what constitutes a good theory, Darwin's Theory of Evolution is great because of the ratio of what it concludes (all the complexity of life) to what it has to assume to get that conclusion (simply the nonrandom survival of hereditary information through many generations)[1]. The creationist idea that a supernatural being (an intelligent designer) instantly created all living things exactly as they are today requires a tremendous amount of assumptions. We'll need to assume that the creator is more complex than we are to accomplish all of that in the given timeframe. We also need to deal with the assumptions and logical difficulties in who designed the designer? Who created God, and if we can figure out who created God, who created the God that created that God? We can follow that to an infinite regression. If someone believes that their God is the only one ever created, what assumptions did they have to make to arrive at that conclusion? How many other gods did they have to eliminate from the equation and on what basis were those gods eliminated? How do we conclusively know? We have to assume that God knew or planned trillions and trillions of details to account for every living thing. Creationism is statistically improbable while evolution can still be observed today.

The term "extinction" refers to the end of a species. For example, the dinosaurs are extinct. The Dodo of Mauritius is extinct. The Passenger Pigeon is extinct. In fact, 99.9% of all the species that have ever lived on our planet are extinct[23]. Extinctions occur all the time and our planet has even seen a few mass extinctions. Species can become extinct for a number of reasons including habitat destruction, genetic pollution, predators, competition, dwindling food sources, disease, and climate change. Extinctions are remarkable, but perhaps not as remarkable as the question that I'm going to pose next. If God created all living things, what does it say about His "engi-

1   Dawkins, Richard (2006), *The Selfish Gene* (3 ed.), Oxford University Press, ISBN 978-0-19-929115-1

2   Newman, Mark. "*A Mathematical Model for Mass Extinction.*" Cornell University. May 20, 1994. Retrieved July 30, 2006.

3   Raup, David M. *Extinction: Bad Genes or Bad Luck?* W.W. Norton and Company. New York. 1991. pp. 3–6, ISBN 978-0-393-30927-0

neering" and "design" capabilities when 99.9% of His creatures are now extinct? If you designed 1,000 houses and 999 of them crumbled to the ground while only 1 remained standing, would you consider yourself to be an intelligent designer? If God is an architect, He is incredibly inept, inefficient, and incompetent. If He simply willed everything into existence as the Book of Genesis claims, God is a pathetically terrible architect. Perhaps He shouldn't have rested on the 7th day...

If every animal and human were designed perfectly, then what need would there be for the animal or human to change? If we were designed perfectly in God's image, how could we possibly be improved? We can find changes in every single species that has ever existed on our planet. For example, if we look at Neanderthals and assume that intelligent design is a superior answer to evolution, what are we to make of the differences between the craniums, muscularity, and other physical distinctions between them and us? If Homo neanderthalensis (one of many subspecies never mentioned by the world's great religions) did not share a common evolutionary ancestor with Homo sapiens (modern man) and was instead intelligently designed, what would be the purpose in changing an already "perfect" design? Why wouldn't modern man have the larger cranium? There is a saying in paleontology that states "fossils do not reproduce." I think we can all agree that two fossils are not going to procreate and make little baby fossils in the same way that we can all agree that fossils clearly show the differences between Neanderthals and modern humans. The genetic makeup of human beings is not particularly special in relation to other animals. In fact we have the exact same types of genes as a mouse, a horse, or a rabbit. Our building blocks are the same. We simply use the genes differently. Our genetic makeup is 99.5% similar to Homo neanderthalensis, and yet that tiny difference is noticeable. Either God was an incredibly inept designer, as I've stated, or we must give honest consideration to the theory of evolution based upon the weight of the actual evidence.

The sad fact is that most people do not fully understand evolution. The time scale over which most evolution occurs makes it a difficult concept for many to comprehend. I could look at a photo of George W. Bush when he was 10 years old and another when he was inaugurated as President of the United States. While I don't have a picture of every single day between those two photos, I can be reasonably certain that he changed gradually during that time. Now, I'm not using the growth of a child into a man as an example of evolution, but rather highlighting the concept that just because changes are gradual doesn't negate the fact that change has occurred.

One of the more popular complaints offered by creationists regarding the validity of evolution deals with replication. If something can't be replicated, then it can't be observed and therefore doesn't qualify as part of the scientific method. It's a silly premise. A scientific theory is a deduction based on evidence, not just the premise of replication. In a court of law, the prosecution doesn't have to replicate a murder to prove that a murder happened. A scientific theory is consistent with all observable evidence. This is one of the more repeated myths; however there are a lot of myths surrounding evolution and I'd like to highlight some of them. Even if someone refuses to believe in evolution, at least they'll become a little more familiar with what it is that they don't agree with.

Myth #1. Humans Came From Apes

I frequently hear this one, and when I do, I know that the person has never taken the time to learn anything about evolution. This is usually followed by the question "if we came from monkeys, why are there still monkeys?" to which the only appropriate response is "if God created man from dirt, why is there still dirt?" All kidding aside, at no point has any evolutionary biologist said that humans evolved from apes. Humans and apes share a common ancestor. This ancestor was neither human nor ape. Just as a tree has branches, our species has branches. From this common ancestor, we'll find our evolutionary branches filled with gorillas, humans, and chimpanzees. We'll also find many branches that have gone extinct including Homo ergaster, Homo neanderthalensis, and Homo habilis. It's truly remarkable that we still have the fossils of these species to examine! I've heard people proclaim (sadly, on too many occasions) that fossils are the handiwork of the devil and that Satan put those fossils in the ground to confuse us. There isn't an appropriate response to an assertion like that.

Myth #2. If I Can't See It, It's Not Happening

I would be willing to bet that nobody has ever seen a real talking snake, and yet billions of people readily accept that premise as true. Evolution cannot be boiled down to a single fossil. Evolution is proven through the comparison of the convergence of fossils along with the genetic comparisons between species. For example, scientists have sequenced both the genome of humans as well as the genome of chimpanzees and have found that humans are 98.6% similar to our distant evolutionary cousins. To put this into perspective, the differences between chimps and humans is smaller than the differences found between mice and rats. Whereas religion points to a holy book as its source of authority, evolution points to a wide combination of scientific practices such as genome sequencing, molecular biology, paleontology, zoology, botany, and geology to reach the conclusion that life on Earth has evolved and will continue to do so.

Most people are familiar with the term "missing link." It's one of the most common terms used to describe a transitional fossil. If evolution is true, we should be able to find evidence of animals (including humans) in most cases that have features from both an ancestor as well as its descendants. Considering the conditions that need to be met just to create a fossil, it truly is remarkable how many of them we have been able to study. We have many transitional fossils for virtually every species. If we include microfossils, there are literally trillions. We have even found fossils showing the transition of fish to amphibians. In 2004, Neil Shubin and Ted Daeschler found well-preserved fossils of the Tiktaalik, a fish that could crawl. Research on specimens of Archaeopteryx suggests that the earliest birds had four wings instead of two making them an ideal transitional fossil between four-limbed dinosaurs and two-winged birds. The Heteronectes chaneti, with its partially migrated left eye, is a transitional fossil of flatfish. The list of transitional fossils is pretty incredible. Every time we find a new one, it's like finding another piece to the puzzle. We can look at the changes from Apidium all the way to Homo erectus and Archaic Homo sapiens. Every time we find a transitional human fossil, it makes it more difficult to believe the Biblical account of God creating man from dirt and literally blowing the breath of life into him—a concept that we have yet to see an equivalent amount of proof for.

The most famous human ancestor is the 3.2-million-year-old hominid affectionately nicknamed "Lucy." Lucy was found in 1974 by paleontologist Donald C. Johanson in Hadar, Ethiopia, and she had a mixture of both human and ape features. Lucy had the long dangling arms similar to apes but a pelvis, spine, and legs similar to humans, which made her better suited to walking upright. Twenty years later, scientists announced the discovery of "Ardi," a fossil skeleton from a human ancestor that walked the planet more than a million years before Lucy. The older Ardi showed us that our lineage included an ancestor that was a biped on the ground but was a quadruped when moving around in the trees. Ardi was unique in that it demonstrated an unexpected mix of traits and showed us what our last common ancestor may have been like. While neither Lucy nor Ardi is the common ancestor between humans and chimps, they are the closest that we have been able to find...so far.

We don't have to look at evolution purely through the lens of time. Evolution through natural selection can be seen every day through viruses and bacteria. Microevolution has become vitally important to medicine. Published August 4, 2010, R. Craig MacLean, a Royal Society University Research Fellow from the University of Oxford, said quite explicitly in *Discovery Medicine*:

> The evolution of antibiotic resistance is an amazingly simple example of adaptation by natural selection, and there is growing interest among evolutionary biologists in using evolutionary principles to help understand and combat the spread of resistance in pathogen populations.

When discussing antibiotics specifically, he says, "resistant cells have higher Darwinian fitness relative to sensitive cells, and natural selection therefore results in an increase in the frequency of resistance in the population." Evolution is why we see antibiotic resistance today. A person doesn't have to believe in evolution, but they should be thankful that enough scientists do so that they can help keep us healthy.

The following is my favorite example of rapid evolution. In February 1988, biologist Richard Lenski began the E. coli long-term evolution experiment. Bacteria reproduce quickly which makes them great test subjects. The experiment is currently tracking the genetic changes in 12 initially identical communities of asexual E. coli bacteria. In February 2010, they surpassed 50,000 generations, which is simply remarkable! To put this into perspective, consider the fact that as of 2008, the average generation length for an American was 25 years. If E. coli were humans, this would be like watching evolution occur over the course of 1,250,000 years! Lenski and his team have painstakingly detailed and reported all of the genetic changes including evolutionary adaptations that have occurred in each of the communities. In each community the individual cells became larger than their ancestors over time. Each became more efficient at using the glucose that they were given. One lineage diverged and evolved to gain the ability to consume citrate (citric acid), which was also available. Leski and the researchers found that evolution occurs in three stages. The second stage involves a mutation at the genome level. "It wasn't a typical mutation at all, where just one base-pair, one letter, in the genome is changed." Leski added, "Instead, part of the genome was copied so that two chunks of DNA were stitched together in a new way. One chunk encoded a protein to get citrate into the cell, and the other chunk caused that protein to be expressed. That is a new trick for E. coli." That's not something that today's E. coli can do, but it becomes possible 50,000 generations later. Just as remarkable are the similarities between evolutionary theory and the results in Lenski's lab. As we would expect with evolutionary theory, there have been hundreds of millions of mutations in these populations but not every mutation survives. In fact, less than 100 reached fixation[1]. This would absolutely be in line with Darwinian evolution.

Evolution is occurring around us all the time and on a massive scale. Macroevolution and microevolution differ in the time scales involved, but evidence exists for both of them. We can and have demonstrated microevolution in our labs. As Professor Lenski pointed out to Andrew Schlafly, a conservative creationist who tried and failed to discredit his work, "In other words, it's not that we claim to have glimpsed 'a unicorn in the garden'—we have a whole population of them living in my lab!"

Myth #3. Evolution Is Random and Life Is Too Complex

When someone says that we are simply too complex to have been a product of evolution, they are making an argument that is commonly referred to as irreducible complexity. I've listened to Christian apologetics like Ken Ham and Lee Strobel make this argument frequently. The term "irreducible complexity" was coined by Michael Behe, who is a biochemistry professor at Lehigh University in Pennsylvania. He argues that humans cannot be the product of evolution because we have so many complex parts. If even one of those parts were missing, we wouldn't be alive. Plenty of examples are given to try and support this theory including watches, mousetraps, the human eye, blood clotting, and arches. None of these things would be functional until all of the parts were there. Using an arch as an example, the arch could not support itself during construction. It can't support anything until it is completed. Sounds valid, right?

---

1 Lenski, Richard E. (2003). Janick, Jules. ed. "Phenotypic and Genomic Evolution during a 20,000-Generation Experiment with the Bacterium Escherichia coli." *Plant Breeding Reviews* (New York: Wiley) 24 (2): 225–65. doi:10.1002/9780470650288.ch8. ISBN 978-0-471-46892-9.

People like Behe, Ham, and Strobel assume that if something is complex, then it "must be" divinely created. I liken these people to audience members at a magic show who chalk up the appearance of a rabbit from a hat to real magic. Science has continually chipped away at the complex and magical to reveal natural explanations. In the arch example, we build scaffolding to provide support while we add the stones to the arch. Once the arch is built, we take away the scaffolding. If you had never seen the scaffolding in the first place, the arch would appear to be irreducibly complex, but when you understand how it's built, the magic disappears. The same process occurs in nature and I think it does a great job highlighting the principles of natural selection. What once may have been considered advantageous can eventually have the ability to become essential. Conversely, something that was once deemed essential can one day be discarded because it is no longer needed. In our own bodies, we see things that we would consider to be irreducibly complex, but that doesn't mean that there weren't components in the past used to "support" the building of these complex things. Just as the scaffolding is eventually removed when it is no longer useful, these support structures in our bodies can be removed as well.

I had once heard someone use the example of Jenga to help explain this concept further. Jenga is a game with 54 wooden blocks that get stacked upon each other to build a tower. Players then try to remove a single block at a time from any level. Creationists and evolutionists could look at the same Jenga tower and see a complex structure and wonder how it could have gotten so tall and not fallen over. Creationists believe that the Jenga tower was instantly willed into existence exactly as we see it. Evolutionists believe that the tower was built block by block over time. The end result isn't irreducibly complex when you know how it's built.

While the argument isn't new, Michael Behe's coining of the term "irreducible complexity" has given proponents of intelligent design false support for their views. His views on intelligent design have prompted the Lehigh University to issue the following disclaimer on its website: "While we respect Prof. Behe's right to express his views, they are his alone and are in no way endorsed by the department. It is our collective position that intelligent design has no basis in science, has not been tested experimentally and should not be regarded as scientific."[1]

Behe has appeared in multiple court cases testifying in support of intelligent design, but none more important than Kitzmiller v. Dover Area School District. In an attempt to show how First Amendment rights were being violated, this case was an attempt to force the subject of creationism to be taught in the classroom. Behe was called as the primary witness for the defense and he was tasked with providing evidence to support intelligent design. It's one thing to present intelligent design as "science" to people who aren't trained to critically evaluate the "evidence." It's something entirely dif-

---

1 Department Position on Evolution and Intelligent Design. Department of Biological Sciences, Lehigh University. Retrieved 7/25/2008

ferent to present the same information in a court of law and doing so while under oath.

The judge in the case ultimately ruled that intelligent design is not scientific and therefore did not have to be taught in public schools under the banner of science. In his findings, the judge used a great deal of Behe's testimony against him[1].

- "Consider, to illustrate, that Professor Behe remarkably and unmistakably claims that the plausibility of the argument for ID depends upon the extent to which one believes in the existence of God."

- "As no evidence in the record indicates that any other scientific proposition's validity rests on belief in God, nor is the Court aware of any such scientific propositions, Professor Behe's assertion constitutes substantial evidence that in his view, as is commensurate with other prominent ID leaders, ID is a religious and not a scientific proposition."

- "What is more, defense experts concede that ID is not a theory as that term is defined by the NAS and admit that ID is at best 'fringe science' which has achieved no acceptance in the scientific community."

- "We therefore find that Professor Behe's claim for irreducible complexity has been refuted in peer-reviewed research papers and has been rejected by the scientific community at large."

- "In fact, on cross-examination, Professor Behe was questioned concerning his 1996 claim that science would never find an evolutionary explanation for the immune system. He was presented with fifty-eight peer-reviewed publications, nine books, and several immunology textbook chapters about the evolution of the immune system; however, he simply insisted that this was still not sufficient evidence of evolution, and that it was not 'good enough'."

The point here is that once the concept of irreducible complexity is properly scrutinized by qualified people, it loses all support. Natural selection can and does provide an elegant explanation for the complexity that we see, and we don't need a great and powerful wizard hiding behind the curtains to create it. For example, spend a few minutes with creationists and you're bound to hear the popular argument of the watchmaker. If you were walking along the beach and found a watch, you could look at all of the complicated parts within it and easily come to the conclusion that the watch was intelligently designed. A higher intelligence designed each part of that watch with a particular function in mind. The watch is too improbable to have been created on its own. It could not have arisen through a purely random process, and if one part of the watch ceases to function, the whole watch stops ticking. We couldn't expect a tornado to blow through a hardware store and randomly assemble a working watch. When this scenario is applied to human beings, the human body becomes our watch and God becomes the

---

1 Kitzmiller v. Dover Area School District

watchmaker. Under this scenario, it is argued that human life could only have come about through intelligent design.

The argument is persuasive, but just like our arch example; this complex design is merely an illusion once we understand the processes that gave rise to it. What Darwin showed us was how the process of replication makes such an illusion possible. Replicators make copies of themselves and these copies will make copies of themselves until we have a long lineage of copies. Since each of these copies has to compete for resources and the copying process itself is prone to error, replicators that can reproduce more efficiently will succeed where less efficient ones fail. These dominant replicators will continue through subsequent generations, and after enough generations have passed, we get the illusion of intelligent design.

Our bodies are so fantastic and complex that it's easy to see how folks can believe in intelligent design, however there's one more item I want to add. If man was created in the image of God and God is perfect, then we should be able to say with certainty that our bodies are perfect—or at least perfectly designed. I'll argue that nothing could be further from the truth. If we look at the human eyeball for example, it is one of our more structurally and functionally-complex organs. It's far from perfect however. We have photoreceptor cells in our retina that sense light and pass that information to other cells that eventually send that to the optic nerve and on up to the brain. If God was an engineer, we should question the wisdom of putting the neural connections in front of the photoreception cells where they can filter and scatter the light. This light also needs pass through a network of vessels before it ever reaches the light-collecting cells in the back of the eye and the image the brain eventually receives from this process is upside down. If all of the sensory wiring of the eye were located behind the photoreceptors, we wouldn't have a blind spot in our retina and yet every human being has this blind spot. If we were created in His image, would it be safe to assume that God has this blind spot as well? Is there anything that God cannot see? Additionally, our eyes can only see a minute fraction of the electromagnetic spectrum. If we likened the electromagnetic spectrum to a football field, human beings would only see the equivalent of a hash mark. When viewed from this perspective, we are actually quite blind.

I question the intelligence of an intelligent being that would design nipples for men, wisdom teeth, the male uterus (prostatic utricle), the tailbone, and the appendix. These are hardly perfect designs. As embryos, each one of us has gill supports, a yolk sac, and a tail that will eventually be absorbed by the body[1]. Our bodies require water to survive and we live on a planet that has three quarters of its surface covered in water, yet our perfectly designed bodies can't process that water because it contains salt. I question this designer's intelligence in creating a creature that has to eat plants or other animals every few hours to survive. Of course the animals must be cooked or else we risk getting sick. We can eat grass, which is the most abundant plant and easiest to find, but we couldn't survive on it. The plants and animals

---

1 *Biology: Understanding Life.* Sandra Alters. 2000. ISBN: 0763708372. pp 521

that we do eat are swallowed through the same hole that we use to breath, effectively guaranteeing that a certain percentage of us will choke to death each year. Our skin protects our internal organs, but every time we get over-heated, we sweat out the very water that we need to survive. The sun that our God put into the sky can turn this same skin cancerous just by being exposed to it. If you were designing a product where its most valuable assets were under the skin, wouldn't it make sense to make it difficult to cut or puncture that skin? Something so important wasn't designed to even with-stand a cut from a piece of paper. Finally, with the exception of the brain, we can find an example of at least one animal in nature with more advanced body parts than us. The eyes of an owl allows it to see better than we can. A dog's nose allows it to smell better than we can. A dolphin breathes and eats out of different openings. A cheetah can run faster than we can. The common household cat can hear better than we can. Kangaroos jump higher and far-ther than human beings. All of this would seem to be in line with the notion that we and the rest of the animal kingdom are the products of evolution. If we were perfectly designed and created by God in His image, then all of this would appear to be less like intelligent design and more like incompetent design. After all, why would he forsake His most perfect creation in virtually every facet of design? We are supposed to be His masterpiece.

When proponents of intelligent design like Behe argue for this type of in-clusion in public schools alongside the legitimate science of evolution, I have to ask how this is markedly different than someone arguing for the inclusion of any other pseudoscientific topic. The request is as inappropriate as it is bizarre. Should we have astrology taught alongside astronomy? Perhaps the syllabus could delve into the scientific facts surrounding horoscopes, tarot cards, and psychic readings after the topics of meteorites, The Big Bang, and terrestrial planets have been explained. Should we have alchemy taught alongside chemistry? Perhaps that syllabus could cover the scientific pro-cess of turning common metals into gold, the process for summoning spirits, and the list of ingredients within the elixir of life after the periodic table of elements, atomic structures, and chemical equations have been explained. Creationism simply doesn't belong in the public school system. For those parents who can't bear the thought of having their children taught evolution instead of creationism, there is a wonderful alternative: parochial schools. As President Ulysses S. Grant said in 1875, "Church and State" should be "forever separate." Faith and the teaching of it should remain relegated to churches, families, and privately-financed schools. Intelligent Design is, as the courts have declared, a pseudoscience devoid of support from the scien-tific community. As such, it should not be presented in a scientific manner within a public school setting. In fact, it hasn't earned the right to be pre-sented in a scientific manner anywhere.

Myth #4. Evolution Is Just a Theory

Yes! Evolution is a theory! There is no doubt that it fits the definition. The problem lies with the common misconception of what that definition is.

How many times have you heard someone say "I have a theory about that"? It's fairly common to use the word "theory" where it doesn't actually fit.

A scientific theory is a well-established principle based upon repeated testing and observation. It is used to explain things in the natural world. In addition to repeated observations, a theory includes laws, predictions, facts, and widely accepted and tested hypotheses. A theory is often made up of multiple hypotheses. Some examples would include plate tectonics, atomic theory, Stockholm syndrome, architecture, Theory of relativity, and yes, Theory of evolution.

A hypothesis is a specific prediction about an expected outcome to a test or study. For example, if I use an appropriate amount of fertilizer on a plant, the plant will grow to be bigger than a plant that doesn't receive fertilizer. A hypothesis is essentially an educated guess. A hypothesis, by its very definition, does not deserve equal weight to a theory.

A good hypothesis is something that can be tested. To be considered "good," we have to be able to measure either the cause and effect or the correlation. Intelligent design doesn't necessarily make a good hypothesis, but if we use a loose definition of hypothesis, we can put intelligent design in there.

Scientific theories are not guesses. A hypothesis is a speculative guess that requires testing. Evolution has achieved the label of "theory." Intelligent Design has not.

Myth #5. Evolution Violates the Second Law of Thermodynamics

Every time I hear this, my first question is "What are the other laws?" I'm usually met with a blank stare. Other than the fact that most people have no idea what the Second Law of Thermodynamics actually states, I don't know why this one keeps getting offered up for denial of evolution. The Second Law of Thermodynamics basically states that randomness (disorder) cannot decrease in an isolated system. The problem with this argument is that our planet is not an isolated system. That's it. It's the simplest and easiest creationist argument to negate.

If you're not familiar with the Laws of Thermodynamics, rest easy. It's not that difficult. The First Law deals with the conservation of energy— energy/matter can be neither created nor destroyed. The Second Law deals with the direction of that conservation—the entropy in an isolated system always increases or remains constant. The Third Law deals with Absolute Zero—energy will stop being produced once you reach 0 K. The Zeroth Law basically says that if two systems are in equilibrium with a third system, then they are also in equilibrium with each other.

What in the world does this have to do with evolution? Creationists frequently misinterpret the Second Law to say that things must go from order to disorder. God created order and now we must have disorder. Evolution is the reverse: disorder to order. Our sun continually provides us with energy, thus we are not in a closed system and evolution does not violate this law. If we plant and grow corn in a field, the ripe corn will have more usable energy than the seed that we initially put in the ground. Evolution is not the only example we have in nature where order can come from disorder. If you've ever seen a sand dune, a stalactite, a snow-covered roof, or lightning, you're watching order come from disorder. All of those things are made up of random disorder (grains of sand, snowflakes, energy) and none of them required any type of intelligent programming to produce that order. If we look closely, we can find many more examples of order from disorder in nature.

-- Evolutionary Conclusion --

Whether we're looking at fossils or bacteria, evolution is all around us. Darwin's theory is stunningly beautiful in its ability to explain a great deal about life. Evolution allows life to adapt to an ever-changing environment. The real difference between evolution and creationism is that one is evidence-based while the other is belief-based. Either we believe the evidence suggesting that we evolved over a long period of time to the state that we find ourselves in today or we believe that God created man instantly from dirt and His breathe. The debate really boils down to those two choices. One deserves to be taught in classrooms. The other deserves to be taught in a church. The most ardent supporters of Christianity will deny evolution but will gladly talk about the infallibility of the Bible...which speaks of mythological creatures as if they were real and had roles to play.

A cockatrice is a mythical creature. It is a two-legged dragon with a rooster's head. It is also known as a basilisk and the New International Version of the Bible translates it to "viper." Jeremiah 8:17 in the King James Version says, *"For, behold, I will send serpents, cockatrices, among you, which will not be charmed, and they shall bite you, saith the LORD."* Isaiah 59:5 says *"They hatch cockatrice' eggs, and weave the spider's web: he that eateth of their eggs dieth, and that which is crushed breaketh out into a viper."* Isaiah 11:8 and 14:29 also reference the cockatrice.

Cherubim are mentioned throughout the Bible and are the second highest rank in the Christian angelic hierarchy. God puts one at the entrance to the Garden of Eden with a flaming sword. Ezekiel describes them as having 1 head with 4 faces. On one side was a human face. The right side had a lion face. The left side had an ox face, and the back had the face of an eagle. Cherubim have the hands of a man, feet of a calf, and four wings—two extending upward and two downward. I think it's safe to say that if you saw one eating plants from your garden, you'd certainly be able to distinguish it from the average rabbit or deer.

In the King James Bible, satyrs are referenced in Isaiah 13:21 and Isaiah 34:14. You would be forgiven for not knowing what a satyr is, as I'm confident that not many modern-day zoos keep them on display. A satyr is essentially a half man–half goat who loves to dance with nymphs and drink wine. Again, if you saw one sitting in your garden, it would be easily distinguishable from other animals.

There are more than 20 references in the King James Bible to dragons. The Bible makes references to witches, which must have been real because God commands us to kill them. Of course, who can forget the talking animals in the Bible? There's the talking snake from Genesis and Balaam's Donkey from

Numbers. I love that story by the way! Balaam's donkey sees the angel of the Lord in the road and tries to turn away from him three times, but Balaam beats the donkey each time. Then the Lord opens the donkey's mouth and the donkey says "What have I done to you to make you beat me these three times?" Every time I read this story, I can just hear Eddie Murphy's voice as the donkey from the movie Shrek. It makes me laugh every time.

While some Christians tacitly agree that these mythological creatures exist, many more reasonably refuse to accept the literal interpretation of those passages. On more than one occasion I have heard a Christian say, "I can still believe in Jesus without believing in cherubim." I find that position to be untenable. It would be no different than someone saying that he/she believes in Santa Claus but not the elves or flying reindeer.

Evolution may be a difficult concept for creationists, but talking animals, cockatrices, satyrs, dragons, and cherubim are difficult for the rest of us to reconcile with reality. Admittedly, even though there are gaps in our historical account of evolution, we do not have a single shred of evidence for the creatures that the Bible purports to be real. We also do not have fossil records for the "crocoduck" or "fronkey" which creationists like Kirk Cameron and Ray Comfort trot out to the uninformed masses as "evidence" against biological evolution. Only those with a misunderstanding of evolution would expect to see a crocodile–duck or frog–monkey. That's not how evolution works nor has it ever been presented in that manner.

Evolution is a scientific approach to explain how we came to be what we are today. It not only explains a great deal about us, it has incredible predictive power as well. It has been put to the test by thousands of scientists and has largely passed these tests each time. Creationism on the other hand does not seek to explain anything. It simply asserts its position. Evolution does not explain how initial life began, nor does it ever make any attempt to do so. It simply explains how more complex organisms developed from earlier simpler ones. That's it. Belief in evolution does not preclude someone from believing in an ultimate creator of the universe, but it does prevent someone from giving honest intellectual weight to the accounts of creation put forth by our organized religions. Any religious account asserting that man and animal were created exactly as they are today simply has not earned the right to be put on equal intellectual footing. Evolution makes the Genesis account of creation less believable, and frankly, that's a good thing.

Chapter 19. Twinkle, Twinkle Little Star

> The president of the United States has claimed, on
> more than one occasion, to be in dialogue with God.
> If he said that he was talking to God through his hair-
> dryer, this would precipitate a national emergency. I
> fail to see how the addition of a hairdryer makes the
> claim more ridiculous or offensive. —Sam Harris

Throughout the course of this book we have looked at religion through the prism of our earthly realm. We have looked at the various claims and assertions put forth by our major religions along with their associated effects on our neighbors from the vantage point of our two feet planted firmly on the ground. To gain another perspective with which to consider these claims and assertions, we need to reach for the stars. If every religion purports to speak on behalf of the creator of the universe, it stands to reason that we would benefit greatly in our understanding of this creator by looking at his creation. If I were to say to you that the universe is a big place, I wouldn't be doing the universe justice by declaring that so nonchalantly. The known universe is not just a big place; it is bigger than anything you or I have ever imagined. Human hubris fueled by religious beliefs about our significance in relation to this creator places us as the single most important part of this expanse and this view has permeated our society for millennia. Even today, we can't seem to convince nearly 1 out of every 5 Americans that our planet is in fact not the center of our solar system let alone the center of the universe. For the rest of us, we can begin to look at things in a new light the moment we change our vantage point. For example, when Carl Sagan requested the Voyager 1 spacecraft to turn its camera towards Earth as it was preparing to leave our solar system, our planet was barely discernible. The image of our planet taken by Voyager 1 is perhaps one of the most humbling images I have ever seen. It takes some effort just to try and find our planet which is essentially no bigger than a pixel in the image. As Sagan once said, "all of human history has happened on that tiny pixel, which is our only home."[1] From just 3.7 billion miles away, our planet was nothing more than a bluish-white dot. I can't stress enough just how small we are compared to the known universe.

This is literally the creation that the God our neighbors pray to has brought into existence. In order to be Christian, Muslim, or Jewish, you have to believe that this astronomically huge expanse of stars, planets, comets, asteroids, black holes, and supernovas was all created and set into motion so that the creator could have a personal relationship with just one specific species of primates living on a single pixel in the night sky. To be a believer in any of the Abrahamic faiths is to believe that all of this was done so that God could impart to us what He considers to be the most important lessons of the universe. Stars are literally exploding as we speak and black holes are swallowing anything unfortunate enough to come too close. In the face of all of this cosmic destruction, we are given some very specific commands and expectations about our terrestrial existence. For example, God does not want us to eat shellfish or pork. He does not want us to wear clothing consisting of linen and wool, plow a field with a yoked ox and ass, cut ourselves, and under no circumstances are we to ever flirt with belief in another divine being. To be a religious person is to believe that the creator of the universe put into motion hundreds of billions of galaxies so that we could know the true virtue of circumcising a young boy. It's hard to imagine how the foreskin of a boy's penis could possibly factor into the functioning of the cosmos, yet here we have religion dictating to us that this is precisely what the creator of the universe desires for us to do. To think in this way is to assume that the purpose of the universe is to provide a fertile ground from which mankind can serve God. If that's the case, then why go to all the trouble of creating the enormity of the universe? This seems a rather obvious question, doesn't it? If we are to believe that the universe was created specifically for us to have a personal relationship with its creator, what purpose does the rest of the universe have that supports this intent? Why does this relationship require the enormous and distant galaxies like Andromeda and Tadpole in order to function? Once we look at the universe as it is and not as we want it to be, it becomes embarrassingly obvious that it's a tremendous waste of space if even one iota of religious dogma is true. There's nothing in the known laws of physics that leads us to believe that life is wholly dependent upon the existence of billions of other galaxies. If God wanted to create human life, He was terribly inefficient at doing so. For much of the 4.6 billion years that our planet has been in existence, we humans have barely been around long enough to qualify as a blip. If our planet were a human being and lived to the ripe old age of 100, our species could have barely been around long enough for a single wink of the eye. If any of this strikes you as odd, it should. In the days of Moses, Jesus, and Muhammad, we knew very little about the cosmos.

---

1 Speech given at Cornell University. October 13, 1994

The authors of the Bible, for example, didn't know just how big the universe really was because they barely had a concept of the universe to begin with. To be a Christian, Muslim, or Jew is to believe that this entire thing was created specifically with us in mind. This is at the very least an audacious and egotistical assertion that strains credibility.

If we gaze through a telescope and look for the next closest star to us after our sun, we'll find a star named Proxima Centauri. It is a mere 4.2 light years away. When we see the light emitted from Proxima Centauri, it was created over 4 years ago and we're just seeing it now. It takes that long to reach us! In Genesis 1:3, the Bible tells us that God created light. God gave labels to both night and day in Genesis 1:5—the dark would be called night and the light would be called day. On the fourth day, God created the sun, moon, and stars. If God created light in verse 3, where did the light that created night and day come from? It certainly didn't come from the sun (or any other star) which hadn't been created yet. Earth would obviously have to be spinning as this is what gives us the concepts of night and day. Where did this mysterious light come from? Let's come back to that in a moment.

When God put the stars into the sky on the fourth day, one would assume that he created all of them at the same time. If someone believes that the universe is less than 10,000 years old, how do they explain the fact that we are able to see stars that are literally millions or billions of light years away when the light that we see was originally created millions or billions of years ago. This is often called the "starlight problem." Let's come back to this in a moment as well.

On the fourth day, God also created the lesser light to govern the night. If the greater light that governs the day is the sun, the lesser light is the moon. So, according to Genesis, God created moonlight. The only problem with this account is that our moon is unable to generate light on its own. The moon's light is actually a reflection of the sun's light, but can we really expect unenlightened men from thousands of years ago to know that? There needed to be an explanation for the moon, and because of our scientific progress, we can reliably say that the Bible was clearly wrong on this account.

Sam Harris, the noted neuroscientist, uses the following example—water is chemically comprised of hydrogen and oxygen. What if someone doubted that? Is there such a thing as a Biblical chemist? In Genesis, God created water before he created light. If there was no light, there were no stars. If there were no stars to fuse helium and hydrogen into heavier elements like oxygen, either the water doesn't contain any oxygen or God created special oxygen. Did God create special oxygen or did Moses simply not have an adequate understanding of how chemistry works? What happens when we apply Occam's razor to this scenario, which essentially says that all things being equal, the simplest answer tends to be the correct one? What is more likely—that the people who wrote the Bible didn't have the same understanding of our universe that we do today or that we have to invoke the Divine Default and say that God suspended the laws of the universe to accomplish everything the Bible says in the order that it proposes? These types of conflicts can and should be expected from texts that are completely man-made.

It's interesting to read the opinions of creationists and religious apologetics as it relates to these conflicts. Most creationists will say that they don't know for sure because the Bible doesn't say. That doesn't mean that they don't have ideas though. I've heard such ideas as the original light from Genesis 1:3 was radiated from God Himself or that the sun was actually created on Day 1. My concern with these answers is that the Bible doesn't say any of it. If the sun was created on Day 1, then why not just explicitly say so? Why bother creating the moon and all the other stars days later? The sun is a star after all, but when the Bible was written, not a single person in the world knew that it was a huge nuclear sphere of plasma. Our understanding of the cosmos at that time was still in its infancy. Assuming this wasn't a metaphor, if the light radiated from God Himself, was God only able to see one side of the planet? If He is everywhere and can see everything, wouldn't His light radiate everywhere? The light was obviously directional. If it wasn't, there wouldn't be the perception of night and day.

I've seen pseudoscientific accounts that suggest that clocks ran at much higher rates during this Creation Week than what they run today. Therefore light from far-flung galaxies would only need days instead of the millions or billions of years that it takes them today. This basically means that time went faster everywhere else in the universe except here on Earth. A day here would be more than a billion elsewhere. This idea only has merit under a creationist framework. There's nothing to suggest that light traveled infinitely faster during God's creation than it does today. This concept is referred to as c-decay and has been thoroughly debunked repeatedly by real scientists. Science has advanced more than enough to detect enough residual decay and yet there is none. In order to make this theory work, light would have to travel more than a million times faster than it does. Dr. Jason Lisle, writing for the creationist organization Answers in Genesis, reminds us that "We should also remember that God is not limited to natural methods as we are."[1] Yet again we are reminded that if we invoke the Divine Default, all of these inconvenient contradictions go away.

Each of us is, or at least should be, familiar with the periodic table of elements. If you've taken a chemistry class, you've seen it. If you had taken a chemistry class one hundred years ago and asked your professor where each of those elements physically came from, he/she would not have been able to definitively answer you. They simply didn't know for sure. That answer wouldn't become available until the past fifty or sixty years. Modern astrophysicists are now able to trace the origin of many of these elements. These elements can be found in stars, and when those stars inevitably explode, they spread those elements in every direction across the vacuum of space. The reason these elements are so prevalent in our universe is precisely due to these explosions. It is quite interesting to compare the most common, abun-

---

1 http://www.answersingenesis.org/articles/am/v5/n2/distant-starlight Retrieved on 3/18/2012

dant elements in the universe to the most common, abundant elements in human beings.

Universe	Humans
Hydrogen	Hydrogen
Helium	
Oxygen	Oxygen
Carbon	Carbon
Nitrogen	Nitrogen

You'll notice that besides helium, which is an inert gas to humans (i.e., it does nothing and our bodies don't require it), our chemical composition is identical to the most common elements in the universe. If God created us, He didn't create us out of anything special. Most of our body consists of water, which is comprised of hydrogen and oxygen. Next we look at carbon which is what life is based upon. Carbon is the most chemically active element in the periodic table so it should come as no surprise that life forms such as ours make such wide use of carbon. We can use carbon to make molecules that have thousands or even millions of atoms. There are more carbon compounds than all of the other elements combined! Because we know that life is carbon-based and carbon, hydrogen, and oxygen are some of the most abundant elements in the universe, it would be incredibly narcissistic to think that we are alone in the universe. The fact that we have been unable to create life in our labs doesn't mean that nature isn't capable of doing it here or elsewhere.

Considering the sheer size of the universe, it would take a lot of stars to spread those elements to every corner. There are an estimated 70 sextillion stars in the known universe. That's 70,000 million million million stars. That number does not include planets, moons, asteroids, or comets. Those are just stars and that is ten times more than all of the grains of sand from every inch of every beach on our entire planet. If you recall from the earlier chapter about the Divine Default, I made reference to the fact that the human mind has difficulty with probabilities. It doesn't come naturally for many of us. The potential for life elsewhere in our universe is one of the best examples of probability. If we took just 1% of the estimated number of stars in the known universe and then took 1% of those stars and then 1% of those stars and then 1% of those stars and then 1% of those stars and then 1% of the remaining stars, there would be potential for 70 billion solar systems orbiting around those 70 billion stars where just 1 planet in 1 solar system needs to support life as we know it using the same abundantly common elements that we use. Just because we haven't found life elsewhere yet doesn't mean that it doesn't exist. Over the past three years, NASA's Kepler Space Telescope has identified more than 2,300 potential planets and has already confirmed more than 100 where the conditions for life could be ideal. Kepler 22b is thought to be in its star's habitable zone where liquid water could exist and perhaps even life as we know it. Additionally, the planets Gliese 581 g, Gliese 667C c, HD 85512 b, and Gliese 581 d have already been identified as potentially life-friendly as well. The Gliese system is only 20 light years away which is, cosmically speaking, just around the block from us. Any of these planets could harbor life. Statistically speaking, life may be inevitable! It's important to note that while I can make a statement like this with little fear of retribution, that wasn't always the case. The Italian monk Giordano Bruno was burned at the stake by the Church for blasphemy when he suggested and refused to recant his belief that life could exist outside of our planet.

The Church can no longer burn you at the stake, so if you are open to the probability that life could exist on another planet somewhere among those 70 sextillion stars, what theological implications do you think this would pose? Our own human history has produced thousands of Gods. What type of deity might an alien civilization believe in? It certainly wouldn't be Jesus Christ! Christians will tell you that Jesus was sent to Earth to save mankind. There's no mention in the Bible that God impregnated virgins from any other planet. If a civilization from a completely different planet has religion, we can be reasonably certain that it won't resemble the specific, organized religions that we have on our planet. The aliens, assuming that they are equally evolved, would most likely have discovered chemistry, biology, and astronomy. These disciplines can be rediscovered using the same methods. No such methods exist for our religions. They would likely not exist in their current forms and this should tell us something about the nature and truthfulness of our religions. If we had to start human history over, we would most likely still have religion, but each would be different than the ones we have today.

CHAPTER 20. DOCTOR, DOCTOR

> Deaths in the Bible—God: 2,270,365 not including
> the victims of Noah's flood, Sodom and Gomorrah, or
> the many plagues, famines, fiery serpents, etc because no
> specific numbers were given. Satan: 10.—Unknown

There a number of famous doctors throughout history that weren't ac-tual doctors. Dr. Seuss, Dr. No, Dr. Claw, Dr. Octopus, Dr. Who, Dr. Dre, Dr. J, and Dr. Evil come to mind. Add another one to that list. As the Reverend Doctor JJ Dyken, I invite you to address me as Doctor, Reverend, or Rever-end Doctor. Both of the titles prior to my name are technically correct, but if you're feeling ill, I'm the last person you should call. I am technically an ordained minister with a Doctorate in Divinity, but neither distinction re-quired the type of effort to obtain as someone who has put in the dedication to achieve an actual medical degree or a doctorate of philosophy. In fact, I look upon these distinctions as evidence for the absurdity of religion's at-tempt at legitimacy. I liken my Doctorate in Divinity to having a Doctorate of Alchemy or a Doctorate of Astrology—utterly useless distinctions encased within beautiful frames. While the certificates look very nice, I didn't have to put forth any significant effort to achieve either of these titles, nor do I think I should have been able to receive them that easily. I am not special. In fact, I am rather common, and that is precisely the point. This distinction of reverend or doctor is unnecessary. Anyone who is willing to read, listen, and contemplate can use their (pardon the pun) God-given common sense to critically evaluate the beliefs and assertions put forth by their chosen reli-gion. No special titles are required.

It should give us cause for concern that literally thousands of people around the world use their titles in religious settings under official situations. These people lead congregations every week and serve in a formal capacity at weddings, funerals, baptisms, and more. Their credentials are just as equally valid as mine, yet they use them as the basis for their moral and religious authority. What does this practice say about a large number of our everyday religious leaders? What does this say about the seriousness with which a title like Doctor or Reverend can be so easily handed out? The ease with which these titles can be obtained is a testament to the mockery that we call organized religion.

We treat the credentials of Reverend Doctor as if the creator of the universe has authorized and endorsed these people to speak on His behalf. This is astonishing as it means that one human being can tell another human with certainty what the creator of the universe expects from us and can tell us with that same degree of certainty what happens to us after we die. The moment we acknowledge that someone has received divine revelation; we have opened the door for them to assume power in the only world in which we can be sure exists. No religion on Earth has such incontrovertible proof to justify such arrogant certitude, but that doesn't prevent religion from attempting to lay claim to that authority. People will hear what they want to hear and the source or basis for the information is often irrelevant.

For example, when 4-year-old Kanon Tipton made headlines in 2011 for his evangelical preaching, believers were immediately awestruck. Non-believers were just as awestruck but for completely different reasons. Kanon started out when he was just 21 months old mimicking the movements of his father and grandfather. Today the pint-sized evangelical is considered the world's youngest preacher, even though Kanon apparently only preaches when the Spirit moves him. The following is part of the transcript from one of his sermons:

> "I'm preaching about . . . I'm preaching about . . . the one God. Like a man's church to the man's church of Pentecost, of Pentecost, of Pentecost. Is going to do for the one Lord. The red hot revival. If the Lord has the words you have the Pentecost Grenada Mississippi. The Lord is here tonight and his name is Jesus. There is only one God. And then he's going to praise out his tears and just worship God and then he's gonna worship God. But the Lord is going to do it, that means God has to do it and then Jesus has to do it and then God is going to do it and then Jesus. I love to preach here tonight."

Kanon is the perfect example of indoctrination. What knowledge and experience could a 4-year-old child possibly have that would allow any adult to seriously consider him a Pentecostal preacher? Can he logically explain the concept of Jesus, the Holy Spirit, or religion in general? If he can, on what basis would he be able to do this competently and legitimately? What life experience outside of the church does he have on which to speak authoritatively on topics where religion seeks to influence us? Have the Tiptons ever exposed young Kanon to any other religion? If not, on what basis can he claim the authority to dismiss all other religions?

Sadly, the story of Kanon Tipton isn't unusual. Samuel Boutwell is a Baptist preacher at his Brookhaven, Mississippi, church. Samuel became a preacher after being "saved" at the ripe old age of 3. It seems a rather obvious question, but what kind of maturity could a child this age have to adequately understand the commitment he's making or the words coming out of his mouth? This type of gimmick has immoral implications.

Hugh Marjoe Gortner is a former Pentecostal preacher who was ordained at the age of 4. He too shared the title of "youngest ordained minister in history." Marjoe (a portmanteau of the biblical names "Mary" and "Joseph") achieved fame when years later he starred in the movie bearing his name. The film provided a behind-the-scenes look at the business side of Pentecostal preaching and ended up winning the 1972 Academy Award for Best Documentary Feature. In the film, Gortner, now a non-believer, allows himself to be filmed preaching during actual revivals. Marjoe explained to filmmakers precisely how Pentecostal preachers like him operated, how they manipulated people, and how much money could be taken in.

Terry Durham was ordained at age 6 and has spent years traveling the country preaching to packed churches. He claims to be able to heal the sick and can apparently speak in tongues. Terry's father Todd markets and promotes Terry Durham Ministry. In a 2009 interview, he told ABC News, "I see Terry Durham as a major icon for the Christian industry. Jesus is the product." Todd's goal is to surpass the earnings of such Christian evangelists as Joel Osteen. "Joel is at 76. One day I am hoping that Terry will be at about $86 million. So you know ministries are profiting these days. Everyone is buying into this."

It wouldn't be such a stretch to find these actions not only a circus of absurdity but potentially bordering on child abuse. Videos of these children preaching are all available online for anyone who wishes to view them. What becomes immediately apparent to those who watch the performances is the style of preaching. Children have an amazing ability to mimic adults in both mannerisms and one-liners. More important, however, is the content of the sermons. Children of these ages are not intellectually mature enough to grasp the serious doctrines coming out of their mouths. Most adults seem incapable of grasping theology, so why should we give legitimacy to a child who hasn't developed the critical thinking skills necessary to put themselves in a position to teach others?

Just as my credentials of Reverend Doctor serve as a testament to the mockery of religion, the fact that people take the preaching of young children seriously serves the same function. Until religion begins to take itself seriously, expect many more Reverends and Doctors...of all ages.

Chapter 21. The Final Word

> We must respect the other fellow's religion, but only in
> the sense and to the extent that we respect his theory that
> his wife is beautiful and his children smart.—H. L. Mencken

The Divine Default is an attempt to highlight not just the often irrational attributions to God but also the corollary that any divine intervention on someone's behalf is deemed worthy where others are not. When millions of young children will die this year because they don't have access to clean water or food (items that we as Americans take for granted), we should be honest about the obscene nature of attributing anything positive to God. When someone says that God has given them the strength to get through a tough situation, we should recognize the egotistical hypocrisy of that kind of attribution because the corollary is that this same God didn't feel it particularly worthwhile to save the ten or so children who died of preventable causes while you read this paragraph.

I believe that we all need to practice a little more cosmic humility because the truth is that we don't understand everything. With a global population of 7 billion and growing, the arrogant certitude of our religious convictions is not the type of discourse that will help us live together in peace. Pretending to know things that are completely unknowable is not the best course of action. With every faith laying claim to the true God(s), the simple fact is that they can't all be correct. Logically, the vast majority, if not all, are wrong. This is perhaps the single biggest reason for making the case that religion is a manmade invention. If there is a God, He is most likely not a personal deity who authors books and occasionally answers prayers.

To be religious is to believe that God created this massive universe for the sole purpose of maintaining a relationship with one species of primate on a small planet orbiting an ordinary sun in an ordinary solar system in an ordinary galaxy which is just one of many galaxies. We're told by the religiously faithful that the universe is fine-tuned for life and meant for us. Considering the fact that the universe is actually extremely hostile to life, it's much more likely that it is our species that is fine-tuned for the universe. If life on our planet were completely wiped out, there is no reason to believe that the universe would care one bit. The universe wouldn't bat an eye at our extinction just as it didn't bat an eye when 99.9% of all animals on our planet went extinct. We can look up to the cosmos and see stars much like our own sun blowing up every second of every day. It becomes an exercise in egotism when we link the merciless destruction occurring in the cosmos to a god who cares about our personal problems and is willing to suspend the laws of the universe—in our favor—to answer prayers.

To believe in the Christian God is to believe that millions upon millions of people throughout the course of human history are literally burning in a lake of fire as we speak because of what they didn't know they needed to know. Through no fault of their own, they were never told the importance of Jesus Christ. Perhaps they were born in a culture where Christianity is not influential. Should a reasonable, moral person believe that someone in a remote part of the world who had never been exposed to the story of Jesus will be penalized for eternity for a crime they weren't even aware of? Surely a being capable of creating something as grand and awe-inspiring as the universe is capable of devising a better solution to safeguard the eternal well-being of human souls.

If God has explained to us our purpose, does it not strike you as odd that we are essentially treated as slaves? Religion dictates how we are supposed to act, what we should eat, what we should wear, and even how we are supposed to think. Islam provides instructions for virtually every facet of life from sex to banking. Christianity tells us that we can be convicted by God for just the feelings we have or the thoughts that might occur to us. Jesus was in essence the first person to enact thought crime legislation. What kind of relationship is this when even thought-crimes are punishable? That is the very essence of a totalitarian dictatorship. Some people are quite content to be slaves and may even feel pride in their shackles, but as the English might say, that's not my cup of tea. For me, the purpose of life is not to worship a celestial dictator and slaveholder. I firmly believe that we must determine our own purpose, and I have determined that my purpose is to maximize my happiness as well as the happiness of those around me. We should attempt to do this by trying to reach the Pinnacle of Morality on our Moral Ladder with every opportunity we get. We can only be certain of receiving this one life so it seems to me that arguing over the validity of the next life is not the best way of maximizing our time.

There has been great effort in the United States to achieve religious tolerance, but toleration is the not the end game nor is it a panacea. We have tolerance not because of divine mandate but rather because we are a secular country with secular rules. In some other parts of the world, the tolerance that we enjoy in the United States does not exist between faiths. To a Christian, belief in Jesus Christ as our savior is the only way to reach Heaven. No matter what else that Christian might have in common with a member of another faith, the non-Christian is going to Hell. Likewise, a Muslim believes that the Qur'an is the perfect word of God, and once a Christian or Jew has been made aware of that belief and rejects it, the Christian or Jew is destined for Hell. The Mormon faith is quite explicit in its belief that every denomination of Christianity was misguided, corrupt, and unacceptable, as told to Joseph Smith by God himself. When God says that non-Mormon versions of Christianity are "an abomination in his sight," how far can we really expect interfaith dialogue to go?

As nice as the concept of tolerance may be, it has to be mentioned that tolerance is clearly not something that is endorsed by the god of the monotheistic religions. Intrinsically indoctrinated into these faiths is the basic tenet that every other faith is wrong and those believers are on the wrong path. Therefore, commandments such as "Thou shall have no other Gods before me" translate into a material belief that every other faith, and by extension the believers, are wrong and represent a potential landmine. Infidels are everywhere as is temptation to be led astray to a foreign god. The term "tolerance" implies a non-judgmental acceptance of other faiths that are, according to scripture, irreconcilable and forever at odds with someone's belief. This becomes even more disconcerting when we recognize that most people didn't even have a say in originally picking their religion.

Why does faith deserve respect? What is honorable about believing something without sufficient evidence for doing so? There isn't a single area of discourse outside of religion where this practice would be respected, and yet we continue to coddle religion in a way that is detrimental to our continued survival. It is socially taboo to question someone's beliefs no matter how bizarre they might be. Sam Harris illustrated this concept by saying that religion "allows perfectly decent and sane people to believe by the billions what only lunatics could believe on their own. If you wake up tomorrow morning thinking that saying a few Latin words over your pancakes is going to turn them into the body of Elvis Presley, you've lost your mind. If you think more or less the same thing about a cracker and the body of Jesus, you're just a Catholic."

The bottom line is that we do not have to respect any religious belief—only the person's right to hold such a belief. Someone may believe they have a personal relationship with the creator of the universe. I think they are wrong, but as long as their belief doesn't infringe upon my rights, I respect their right to hold that belief. Unlike Christianity, I don't believe we should legislate someone's thoughts nor do I think it appropriate to invade the sanctity of another person's mind. A human being has the right to believe whatever they like as long as their actions do not negatively impact someone else. For this reason, I question the legacy of extending tax exemptions to churches. Churches in the United States own between $300 and $500 billion in untaxed property[1]. In an age of austerity, why are we still giving up in excess of $71 billion dollars a year in tax revenue?[2] If God will provide (as it states in multiple Biblical passages), we shouldn't be forced to extend tax breaks to churches when that money could be used for education, research grants, or infrastructure. Religious organizations often provide useful social welfare functions, but these tax breaks are fiscally irresponsible.

Because of its pervasiveness, religion should not be taboo. It should not be a topic that is sheltered and unapproachable. Religion has historically been a prime source of hatred in our world. When people will literally kill others over the publishing of a religious cartoon, we have to question the sanity of religion. When people believe that temple garments can protect the wearer both physically as well as spiritually, we have to question the sanity of religion. When a televangelist screams that tornadoes are God's way of telling people to come to Him but overlooks the fact that "tornado alley" is right in the heart of America's Bible Belt, we have to question the sanity of religion. When a person believes that a spirit or soul (called a thetan) can be cleansed of spiritual impediments from past experiences using a modified ohmmeter and that a galactic ruler named Xenu kidnapped 178 billion people, flew them to Earth in spacecraft resembling a DC-8, buried them near volcanoes and blew them into the air with hydrogen bombs, we have to question the sanity of religion. When a woman will not leave an abusive husband because she fears that it will make God angry, we have to question the sanity of religion. When a gay teen commits suicide because of Biblically-justified persecution, we have to question the sanity of religion. To do otherwise would be a dereliction of duty to our brothers and sisters.

The usefulness of the holy books from the world's "great religions" has run its course. There is nothing of value left in the Qur'an or the Bible, for example, that we can't derive from a more secular source. Faith makes tremendously spectacular claims with tremendously insufficient evidence to do so. As I've shown in this book, we don't need the Bible to form the basis for determining our morals; this is evidenced by the fact that the vast majority of us are not fundamentalists. It is absolutely possible to be moral without worshiping a god that purports to be all-loving, all-powerful, and all-knowing but can't seem to be all three at the same time. I've also shown that it is possible to be charitable, kind, just, and tolerant without being religious. Religion isn't going to help us find cures for any diseases. It isn't going to help us find alternative energy sources. It isn't going to help us explore the wonders of the universe. Religion concerns itself with the intangible by placing tangible demands and pretending to be anything but a collection of flawed books written by imperfect human beings with limited knowledge.

Consider the fact that, for centuries, we believed that the world was flat and that we were the center of the universe (sadly some still believe this). For much of human history, we believed that sickness and disease were pun-

---

1 Jeff Schweitzer, PhD, "*The Church of America*," Huffington Post, Oct. 11, 2011
2 *Research Report: How Secular Humanists (and Everyone Else) Subsidize Religion in the United States.* June/July 2012 issue of Free Inquiry. Ryan T. Cragun, Stephanie Yeager, and Desmond Vega

ishments from God, and we believed this because we didn't have a better explanation. After all, Germ Theory wouldn't be validated until the late 19th century. We are learning more about our world every day and at a pace that exceeds anything that we've ever seen in human history. The Bible, Bhagavad Gita, Qur'an, and Tanakh have been wrong on virtually every important fact about us and our world that there is no reason to believe in any of their metaphysical claims. Not a single line in any of these books suggests that they were written by an omniscient being. In fact, there isn't a single line that couldn't have been written by a first-century person. For example, when Muhammad is asked to explain why a child will look like one parent instead of the other, he is told by the angel Gabriel that it is wholly dependent upon which parent sexually climaxes first during intercourse (Sahih Bukhari 4:55:546). If the male climaxes first, the child will look like the father. A claim like this is almost comical today. Our knowledge of genetics renders this type of claim absurd. Each time we learn something new, religion is forced to give a little bit more. History has shown that religion has been forced to cede a lot of ground in both scientific and moral matters over the course of the past two millennia and it will be forced to continue to do so. It's your choice whether to believe in scientific accounts or religious accounts. It's your choice to decide which method is a better way of determining fact from fantasy. We should no longer feel obligated to make intellectual accommodations to irrational religious beliefs. The man who is blind to the atrocities committed in the name of religion is a man who is blind to reality. It's time for mankind to open its eyes and determine whether or not its perception of reality is reasonable and intellectually honest.

Kierkegaard once said, "There are two ways to be fooled. One is to believe what isn't true; the other is to refuse to believe what is true." As a species, we have not found a better, more consistently reliable way of determining the truth than the scientific method. I will be the first to admit that science isn't perfect—not by a long shot. We've gotten things wrong. We've even gotten things spectacularly wrong, but therein lay the single biggest difference between science and faith. Where science has failed, the failure was discovered and corrected by science. Science evolves by building upon truths. The same cannot be said about religion. Religion does not change. Everything that was written thousands of years ago must remain the same regardless of any evidence to the contrary. The Bible and the Qur'an are not open for editing. Those of us who elevate science over faith do so because we understand that the self-correcting nature of science makes it more useful and accurate over time. Scientific conclusions change whenever new evidence is presented warranting such a change and the change is always upward. The direction of that change is a very important distinction. Scientific changes rarely lead to a less trustworthy conclusion. Science may be flawed at times, but the scientific process is not. The same cannot be said about our holy books. Over the course of centuries, we have seen the differences in these directions become more pronounced. I'm reasonably certain that you cannot name me one thing where religion has demonstrably proven modern science wrong.

We understand more about the world and our place in it than the character of Moses could have possibly dreamed. Knowledge obtained by observation will always be superior to knowledge obtained through revelation.

Instead of spending time and energy on reverence for our religious figures, that admiration should be applied toward scientists—real life humans who are much better equipped to uncover the actual truths about the universe. If we are to stand in awe of anything, it should be the fruits of their labor. The actual universe is so much more beautiful, complex, and awe-inspiring than any superstitious belief in Heaven or Paradise could ever be simply because the universe is real. Science is real and it shouldn't be so easily dismissed when a religious contradiction arises. If human beings have the ability to think critically using rational arguments, intelligent communication, and emotional maturity, then we have the ability to evaluate specific claims of truth. We do not have to accept any religious claim because we want it to be true, it makes us feel good, or because it simply is being asserted. We can ask for the evidence. We already do this in every other discourse of our lives. Religion does not deserve an exemption.

In the spirit of intellectual honesty, it is imperative that we not only admit but embrace our ignorance. We shouldn't claim to know something when we don't. This means being open to changing our minds when new facts warrant the change. If we are told that God stopped the sun in the middle of the sky for nearly 24 hours to allow Joshua to finish his battle, we would do well to question the evidence before accepting it as fact. That type of claim is not just religious—it is also a cosmological claim about the way in which our universe and our solar system work. Our scientific knowledge is advanced enough to realize just how impossible that claim really is without invoking the Divine Default. As such we should be open to changing our minds on the historicity of the claimed event and at the same time recognize the deterioration of credibility for the original source. Far too many people refuse to change their beliefs even in the presence of invalidating evidence. Refusal to change belief is a refusal to make an honest attempt at finding the truth. The Dalai Lama once said "If science proves some belief of Buddhism wrong, then Buddhism will have to change." Imagine if every religion took that same position.

In the end, it all comes down to choice. We can choose to believe in things because the evidence suggests it or we can choose to believe in things precisely due to a lack of evidence. We can choose to be open to reason and logic or we can be closed off from it. We can choose to indoctrinate our children into a specific faith or we can choose to let them decide for themselves. We can choose to discuss differences rationally or we can choose to use violence to get the results we want. We can choose to be good out of compassion for our fellow man or we can choose to be good out of divine fear. We can choose to seek knowledge or we can choose to be content with what we know. Ultimately, the choice is ours.